BE THE
CHANGE

WITHDRAWN

BE THE CHANGE

How Meditation Can Transform You and the World

|||

ED and DEB SHAPIRO

STERLING
New York

To Deb's mother, Anne, and to our teachers.
May all beings be happy!

STERLING
New York

An Imprint of Sterling Publishing
387 Park Avenue South
New York, NY 10016

ISBN 978-1-4027-8239-8 (paperback)
ISBN 978-1-4027-7670-0 (ebook)

Library of Congress Cataloging-in-Publication Data

Shapiro, Eddie, 1942-
   Be the change : how meditation can transform you and the world/Ed and Deb Shapiro.
      p. cm.
   Includes index.
   ISBN 978-1-4027-6001-3
   1. Meditation. I. Shapiro, Debbie, 1953- II. Title.
   BF637.M4S515 2009
   158.1'2--dc22
                  2009013194

Distributed in Canada by Sterling Publishing
C/o Canadian Manda Group, 165 Dufferin Street
Toronto, Ontario, Canada M6K 3H6
Distributed in the United Kingdom by GMC Distribution Services
Castle Place, 166 High Street, Lewes, East Sussex, England BN7 1XU
Distributed in Australia by Capricorn Link (Australia) Pty. Ltd.
P.O. Box 704, Windsor, NSW 2756, Australia

For information about custom editions, special sales, and premium and corporate
purchases, please contact Sterling Special Sales at 800-805-5489 or specialsales@
sterlingpublishing.com.

Manufactured in the United States of America

2   4   6   8   10   9   7   5   3   1

www.sterlingpublishing.com

Author photo by Erich Pregler

Contents

|||

Foreword by His Holiness
the Dalai Lama

|||

The very purpose of our life is to be happy. There are two kinds of happiness—one that mainly comes from physical comfort and another that involves the mind. Obviously, of the two, mental comfort is superior and more influential. We can see this in our own lives because when our mental state is calm and happy, we can easily put up with small physical discomfort or pain. On the other hand, when our minds are restless and upset, the most comfortable physical facilities don't make us happy.

Since our state of mind is so important, the question arises whether we can train or improve it. Over a very long time, human beings have developed ways to shape the mind; we usually call these methods meditation. Generally speaking, there are two types of meditation. Analytical meditation mainly employs reason. Another kind of meditation simply involves placing your mind at a certain point, without changing it or undertaking any investigation, letting it rest on that single point.

Meditation is an important instrument for shaping or transforming our minds. As a simple Buddhist monk, I have meditated for a long time. As I have gotten older, I have noticed that, even though many problems I have to deal have become more serious and my responsibility for them has become greater, my mind is nevertheless calmer. But don't get the impression that meditation needs to be a religious subject; simply training the mind is a kind of meditation and, while simple single-pointed meditation doesn't necessarily lead to firm convictions, analytical meditation is much more effective in achieving this.

By and large, the mind always looks out critically and deals with external events, but rarely bothers about itself. Therefore, we have to give it new instructions. Up to now, you have dealt with what's going on outside; that's well and good, but now the time has come to explore within and find out more about the mind itself. In doing so, we also have to make an effort to restrain the way our thoughts follow memories of the past and speculations about the future. We need to find the space between such thoughts, which, like the water deep in the ocean, remains clear and undisturbed even though there may be waves on the surface. This is one way to look at the mind itself; it's not easy, but I think it is worthwhile to try.

In this book, Ed and Deb Shapiro have gathered together the thoughts and reflections of a wide range of people with a variety of experiences in meditation. Anyone interested in meditation should not only read what these people have to say, but also try it out. If you like their suggestions and they are helpful to you, use them; if they aren't, disregard them. Treat this book as you would a cookery book. You wouldn't merely read recipes with approval; you'd try them out. Some you'd like and would use again. Like cookery, meditation only makes sense if you put it into practice.

July 17, 2009
HH the Dalai Lama
Nobel Peace Prize recipient

Foreword by
Robert Thurman

|||

Thank goodness Ed and Deb have so beautifully enfolded the gifts of all the fascinating individuals in this book within the moving stories of their own lives and transforming experiences! In this living book, Ed and Deb have masterfully woven the many voices into a symphony; the insights and stories harmonize and contrast with each other in a marvelous rich flow that is both calming and energizing, creating a single collective yet selfless voice.

Reading this book is itself a powerful meditation. Without even trying, you effortlessly go deeper into the best places of your mind and heart, by flowing along page-by-page, teacher-by-teacher, insight-by-insight. You will find you are naturally developing mindfulness as you read the words written here and share in the thoughts and lives of these beautiful people, who are honestly and vividly reaching out to you by telling their stories and revealing their insights, their practices, and their performances regarding meditation.

The great mystics of Buddhism, Judaism, Christianity, and Islam were all blown away when they found nirvana or the kingdom of God within. We need not think they are so far beyond us. All of them patiently told us we could find our true purpose, discover our real meaningfulness, and actually enjoy happiness. And all of them provided us with methods to move us toward these goals. We can, must, and will *be the change* we long to see the world enjoy! We *can* recover from helpless addiction to externalities, impermanent possessions, distracting entertainments, and disappointing preoccupations by turning on our freely intuitive intelligence, tuning in to our deepest hearts through mindful meditation, and dropping out of despairing self-centeredness into the embrace of the lovingness of creation!

In saying this, I make no pretense of having realized more than a hint of all that is possible for us, the wonders we were born to enjoy; I do not claim to have won the super prize of enlightenment yet in this life! But I know by sound inference that each one of us will, sooner or later, experience the bliss of awakening to our authentic selves. When we do, it will be like "coming home," a realization that we always already knew this place.

After all, we know from the highly credible testimony of Buddha and Jesus and the other great teachers that nirvana (the kingdom of God) is the *real reality* of the world, right here and now! And so we can enjoy this moment, reading the words in this book while experiencing the gentle but ecstatic, consciously mindful and inconceivably blissful nature of nirvana!

What an honor to join His Holiness the Dalai Lama with a foreword: He is the sun and I am a firefly in his rays. What a privilege to strike a key chord at the opening of this treasury of heartfelt advice by many of the greatest people you would ever hope to meet, all seasoned and realized meditators, way beyond me! And what a challenge to partner with Ed and Deb to move this magical mystery meditation train along toward the meaningful life that is the destination for every single one of you dear readers!

I only dare proceed because I find a job for myself here with this miracle train, where the engine is the great heart of all spiritual teachers, visionaries, and poets throughout the world from all times, the kind and skillful engineers are Ed and Deb, and the cars you ride in so comfortably are the spacious realizations of all the great meditators who carry you along.

I am just the conductor who sees you up the steps, shouts out "Aaaalll abooooaaaard!" and then swings up alongside you all! Congratulations for embarking on this very special and magical journey.

"Tenzin" Bob Thurman
Jey Tsong Kappa Professor of Indo-Tebetan Buddhist Studies,
Columbia University President, Tibet House, United States

Part I

||||

THE GREATEST
ADVENTURE OF ALL

I

| | |

Changing Me, Changing Us

*If you do not change direction, you may end
up where you are heading.*

LAO TSU

When we look at the world from the moon, as astronaut Edgar Mitchell explained to us, it is just a small round ball. As *Apollo 14* moved closer and the earth became larger, Mitchell's life changed forever. From exploring the far reaches of outer space, he began to seek a deeper meaning for his experience and turned to explore his inner world, which came to include meditation.

In a similar way, we both realized the importance of meditation early in our own lives in response to the need to find meaning in the midst of chaos. Ed was in his twenties; Deb was just fifteen. But even at that young age, we had already realized that some place of understanding and insight was missing.

More recently, when we first thought of this book, it was in response to a comparable need to make sense of what was happening all around us. At a time of economic downturn, with corruption on the rise and countries at war, we wondered what could bring greater awareness, kindness, and compassion to a world in so much chaos. Could something as subtle and understated as meditation possibly have any affect on business, the environment, conflict, or even politics? Could meditation make a big enough change in consciousness to transform the way we see ourselves, each other, and our world? And what change could happen if something so simple were to become a global movement?

Although we have personally had many years of meditation experience, in this book we wanted to paint a more colorful and varied picture by including other viewpoints and voices. So we spoke to more than one hundred meditation practitioners in various walks of life. They included teachers, activists, scientists, religious leaders, professors, businesspeople, film actors, artists, musicians, environmentalists, yogis, therapists, doctors, authors, and others. Our questions focused on how meditation had changed them, how it can change us, and how as a result we can then transform the world. Talking with so many remarkable people was truly mind-blowing! Everyone was deeply passionate about this subject and had something different to say, each experience of meditation was unique, and the understanding of how we can make a difference in this world was inspiring and expansive. Their valuable insights and answers are interspersed throughout the text, and you can read their biographies at the back of the book. In particular, what we learned from these multidimensional voices is that meditation is a very cool thing to do.

And we are not alone in thinking this. Cross-legged yogis and Buddhist monks can be seen in advertisements for everything from computers and credit cards to herbal teas, major newspapers and magazines carry stories on the benefits of meditation with tips from famous film stars, and no self-respecting bookshop is without a how-to-meditate section. In our local post office, on the wall behind the counter, fliers advertising meditation and yoga classes hang next to overseas postal prices.

Meditation has been the main focus of spiritual practice for thousands of years, but it is only in the last few decades that the general population has begun to realize how important and valuable this practice really is, regardless of spiritual or religious interests. We do not have to be a hippie or on a spiritual quest to meditate. We have taught everyone from housewives to athletes and musicians, and therapists to CEOs, in yoga centers and town halls, high school gymnasiums, corporate boardrooms, and on television.

However, this poses a conundrum. If meditation is so available and as well known as it seems to be, why is it not already an integral part of everyone's lives? If health reports are saying how good it is as a way to cope with stress, why do we ignore it or find excuses not to do it? And why do we think of something as a waste of time when all the research tells us it is of such immense value?

We Are Not Who We Think We Are

Perhaps you have heard this story about a frog and a scorpion:

One day a frog was sitting happily by the side of the river when a scorpion came along.

"Oh Mr. Frog," said the scorpion, "I need to get to the other side of the river to be with my family. Will you please carry me across?"

"But Mr. Scorpion, if I do that, then you will sting me!" replied the frog, somewhat aghast at the request.

"No, I won't," said the scorpion.

"Do you promise?" asked a rather doubtful frog.

"I really promise—I will not sting you," said the scorpion.

"Do you really, really promise?" asked a still-dubious frog.

"Yes, I *really* promise," replied the scorpion, very sincerely.

"Okay," the frog said reluctantly. "Hop on."

The scorpion climbed on top of the frog's back and they set off. Halfway across the river, the scorpion stung the frog. In horror, the frog, unable to continue swimming and with both of them about to drown, finally managed to gasp, "Please, Mr. Scorpion, just tell me one thing before we both go under. Just tell me why, when you promised you would not, why oh why did you sting me?"

"Because it is my nature," replied the scorpion.

With no intention of being derogatory to scorpions, this story shows how the nature of the scorpion appears unchangeable and fixed. It has no choice regarding its behavior because it is a scorpion; that is simply the way it is.

And most of us think we are just the same. We think we cannot change, that we are the way we are and that's that—this is who I am and I cannot change and I won't change! But where a scorpion is not necessarily able to act any differently, we can. We do have choices. We do not have to be the way we think we are; we can actually be and act differently. In the nineteenth century, philosopher William James said, "The great revolution in our generation is the discovery that human beings, by changing the inner attitudes of their minds, can change the outer aspects of their lives."

Dancing with the Ego

And we do so long for change, to be different, to be healthier or happier than we are—the grass always seems to be so much greener elsewhere. Or we want to change the world so that that women are not abused and there is less violence and poverty. This desire for change was the overriding message of the 2008 election when we witnessed a collective yearning for honesty, decency, and integrity.

It can appear relatively simple to make changes in the world, while making changes in our own lives can seem far more overwhelming. It takes courage to move from a familiar and known place to one that is different or without reference points, as it means stepping outside of our usual comfort zone.

So what is it that stops us from changing? What keeps us locked in ourselves, stuck in small-mindedness, thinking our view is the only view that matters? Invariably, it is the ego, the most talked about yet least understood of all our human features. The ego gives us a strong sense of ourselves; it is the "me" part. This is neither good nor bad, except when self-centeredness dominates our thoughts, feelings, and perceptions of life. A positive sense of self gives us confidence and purpose, but a more negative and selfish aspect of the ego makes us unconcerned with other people's feelings; it thrives on the idea of me-first and impels us to cry out, "What about me? What about my feelings?"

| ROBERT THURMAN |

"I think I'm the most important being in the world, but nobody else thinks it is about me, time doesn't think it is about me, space doesn't think it is about me, the planet doesn't think it is about me. It doesn't take much to get the message that it is actually not about me! But if somebody comes and steps on my toe or wants to take away my strawberries, then suddenly it is all about me again!"

By watching how we equate ourselves with images of who we think we are, or with labels that reinforce that image and make us appear special—"I am an American, Russian, Christian, Muslim; I am a teacher, doctor, divorcee, recovering alcoholic"—so the many manifestations of the ego appear before us. In the search for meaning, we hide behind our title, profession, or religion and become attached to the story the label creates, even introducing ourselves in terms of labels or only relating to others who identify themselves in the same way. Seeing through these illusions and being willing to give up our story is no small step. "There is such pressure to keep each of my identities, each of my labels intact," writes Joan Tollifson in *Bare-Bones Meditation: Waking Up from the Story of My Life.* "Why do I feel as if no one really knows me until they know my story? Tremendous fear arises at the thought of losing my labels, and at the same time there is immense peace in living without them."

The nature of the ego is to stay in control, and so it does all it can to keep us in the realm of me-ness. It is a remarkably good shape shifter and can take any number of disguises or appear in many varied forms, but its main job is to keep us distracted. For instance, it can make us believe we are the cleverest, the best informed and most important, as easily as it can make us feel unworthy, unlovable, not clever, or good enough to be happy. And it is this sense of self that is the root cause of so much distress, both in our own lives and in the world, as in its name wars are fought, families split, and friends forgotten.

| MINGYUR RINPOCHE |

"I think the main issue is the negative ego. If we do not understand other people's feelings, their suffering or behavior, then what we perceive, what we are concerned with, is only our own ego and image. If the ego becomes too strong, then it causes a lot of other emotions, such as anxiety, loneliness, depression, anger, jealousy; if we feel insecure, then our ego becomes even bigger in order to protect us. In this way, we harm others, as we have no respect for them. And that leads to fighting. Then the ego thinks that to defeat others is the way to survive: 'I have to be tough in order to reach my goals.' Maybe we will succeed once or twice, but eventually we will lose if we follow the ego."

Self-centeredness and selfishness, which are hallmarks of the ego, affect not only our own lives and relationships but also influence the way we behave in the world. There is no limit to the damage a strong ego can do, from the arrogant conviction that its own opinions are the only right ones and everyone should be made to believe in them, to wielding and abusing power at the expense of other people's lives or liberties.

The ego also makes us believe that we are the dust on the mirror, that we could never be so beautiful as the radiant reflection beneath the surface. Yet how extraordinary to believe that we cannot be free when freedom is our true nature! When we begin to see that such self-centeredness does not lead to happiness and we yearn for something more genuine, when we realize that the pit of meaninglessness and emptiness inside is never truly satiated no matter how much we feed it, or when we have just had enough of chaos and suffering, then the longing for change arises.

| LINUS ROACHE |

"I gave up acting so I could be real. Actors are full of pretense and I wanted to be more authentic. When performing the classics like Shakespeare, there is a unified consciousness with the audience where the inner and the outer are all one and you are sharing that one experience. It is quite profound. There are a lot of artists who reach such transcendence, but they have screwed-up lives. Actors are inherently full of ego and narcissism and so acting appeared contrary to the path of meditation and freedom that I was yearning for. So I stopped acting for two years.

"Until I realized that it is not just actors who are full of ego, everybody is! Everybody has their layers of pretenses and images of who they think they are. I finally saw that acting was not the problem; rather, it was my relationship to it that mattered. I could actually be a real, authentic person who also happened to act. The difference was the awareness of seeing that I am playing an ego, rather than being stuck in an ego. There is no separate spiritual life and working life and personal life. There is only one life. Without access to the inner dimension of freedom, I cannot be either an actor or a fully authentic person."

Hypothetically, all we need to do is to let go of the focus on "me," which is our sense of separateness, our need for distinction, the grasping and clinging to our story. Then we can retire the ego. But this is far easier said than done. In India, the ego is represented by a coconut as this is the hardest nut to crack. Traditionally, the coconut is offered to the guru or teacher as a sign of the student's willingness to surrender his or her ego and to let go of self-obsession. Such a symbolic gesture shows that the ego is considered to be a great obstacle on the spiritual path and an even greater impediment to developing true kindness and compassion.

Embracing Change

Mahatma Gandhi famously said, "You must be the change you want to see in the world." In other words, change has to start within ourselves; we cannot expect the world to change if we do not. If we want to have more love in our lives, we must become more loving; if we genuinely want to end terrorism and to bring real and peaceful change to the world, then we must start by ending the war within ourselves.

Emerging from three years in the Auschwitz concentration camp, psychiatrist Victor Frankl said that after his imprisonment and the destruction of his family, he had been left with only "the last of the human freedoms, to choose one's attitude in any given set of circumstances, to choose one's own way." That is the choice that each one of us has—a choice in how we live our lives, how we care for each other, and how we treat our planet. When we open to transformation within ourselves, so society also transforms—every change that each individual makes creates a chain reaction that is beneficial to all. Then, instead of focusing on the problems, we can start to live the solutions.

This brings us to the importance of contemplation and meditation. Without such a practice of self-reflection, we are subject to the ego's every whim and have no way of putting a brake on its demands. Meditation, on the other hand, gives us the space to see ourselves clearly and objectively, a place from which we can witness our own behavior and reduce the ego's influence.

| MARSHALL ROSENBERG |

"Meditation is staying conscious of one of the most important things to stay conscious of, and that is my internal programming in this moment.

There are four things that tell me it is time to meditate—depression, anger, guilt, and shame. They tell me my thinking is not where I choose it to be. When I stop, I can see what I am telling myself and I can translate this life-alienated, violence-provocative thinking into a life-serving consciousness and communication."

Instead of thinking that we have to somehow eradicate or annihilate the ego, through the practice of meditation we find that the more positive aspects are enhanced while the more self-centered aspects begin to fade in importance. As the need to be constantly engaged in the details of our own story loses its relevance, so the ego releases its grip and becomes less demanding. This does not mean that we become just like a doormat and let people walk all over us. Rather, we are able to communicate more openly and honestly, and to love more unconditionally. Where the ego makes us believe we are immutable and unchangeable, in truth our true nature is completely free, unbound and unfettered.

Peace in Action

Meditation changes us. From being self-centered, we become other-centered, concerned about the welfare of all equally, rather than being focused on just ourselves and our families. We become more acutely aware of how we affect the planet, how we treat each other and our world, and seek to become a positive presence rather than a negative one. As we find our own peace, we want to actively help others to also be at peace.

We were in India in 1986 when we first met HH the Dalai Lama, the spiritual and political leader of Tibet, winner of the Nobel Peace Prize, and probably the world's most famous meditator.

| DEB |

"We were waiting for our meeting in a room that led off a balcony at his residence, beyond which rose the Himalayas resplendent in the morning sunshine. Ed wandered outside to enjoy the view. At that moment, he saw a monk further along the balcony waving for us to come. We presumed this monk would bring us to our meeting. But as we came closer, we realized that this simple and unpretentious man was HH the Dalai Lama himself. Ed and I immediately began to prostrate on the floor, as this is the respected way of greeting such a revered teacher. But HH the Dalai Lama took our hands and made us stand, saying, 'No, no. We are all equal here.' At first, I thought, Oh sure! You are the great Dalai Lama, spiritual leader to millions, and I am just a student. How can we possibly be equal? But over the following months, I felt his words in the core of my being and experienced the true equality he was referring to—the equality of our shared humanness and, simultaneously, our shared heart."

In our ensuing conversation, we asked HH the Dalai Lama what we could do to encourage greater peace. He urged us to talk with people, to communicate with those from other religions, and to enjoy the richness of different cultures by bringing diverse viewpoints together. In this way, he believed, peace through understanding could become a reality. We can apply this same approach to our everyday experiences as, through meditation, we become more acutely aware of our own limitations and prejudices.

| CYNDI LEE |

"The effect of meditation can show up in real-life situations where maybe somebody is pushing our buttons and we would normally respond in an aggressive way, with a habitual response. When we have trained our mind, we can recognize what is arising in time to let it go, we can rest in spaciousness. In that gap, we can make a choice of the action we want to take, instead of thoughtlessly reacting. Without that awareness, we have no options."

Just as science propelled Edgar Mitchell to be able to walk on the moon, so science is now proving that meditation is a genuine way to generate peace by reducing potentially harmful emotions, such as fear and anger. We usually think of such mind states as a fixed part of life, but they do not need to be. Many negative emotions arise from the emphasis we place on success and achievement, which is a left-brain activity. During meditation, we engage the right side of the brain, which encourages us to communicate in a more positive and caring way.

| MINGYUR RINPOCHE |

"Over the past three years, I have been in discussion with professors from different universities and I have found out three things. Firstly, neuroplasticity shows that even if you are born with unhappiness, change is possible. Secondly, the best way to change the behavior of the brain's neurons from negative to positive is through daily meditation. Studies have shown tremendous changes in the left side of the brain of long-term meditation practitioners. And thirdly, the change in the brain from negative to positive is also very good for the physical body, such as the immune system or high blood pressure. All of this leads us to a deeper sense of peace within ourselves."

Integrating Change

To bring peace to those around us and to our world, we have to change from being concerned with our own needs to reaching out and helping each other. But for kindness and compassion to become a natural expression of who we are, we need tools— help, guidance, and support. Meditation in its many forms is the one tool we have found that does all of this. By getting to know ourselves, discovering that we are more than we thought we were, and by connecting more deeply with our essential self, we find that we have the resources, strength, and wisdom to not only make changes, but to become the change we so long for.

| MARIANNE WILLIAMSON |

"Einstein said that we cannot solve the problems of the world from the level of thinking that we were at when we created them. I think a lot of people embrace this concept, while underestimating what it really means. A different level of thinking means a different level of thinking. It does not even mean just a different kind of thinking. It does not mean a different emphasis in our thinking. It does not mean a more loving kind of thinking. It means what he said, a different level of thinking, and to me, that is what meditation brings.

"Meditation can change the world because meditation changes us. That is the point. The world will not change until we change. The state of the world is a reflection of who we are. The state of the world is the effect; the state of consciousness of human beings is the cause. Mahatma Gandhi said the problem with the world is that humanity is not in its right mind and that is what meditation addresses. It returns us to our right mind, and until there is this evolution in consciousness, we will stay locked in a fear-based perspective in which we continue to see ourselves as separate from each other, and in which we continue to think that we can do something to someone else and not reap the result ourselves."

In the following chapters, we explore the sanity and brilliance of meditation, how it affects the many aspects of our personal lives, and how it can change the world for the better. From reducing stress and illness, taming anger, and encouraging kindness and forgiveness, to confronting environmental issues and problems at work, to diffusing violence worldwide, meditation brings greater understanding and compassion wherever the meditator goes. It is a journey, sometimes a roller coaster, sometimes a walk in a gentle glade, but always an adventure to be enjoyed!

2

|||

So What Is Meditation?

To go out of your mind at least once a day is
tremendously important. By going out of your
mind, you come to your senses.
ALAN WATTS

| DEB |

"When I was fifteen years old, my mother took me to a meditation retreat. I have to admit I was a pretty wild teenager, my siblings were all elsewhere, and my mother had no intention of leaving me in London on my own. As I knew some of the people who would be there, and as she was only going for three days, I agreed. I had no idea what would happen or that it would change my life. I really didn't understand the teachings, the practices, or what I was meant to be doing, but the experience of sitting in silence was one of coming home, of feeling that I was exactly where I was meant to be. I sat for hours. My mother stayed for three days, but I stayed for ten. I did not want to leave; I did not want to be parted from this place of belonging. I was home again, and it was as if I had never left."

As it has gained popularity, so a huge amount has been written about meditation—what it is and what it is not, how to do it and how not to. Meditation has been associated with everything from affirming ourselves as thin/rich/in love to visualizing ourselves bathed in white light to sitting cross-legged with closed eyes and doing nothing but contemplating our own navel. Yet meditation is none of these. Rather, it covers a vast arena of experiences and activities, including opening our heart to all beings, realizing the truth and becoming free, counting our breaths, gazing at the flame of a candle, intoning different sounds, or moving rhythmically. It enables us to see our own limitations and self-centered nature more clearly, and to discover the depth and beauty that lies within us. In other words, it is both an experience and a practice—an experience of oneness, of being with who we really are, as well as the practice that enables us to be in this state.

| JOEL LEVEY |

"Meditation as a general term refers to practices developed in all the world's wisdom traditions that encompass many different forms. It is also about recognizing and being liberated from delusion, confusion, and an unrealistic view of reality, which helps free us from the forces of habit and addiction so we can awaken to our highest potential. The practice allows us to abide in harmony and congruence, with a sense of reverence for the mystery and majesty of the world in which we live."

THE EXPERIENCE OF MEDITATION

What is the experience of meditation? What does it feel like? What does it taste like? What are its effects? Does it change us? Why is it so special? Should everyone meditate? Further on in this chapter, we look at what the practice of meditation means, while later in the book we explore how to do it, in all its many forms and flavors, so that it can become an integral part of our being. But first we want to enter into the experience as deeply as the written word allows.

Merging into Oneness

Many of us experience meditation without necessarily realizing it. It can arise spontaneously in moments when a sense of ourselves as a separate individual appears to merge into a oneness with all life, as if our boundaries dissolve and we become one with all things—with the clouds in the sky and the birds swooping and the tree the birds are sitting on and the flowers at the foot of the tree and the rocks and the earth. This is a feeling of no solid self, as if all the ingredients that form this solid sense of "me" have dissolved and there is just a merging into or becoming one with everything. Yet this also feels very grounded, as if we are more ourselves than we have ever been before.

In such moments, there is no separation between ourselves and anyone or anything else because there is no longer a clearly defined, separate, ego-bound being. There is no longer an "I" being aware—there is just awareness. For Deb's mother, it occurred when she was washing the dishes and heard the sound of a wild bird's song; in that moment, she became the sound and lost any sense of being apart from it. For **Deb**, it occurred when a worm crawled over her foot:

"I was barefoot and had been walking slowly in meditation across the lawn. I stopped and was standing very still and silent when this worm crawled out of the earth and traveled across my foot before disappearing into the grass. I had never liked worms that much, but in that moment I firstly felt intense gratitude that it had deemed me safe enough to walk over, and then I suddenly became it; there was no difference or separation between us. I too disappeared into the grass."

For others, such an experience may occur while walking in nature or sitting in stillness and silence.

| JANE FONDA |

"I could never still my mind. And then as I was approaching my seventieth birthday, I thought the time has come. Part of the thing of getting older is that as the externals begin to fray, you are beckoned inward. As my mind became quieter in meditation, I discovered this place that seemed to be suspended behind my forehead, like a chandelier hanging from the top of my skull, where everything stops. It is this place of nothing, of stillness. I am aware of being there, but it isn't the same as thinking. And it is not like I can stay at that place all the time; I feel lucky if I can stay there for three or four minutes. There are sixty people in the hall, sitting silently, and I feel the power of their presence. I realize that we are all the same, as is the cat screeching in the backyard, the bird chirping, and the shiny black floor. I experience everything as ultimately one, that there is no separation. Meditation connects me to this great inwardness and unity, and at the same time there is also a great expansion into everything."

Moments of unity or merging might be fleeting, but they radically change consciousness, awakening us to a reality of oneness, connectedness, and inter-beingness. This affects our whole understanding and, in turn, our beliefs and behavior. In that space of sitting quietly, we meet ourselves in a different way, no longer bound by limitations but as a part of a much greater whole.

| DEBBIE FORD |

"Meditation is connecting to something bigger than myself. We meditate to have a shift in consciousness, to take us out of the limitations of our individual self, and to tap into the greater Self, where we are all one. It might sound like a cliché to say that because we have little clue what it means, but when you meditate, you do feel that connection. You know that to walk by somebody starving is to walk by yourself. You know that to judge somebody else is to judge yourself. In this place hope exists, possibility exists. This is where you know that we are here to have this human experience. Meditation is a process that makes the trip not only possible but also a little gentler."

The experience of releasing boundaries and merging into wholeness is one of great joy and immediate familiarity. It reminds us so completely of who we really are that we forget we had ever forgotten. There is just this, and it is far more real than our normal everyday reality. Consciousness is moved into greater awareness. We see the world in a new way.

| CHLOE GOODCHILD |

"When I think of meditation, it is self-remembrance; a remembering of myself behind the polarity of all the conflicts that I am faced with on the surface of life. Meditation involves the disappearing of the ordinary mind. It is a direct encounter with the spaciousness that exists within and between and beyond things. It is focusing and harnessing the mind in such a way that you just disappear into it."

When we have this experience of merging or being without boundaries, it brings with it not only a sense of deep relief and recognition, but is also something we can find very hard to name or express in words. We know it intimately in our every cell, but how do we explain the expansion of the identifiable self into all things? Is it possible to explain the smell of a rose to someone who lives in a desert? But where meditation may leave us wordless, recent scientific research can now speak for us by explaining what happens in the meditative process.

| SHANIDA NATARAJA |

"During meditation, we see an increase of activity in the area of the brain associated with focused attention and a decrease of activity in the parietal lobe area that really defines our sense of orientation in time and space. For instance, many people experience a loss of really knowing where the boundary is between self and non-self. Then there are brain cells in the parietal lobe that convey the ability to express ourselves in language, and so the decrease of activity here explains the indescribability of mystical experiences and why those who meditate say it is very difficult to put their experiences into words.

"Meditation is a particular brainwave pattern that brings about optimized brain performance and encourages a shift from the left side of the brain to the right side. The left-brain view of the world is, in essence, very fragmented—an isolated ego in a threatening world. The right side of the brain mediates more abstract and holistic thinking, so as we switch over, we become more aware of our interconnectedness with all life, and also more aware of who we are, what makes us tick, and of our strengths and weaknesses. There is a greater acceptance of self. From that stems a greater acceptance of and compassion for other people. These benefits are the result of a different way of perceiving, accessed through this switch from the left to the right side of the brain."

|||

Present Moment Awareness

Sitting still can easily appear boring, and at times we may even ask ourselves, "Why am I doing this? Why am I paying attention to myself? I have devoted my whole life to running away from my mind, engaging in every distraction, and now I am being asked to pay attention to this maddening thing?" Normally, we spend our time either living in regret and what-could-have-been or what-might-have-been or if-only, or in expectation of potential—the what-could-be or what-might-be. Just being in the present moment can feel a little disconcerting or contradictory; we are not used to just stopping and being aware of now.

| SEANE CORN |

"Meditation has always been simply (simply? Huh, I wish it was that simple!) the act of getting my mind focused in the present moment without being influenced by the past or the future. It is recognizing that the thing that so many of us seek we are seeking outside of ourselves in past relationships or future events, and that the thing that we are trying to embody is actually already embodied."

Of course, we can learn from the past. Often the most painful experience turns out to be our best teacher, and we can feel great gratitude as it taught us so much. However, memories can also be like comfortable old shoes we are reluctant to part with. There is no reason why we cannot put them on now and then and enjoy the familiarity, but we do not have to wear them every day. Constantly living in either the past or the future limits our capacity to be in the present with what is happening now.

| MICHAEL CARROLL |

"Ultimately, meditation is resting in the present moment and discovering how to be fully human. I think it only takes a few moments of sitting to realize that we spend a tremendous amount of time out of touch with our life, that we are typically rushing past our experience rather than actually living it, we are rehearsing what we want to say, recollecting what we should have done, hoping, fearing, having all kinds of internal dramas. Meditation trains the mind to recognize this internal drama, chatter, and panic; it gives us an opportunity to observe the charades. In so doing, we can discover a profound depth to our life that had gone overlooked."

The development of present-moment awareness, also known as *mindfulness meditation*, enables both the past and the future to drop away. It can be immensely liberating to have nothing going on but this very moment, to realize that nothing is happening, that nothing more is required of us than to just be fully here now. What a relief! Finally, we can really experience this reality just as it is, without expectation, prejudice, or longing. Someone once asked Ed if he had ever experienced another reality. He replied, "Have you ever experienced this one?" Have you noticed the dew on a spider's web, the taste of honey, or your own heartbeat?

| JON KABAT-ZINN |

"Mindfulness is the awareness that arises when we non-judgmentally pay attention in the present moment. It cultivates access to core aspects of our own minds and bodies that our very sanity depends on, as does our sense of well-being and our capacity to live wholeheartedly in this crazy world. To look deeply into this is where mindfulness—which includes tenderness and kindness toward ourselves—actually restores dimensions of our humanity. Because these dimensions of our being have never actually been missing, it is just that we have been missing them, we have been absorbed elsewhere. When your mind clarifies and opens, your heart also clarifies and opens. The whole world is already different, in a small but significant way.

"And mindful awareness is not missing the light shimmering in this moment from the snow hanging off the roof outside the window and from the hemlock tree beyond it, forming this incredible shape as it descends. It is not missing a look of delight in a child's eye because you are preoccupied with your own thoughts. And it is not being so self-centered that you fail to notice what is going on around you."

When we are fully present, the world in which we live becomes extraordinary, as if being seen and heard and touched for the first time, for we are without preconceived ideas or desires. There is just the experience. Like a child making the unknown known, we are simply with what is, while also impelled to know it more intimately, to explore and understand, even to become it.

| ANNE BANCROFT |

"Meditation for me is an amazement that whatever I am contemplating is there at all. How incredible that spring comes and the grass grows, or that a cup of coffee awaits me on the table, even that a table exists! It is awareness of the miracle that anything is. And I experience *that* it is, before I come to *what* it is. It is totally important in my contemplation to be filled by that it is. But whatever the mystery of its beingness, it also has a conventional existence here and now, an existence within language. So the second part of my contemplation is to do with knowing its everyday life: A table that is both a mystery and a table that is here and now."

Such presence defies our limited understanding of the world; it takes us out of the logical rational mind and into a place of just being, without judgment or idea of what should be. Stepping out of the thinking and conceptual mind, however, does not mean stepping into nowhere or nothing; it does not mean that there is no connection to a worldly reality. We do not become disconnected or cast adrift. Rather, it is stepping into sanity and, more importantly, into even greater connectedness.

| CONSTANCE KELLOUGH |

"To define meditation is to limit it by reducing it to a mental concept. You cannot define meditation just like you cannot define presence or grace or God. We know the mind always wants to define things, but the mind is conditioned by the past and so can only see the projected condition, rather than what is fresh and new in the moment. It also only sees in fragments, not in the whole, so anything that can be grasped by the mind is not the whole truth. To find truth, we come into stillness, for stillness is not personal. We cannot say, 'This is my stillness, and that is your stillness; I have this presence, and that is your presence.' We cannot claim ownership of stillness because it is everything. It pervades all that is. When we can move from separate, ego-based consciousness to unity consciousness, then we know the other as ourselves."

Simply being still in this moment, without attachment to or thought of before or after, invites a deep sense of completion, that there really is nowhere else we need to go. There is just awareness, now, here, in the moment, nowhere else. It is impossible to think of somewhere else as being better—the grass is vividly green exactly where we are.

Happiness and Compassion

A few years ago, we were in Thailand, attending a ten-day silent-meditation retreat in the middle of a coconut grove. Each day a Thai monk would come to teach, and each day he would ask us the same question: "Are you happier today than you were yesterday?" As he said this, a wide smile would fill his face because he knew that we were confronting numerous obstacles to happiness, and not just the ones in our own minds. As beautiful as the coconut grove was, we were living with mosquitoes, centipedes, and snakes, sleeping on wooden pallets, and had no food after midday. How were we expected to find happiness amidst such extremes?

Yet despite his humorous tone, the monk's question was a genuine one. We were on a meditation retreat. If we were not beginning to feel happier as a result, then what was the point of being there?

Every day for ten days, he asked us: "Are you happier today than you were yesterday?" This had the effect of highlighting the extent to which we were preoccupied with our own concerns, doubts, and conflicts, and even how difficulties can actually feel more meaningful than joy. How simple it was to blame physical discomfort for our lack of happiness! The question exposed how negative mindsets can dominate our way of thinking and how easily self-obsession can go unnoticed. It showed us how hard it was to trust happiness, even that we had forgotten what happiness meant.

But our monk was not just asking us if we were happier; he was teaching us that the very purpose of our being is to find the inner peace that is our deepest joy. He was saying that there is enough pain and suffering in the world already—the very nature of life includes change and unfulfilled desire and a longing for things to be different from how they are, all of which brings discontent and dissatisfaction. He was constantly emphasizing that through meditation, we could find a deeper contentment, one that is not dependent on anything or anyone, but arises naturally from within us.

| HIS HOLINESS THE KARMAPA |

"Meditation is very important and meaningful in my life, it is a very practical tool, but we need a clear understanding of why we are meditating. Generally, it is to cultivate the ability to place our attention one-pointedly on any given thing without distraction, and this is essential for traversing the path as it results in greater wisdom and realization. Meditation can also be of benefit to all our problems, but it has to be put to good use. We are all the same in wanting to be happy and not wanting to suffer, in that there is no difference between us, so we can help each other and all sentient beings. When we can live from this deeper level of awareness, it helps us go beyond attachment to immediate forms of happiness and to finding a more universal happiness."

From this place of inner cheerfulness, we awaken compassion. There is a reservoir of basic goodness in all beings, but although it is an innate part of our being, we often lose touch with this natural expression of caring and friendship. It is as if we become caught in quicksand, drawn or pulled into situations that are not always pleasant and can even cause suffering. In meditation, we see ourselves as we are, neuroses and all, but as the experience deepens, so too does our perception. We go from seeing our essentially selfish and ego-bound nature to recognizing that we are an integral part of a far greater whole, and as the heart opens we can bring compassion to our fallibility and humanness. From embracing ourselves with kindness, that compassion moves to embrace all others.

| ROBERT THURMAN |

"Meditation is a neutral and very powerful tool. The choice is what are we going to meditate on? Most people let themselves be guided by a culture that is trying to make them buy things or make them afraid through the news. When we watch television and we see a commercial, it is like a guided meditation on dissatisfaction. We have to guide our meditation in a positive direction. We do this when we meditate on freedom, on penetrating to the deep nature of reality. In other words, if we meditate on being egotistical, we will become more egotistical, but if we meditate on being selfless, we will become more caring and altruistic. When we experience ourselves as totally integrated with everyone, we are naturally going to be compassionate and kind to them."

In this way, meditation has the effect of lifting us out of the quicksand, out of misunderstanding and suffering. Through it we find our freedom from reactive, rash, and self-serving behavior. It is, therefore, the most compassionate gift we can give to ourselves. Having a more compassionate understanding is also vital to our development as a human race, as we emerge from ignorance into wakefulness.

| MATTHEW FOX |

"Meditation is calming the reptilian brain. We have all got three brains in us: One is a reptilian brain, which is about 420 million years old, our mammal brain is half that old, and our most recent one is the intellectual creative brain. The reptilian brain is very prominent; it runs our respiratory and sexual systems; it is action and reaction. We have to calm this reptilian brain so that the mammal brain, which is the brain of compassion and is here to bring kindness and kinship and bonding, can function. I mean, reptiles do not make good lovers; that is not their thing. Meditation allows us to treat the reptilian brain well: 'Nice crocodile, nice crocodile.' When we calm the crocodile, then the mammal brain can assert itself. Meditation is not just for professional monks; it is a survival mechanism for us all, especially in this time of crowdedness and rubbing shoulders with people of different faiths and traditions. We all have to learn to calm our reptilian brain."

III

Form and Emptiness

We live in a world that appears very real: I see the trees, I hold a glass, I drink my tea, gravity keeps us from flying into space, and the oceans are not in the sky. From this perspective, "form" applies to everything meaningful, graspable, discernible, and real. Emptiness, on the other hand, seems to imply an absence of anything meaningful, a state of nothingness that we do our best to avoid. It is often identified with fear and loneliness, even despair. Emptiness is something that we feel somewhere in the pit of our belly, and we spend a lot of time and money trying to fill this inner emptiness, to find meaning, to feel connected.

When we experience form and emptiness in meditation, however, a very different picture emerges, one that sees the inherent limitation in thinking of form as solid and real and the delusion that emptiness is either meaningless or void. Instead of solid, the world of form appears transient and impermanent, and rather than being pointless, emptiness appears rich, full, and inclusive of everything.

| JACK KORNFIELD |

"Emptiness is always here. It is the emptiness in the cup that makes the cup valuable, because into the emptiness, we can put our tea or coffee. It is the empty space in the room that allows us to move around. All things come out of emptiness. Form and emptiness are two sides of this mystery of existence itself. When we only focus on the world of form and hold onto things, we suffer. When we let go and rest in spacious awareness, and return ourselves to the emptiness from which things appear, we find a greater sense of ease and grace and flexibility and wisdom."

Sitting in the stillness of meditation we become very aware of emptiness, of the space within which everything is contained. Simultaneously, there is the awareness that form is both real and yet is constantly changing and dissolving. All life is being born, living, and dying in an endless continuum. HH the Dalai Lama suggests that we look at ourselves as we would look at a table, for instance, "Investigating its nature, searching among its various parts, and separating out all its qualities, we see there is no table to be found as the substrate of these parts and qualities."

When we do this with ourselves, we find that not only is there no definable, tangible self, but we also see how nothing can be owned or grasped. In truth, when we look closely at anything, from a piece of paper to an eighty-year-old man, we see that it is impossible to find a separate self that is entirely independent of any other conditions. Yet while empty of separate self, it is also full of everything. All things are contained in every single thing—the weather, the trees, people, and fish. All are involved in the making of every other thing or being.

This is the relationship of relative and absolute reality, where each one is contained within the other: Emptiness is in form and yet form is in emptiness, while all things are both form and emptiness at the same time.

| PONLOP RINPOCHE |

"Because of emptiness, everything is possible; if it is not empty, nothing is possible. Emptiness encompasses all existence and all nonexistence. But at the same time, everything is here. I was teaching emptiness and someone asked me, 'Does that mean your chair is also emptiness?' I said, 'Yes. Everything is emptiness.' So then he asked, 'Then how can you sit on the chair? Why don't you fall right through?' So I explained that he was mixing the two truths. He was putting my relative body on an absolute chair. This is a pillar, and that is the lawn, and this is a tree. We all agree on that. The pillar can help to lift the roof. There is no debate on that, no argument. Trees can give us oxygen; there is no doubt about that. Just as long as we do not look too closely, that can work perfectly fine. But as soon as we do look closely and clearly, then not even modern science can find anything solid and tangible; there is just emptiness."

Normally, attachment to form is the idea that there is separateness: A separate you and a separate me, and all emotions—both negative and positive—grow out of this assumption of duality. We identify ourselves with our thoughts and feelings and believe they constitute "me," just as we think that our body is "me" or my voice is "me." And we get very attached to the belief in who we think we are, so much so that we see this solid self as separate from anyone else, for they are not-me. But when we see such a solid sense of self as impermanent, constantly changing and interconnected, it means we see that not only is there no solid "me" but there is no solid "you" either.

| ROBERT THURMAN |

"I thought inside was a solid Bob, that there was a solid Bob-person in here, but when I look for that Bob, I cannot find any such thing. Bob is a word; it is a name only. I am empty of a solid Bob, but I am full of the incredible rich process of body and mind as multiple perspectives and angles. The fact that we are empty of any separate essence means that we are a totally inter-relational process. The material like this table that I can put my knuckle on now is just as much emptiness as the air between my knuckle and the table where my hand is poised. The seemingly solid knuckle and table are also emptiness. There is no absolute solid, and there is also no absolute intangible. When you look for the solid core of anything, you will find only emptiness, or non-duality."

We can see the mind as being like the sky that is inherently empty. Whether the sky contains clouds, rain, tornados, thunder and lightning, or sunshine or stars, it never stops being the sky. Behind all the various manifestations, the sky is simply the sky, always transparent. In the same way, we contain all thoughts and feelings, and yet we are not them either.

The great Indian sage Ramana Maharshi taught through stories, and one of our favorites that we often teach in our workshops is the one we call *movie theater*. When you go to a movie theater, before the movie starts, you see a blank screen. Then the lights go out and the projector goes on, the movie plays, and the drama begins. You may feel passion, sad or happy, angry or uplifted—all the emotions in the movie. Then the movie is over, the projector is turned off, the lights go on, and again there is the blank screen. Maharshi says how that blank screen is like our consciousness that is empty of content, while the world and all our feelings are the dramas that play in our minds.

| TIM FREKE |

"Meditation is simply being conscious of being conscious. It is recognizing that I am awareness witnessing sensations and thoughts coming and going. Awareness is this big empty space within which the moment is arising. When I recognize this, I stop seeing myself as just a body in the world, and I start becoming conscious of my essential nature as an emptiness that contains the world. As Tim, I am in the world, but as my deeper being, as the impersonal 'I' of awareness, the world is in me. So I am in this paradoxical state where I see I am both in the world and not of it. If I get lost in identification with my separate self, then I experience suffering and selfishness. But when I am conscious of my essential nature as the spacious emptiness of awareness, I experience a profound sense of oneness with everything and everyone. Awareness is the emptiness that contains my experience; I am this big space within which everything is arising just like in a dream. There is no difference between the presence of awareness and what it is aware of. They are not separate any more than space is separate from the things it contains or a dream is separate from the dreamer."

THE PRACTICE OF MEDITATION

Ultimately, meditation is spontaneous and natural, just as when we go to bed at night and sleep seems to come without warning. But the practice of meditation enables us to enter into the experience more deeply and easily. Practice is not an end in itself; rather, it is the means, like a ferryboat that takes us across a river. It enables us to meet and make friends with ourselves

| MARIANNE WILLIAMSON |

"It is not just that meditation practice helps me, but it is my maintenance. I can be as nuts as the next person without meditation; living in a world like we live in with the craziness and chaos and speed and technology, it takes work to retain our sensor in the midst of all that, and to me this is the most powerful tool for doing so. It is like physical exercise—you never get to the point with physical exercise where you actually like how your body looks, so you don't have to exercise anymore. Rather, if you like what exercise does for you, then you have to keep going because it is a good maintenance program. The same is true with meditation. If it has brought us to some place that feels good, it does not mean we can stop. Daily meditation is a daily visit to the truth about ourselves. When we meditate, we burn through the layers of delusion and the layers of fear that dominate consciousness. And we need to keep doing this on a regular basis."

The beauty of a regular sitting practice is the constant return to quiet stillness in a world of so much noise and distraction. Just as Deb first experienced it, the term *coming home* is often used to describe this feeling, as if we are returning to a place we did not know existed before, yet which feels instantly and intimately known and familiar. We can let go and just be here.

| GANGAJI |

"Meditation can mean really being focused on something, or it can mean letting go of all focus and simply being still. It is not a matter of saying, 'I am going to meditate,' it is more like 'I am just going to be here for a moment without doing anything, without following any thought.' And, in that, there is peace, a surrendering the mind's activity to this huge vast silence and spacious awareness. It is not anti-mind activity; it is simply that usually the mind is spinning round and round, so it is a stopping of that spin."

We usually think of freedom as a release from discipline and structure, yet the organization, routine, and order of a regular sitting practice creates a space within which we can find a truer liberty. A guided format gives us a place of grounded reference, while the repetition of practice acts as both a mirror reflecting those places where we are limiting ourselves and is a constant reminder of our true nature.

| TAMI SIMON |

"The formal practice of meditation is, for me, very important. It serves as a truth-teller, for without it, I can easily fool myself. As a driven-achiever kind of person, before I started meditating, I was unaware that most of the time I was driving situations, trying to push to do more. What I have found through the practice of meditation is that I can actually choose, at any given moment, to lean away from that need to be pushing and to rest in the back of myself. When I do that, I create the space for all kinds of things to happen, and for other people to be heard, and for the whole world to actually be heard through me, instead of living some sort of ego-driven self-centered existence."

|||

Thinking and Being

Although meditation is described as a practice that allows us to stop, be free from distracting mental chatter, to cut through our preoccupation and self-obsession, and to be at peace, in the process we also become aware of seemingly endless random-thinking patterns. Those wonderful moments of experiencing our true Self are invariably interspersed with what has been called a mind that is like a monkey bitten by a scorpion. In other words, the still spaces are edged by busy ones. Such busyness, however, need not become a distraction from meditation—instead, it can be an integral part of the experience.

| LAMA SURYA DAS |

"Meditation is not about getting away from it all, avoiding anything, numbing out, or stopping thoughts. Without trying to be rid of pesky thoughts, feelings, and sensations, we learn how to practice being mindfully aware of them in the immediacy of the very moment in which they fleetingly present themselves. We can cultivate mindfulness of any object: sounds, smells, physical sensations, perceptions. Everything is grist for the mill—even those things we find totally unpleasant."

As thoughts are a natural part of the mind's activity, we have little choice but to find a way to live with them. Trying to stop or repress them is impossible, but if we follow the thoughts, they soon multiply into chaos and we lose our stillness and become disheartened. Instead, we can cultivate the ability to simply witness and be aware of the flow of thoughts without getting caught up in the images or dramas they are leading us to.

| DAN MILLMAN |

"Many of us have tried meditation, but grew discouraged and, after a time, stopped practicing, maybe because it seemed boring or, more likely, we decided that we weren't good at 'quieting the mind.' But we don't need to quiet the mind any more than we need to plug up a bubbling hot springs. Hot springs bubble; it is their nature. Thoughts happen. Emotions happen. Weather happens. We may prefer certain thoughts, emotions, or weather over others, but none are directly controllable by our will. As we sit, we simply observe, we become awareness itself, we become the witness, aware of arising thought-stuff, emotions, images, physical sensations. Yet we do not react to any of it; we merely bear witness to passing phenomena."

As our attention is normally very externalized, so every moment is filled with distractions and activity. We rarely have the spaciousness to internalize, and, therefore, to see how full of thoughts and emotions our mind really is. As such, when we first witness the busyness and clutter of our internal world, it can be a bit disturbing. And yet this noise is quite natural—it is just the noise of the mind at work.

| SAKYONG MIPHAM |

"Even though our mind is always like this, when we first begin to meditate we might say, 'Meditation is terrible. It has made things worse for me.' Nothing got worse; we just stopped and noticed our mind. That is all. It is like getting out of the car on the highway and realizing how fast the traffic is moving."

As meditation is not separate from life, we find that it includes everything that life does—every mood, feeling, and distracting thought—all will arise and make themselves known. A meditation session challenges us to find our way through such discursiveness to the peace that is behind and beyond, just as we can see beyond the clouds or raging storms to the sky that holds it all. We find our way by being the observing witness, and through present-moment awareness.

| JOSEPH GOLDSTEIN |

"I experience a settling into the body, becoming aware of the simple process of breathing, of the different energy sensations in the body, and then of what is arising in the mind—thoughts, feelings, and emotions. I try to stay present to all of it, instead of being lost in all the movies of the mind. At times, I become aware of awareness itself. It is quite an amazing experience not to be lost in the content of the mind but to simply experience the nature of awareness."

There are always moments, however, when it can be difficult to stay connected to being the witness. Sitting quietly creates the space for unfinished or unhealed issues to be seen, and they can, at times, dominate our meditation session. This provides a great opportunity to work more closely with ourselves in order to resolve and heal emotional or psychological concerns.

| SAKYONG MIPHAM |

"In this culture, if we sit and do nothing, people think we are strange. In places like Tibet, where there is a tradition of meditation, sitting still is considered to be courageous. People appreciate that when someone is meditating, he is working with his own mind, which can be challenging. Meditation is proactive. We develop a stability of mind with the intention of making that the basis of our activity. Sitting in silence, we observe thoughts and emotions pouring through our mind like a waterfall. Aggression, jealousy, and desire; they all come and go."

With a practice of self-reflection we have an opportunity to see such strong emotions in a clearer light. In mindfulness meditation, awareness shows how our thoughts are reflected in the world around us, that we are not separate from each other, that what affects one person affects us all. Releasing attachment to ourselves by seeing the illusion of solidity means that we are then able to heal negative thinking and transform it into care and kindness, both towards ourselves and others.

| BYRON KATIE |

"For me, meditation means questioning the stressful thoughts that cause all the suffering in the world. Eventually, we come to see that everything outside is a reflection of our own thinking. Our mind is the storyteller, the projector of all stories, and the world is the projected image of the thoughts we are believing. When the mind believes what it thinks, it names what cannot be named and tries to make it real through the name. It believes that its names are real, that there is a world out there separate from itself. That is an illusion. The whole world is an effect of mind. Inside and outside always match—they are reflections of each other. When we are shut down and frightened, the world seems dangerous or in peril; when we love what is, everything in the world becomes the beloved. After the mind deeply questions and sees its own thoughts, it surrenders to itself and experiences a world that is kind and absolutely saved, the benevolent mind projecting a benevolent world. The mind can no longer validate suffering on this earth, because it has ended suffering within itself. It becomes completely loving, completely free of identification."

|||

Religion, Contemplation, and Prayer

The Buddha sat under a Bodhi Tree and made a declaration that he would not move until he had conquered his own mind. He was committed to awakening to freedom—to be fully, unequivocally enlightened—and that commitment was unshakable. His method to realize such awakening? Sitting in stillness and silence. Among the world's religions, he is known as a master of meditation, and those who live according to his teachings are encouraged to meditate every day.

Other religions also have, at their core, a practice of meditation, silent contemplation, or prayer. For instance, Quakers sit together in silence at their meetings. There is no specific leader, but if anyone at the meeting is moved to say something, then they simply stand and speak into the silence. **Deb's** grandparents were Quakers:

"As a child, I would sit with them in meeting for the last fifteen minutes, when the children came from their Sunday School and joined the main group. I used to squeeze in next to my grandfather, and instantly I felt I was merging into the silence. One day my grandmother was moved to speak. She stood up and said quite emphatically, 'Even if it is a cloudy day, the sun is always shining!' Then she sat down. Being a child, I was highly embarrassed and longed to giggle, but the silence simply absorbed both her words and my laughter."

Although the religion and the form may differ, in practice the result is often very similar. This is one of dissolving the ego or individual self into the greater whole or true Self.

| FATHER THOMAS KEATING |

"For me, meditation is non-conceptual prayer, a relationship with God that emphasizes the heart rather than the mind. It presupposes a certain preparation of all the other faculties, so that our whole person with all our knowing and loving is persuaded to join in the transformative pursuit. It is the search for higher states of consciousness or the presence of God. Contemplation is a form of non-conceptual prayer, and it emphasizes being rather than doing. It is the intimacy that arises in the practice of cultivating interior silence."

The few differences that there are between prayer and meditation are both subtle and yet important, for they demonstrate a recognition of the many forms in which stillness and silence can manifest.

| MATTHEW FOX |

"The essence of prayer is gratitude and praise and thank you. As the German mystical theologian, Meister Eckert, says, 'If the only prayer you say in your whole life is thank you, that would suffice.' The essence of meditation is being still, and out of the stillness there comes a new level of prayer. It works the other way too, as all healthy prayer encourages stillness and silence. So it is not as if prayer and meditation are in competition at all. They both need silence. That is why meditation is a very important dimension of prayer.

"If you think of God as a being in the sky, if you think theistically that I am here and God is out there some place and I am talking to this being called God, or I am asking this being called God as some kind of Santa Claus, then that is theism. I prefer to say that all is in God and God is in all. It is like fish in the water and water in the fish. So what is prayer in that context? It is not about asking for something or projecting onto another being out there someplace. Jesus taught this when he said the kingdom of God is among you and is within you, or, as in the Gospel of Thomas, the kingdom of God is spread out in the world. It moves beyond dualism. So prayer in that context is about swimming in the presence of the divine, or like being on a raft on a rushing river. You are not steering; you are going along for the ride. And you know that something greater than you is working through you, and it's a trip. It's a spiritual trip. It is meditation in its deepest form."

Meditation practice can also take the form of recitation, whether it be chanting a sacred name or word or intoning scripture, and allowing the words to permeate every cell of our being. The silence that follows such intoning can be both moving and deeply profound.

| RABBI TIRZAH FIRESTONE |

"My practice is using the sacred word, but then taking it as a springboard into the deeper states. Because I was raised with Hebrew and I know the power of each letter as a mystical being, the words themselves are an immediate lift-off. My meditation starts with enunciating these powerful words in God's name, and then falling into silence, and it means accessing the oneness where I am no longer Tirzah with my busy mind, my shopping list, and all the things I have to do. Flipping into an impersonal zone is what I call big mind, the *mochin d'gadlut*, or accessing the oneness, which is what all prayer in Judaism is about. It is about going there. Listen. Get quiet. Remember. Go into this place."

Whatever the form, eventually it is simply finding that which works for each of us. It may be through silence or prayer or quiet repetition of a sacred word, through following the breath, through walking or moving with awareness. Or it may be a combination of them all. Or it may just be sitting with whatever presents itself.

| ELLEN BURSTYN |

"Wherever I go, I always have a little altar with candles and some kind of icon. Sometimes my icons are Christian—Jesus, Mary, or both—sometimes they are Hindu, like Ganesh, sometimes they are Sufi. I might read scripture or poetry before I meditate. After a long time of being in Sufism, Jesus kept coming back to me. Every time I sat down to meditate, whatever I was doing, Jesus always came and sat in my mental screen or sat in a lotus in front of me like a yogi. Whatever else was going on, Jesus was there. So finally I said to myself, 'Let's face it, you are a Christian.' So then I kind of stopped doing the other practices so much, and now I just sit with Jesus. I close my eyes. He always approaches, sits in front of me, and we kind of sit knee to knee. We sit quietly together and I breathe in his presence. Sometimes I actually ask a question, and sometimes he answers in words, and sometimes he just breathes with me. The answer to every question always seems to be love and it is always a deepening of peace."

|||

3

|||

How We Got Here

*As the philosopher Socrates once said, the unexamined
life is not worth living. But the opposite is also true. The
unlived life is not worth examining.*

SWAMI BEYONDANANDA

We all have a story to tell, a unique and very personal history.
Some are sad, others happy, some contain something we over-
came that made us a better person: a difficult childhood, an
alcoholic father, a mother who raised us on her own. But what
is the difference that makes one person a hero and another
a threat to society; what brings someone to meditation and
takes another to war? What is the motivation or circumstance
that impels us to do something like meditation, something that
appears so inactive or even self-centered? Why would anyone
want to sit on a cushion, close their eyes, and count their
breaths or beads, or stare at a wall? When Ed was living at the
ashram in India, a young monk would often tease him, saying,
"You are always sitting in meditation; why don't you get up
and do something constructive!"

And why would someone travel as far as India, Thailand,
or Japan to train? What is the impulse that draws us to search

out places to sit still and contemplate the endless chatter in our own mind—a mind that can, at different times, feel equally depressed, anxious, frustrated, and meaningless? It seems like it would be much easier to ignore all this in the hope that it will just go away. Why is it that we go in search of something that often appears inane and unexplainable? And how can sitting on a cushion with our eyes closed be beneficial to us or to anyone else?

Many of the people we spoke with for this book have a personal history of emotional dysfunction, drug abuse, illness, or depression; some were suicidal or spent time in jail. When such a background is used as fuel for personal transformation, then it is known as *spiritual boot camp*, as despite, or perhaps because of, the inner torment, it becomes the impetus for real and meaningful change. Meditation can be integral to that change as a catalyst that enables us to move from a place of suffering to one of awareness, healing, and clarity.

This does not mean, however, that a conflicting childhood or extensive drug use is necessary in order to be motivated to discover meditation or to become more self-reflective. It is an incentive, yet so also is the quest for a deeper understanding of life. There are many who have had perfectly uneventful lives, yet who have a yearning to find a more significant purpose, or to look more closely into the eternal question: Why am I here?

| ED |

"From an early age, I always questioned the absurdity of life being so capitalistic, the materialistic dream of acquiring more and more things. It always appeared so inane. No matter how much people had, they still didn't seem happy or content. There had to be something more."

Conflicting Childhood

Growing up with an abusive or absent parent, in poverty, or without any emotional stability are just some of the ways emotional dysfunction manifests. When this happens, in general we have three choices: to perpetuate the same type of behavior in our own life, to ignore or deny our feelings so that we live without really knowing ourselves, or to use the experience as a means for transformation.

Both of us fall into this latter category. At times, we have needed help to understand and open to forgiveness, but we have both come to realize that by experiencing what love is not, we were able to discover what love is.

Ed grew up in a small, one-bedroom apartment in the Bronx in New York City. He recalls:

"My mother died five days after I was born, so then, according to an old Jewish custom, my father married her older single sister, my aunt Mildred. It was primarily to look after his children. I only found out that my mother had died when I was about nine or ten and we were at our neighborhood synagogue. We went to an orthodox temple where the men sat in the main area and the women sat on the side, separated by a curtain. I was sitting with the men when an elderly man approached me and insistently asked, 'Why are you here? Now is the time to say a prayer for the dead. Is your mother alive? Is your father alive?' I said 'Yes.' So he shouted at me to get out. But as I walked past my aunt Rose, she yelled at me, 'Where are you going?' When I repeated what the man had said, she again shouted, 'Go sit down; you don't have a mother!' I was totally blown away, shocked and confused. Who was the person I was calling mom? I can still see the scene today.

"There were five of us living in this very small Bronx apartment. I don't know how we did it. There was no apparent love between my father Harry and stepmother-aunt Mildred, so I did not know that love existed in a family setting. Mildred was known as the neighborhood screamer; you could hear her shouting at us from down the block. I would always pray no one could hear. My father worked nights at the post office, leaving for work when I came home from school. It was probably so he could avoid being with Mildred, but it also meant I rarely saw him and even more rarely had a conversation with him. At the dinner table, we always fought to be heard; it felt like constant chaos. I never had a toy. One day, I was given a gun and holster set, and Mildred returned it for a school briefcase. All I wanted to do was play outside in the street, but I would be punished for anything a neighbor said I did, even if it wasn't true. One of my greatest embarrassments was that Mildred seemed so old with gray hair and, at that time in the 1940s and early 1950s, woman dressed like older ladies. People would always say to me, 'Little boy, is that your grandmother?' I would cringe and say no; she is my mother. I didn't know that she was not.

"By the time I was in my early twenties, LSD and flower power had come on the scene, with Tim Leary telling us to tune in and drop out and spreading the word of the League of Spiritual Discovery. I innocently and happily found myself a part of the hippie generation as it was in such contrast to my childhood. I would hang out at Studio 54 or go to be-ins with Allen Ginsburg. Acid trips were awakening my consciousness, and I was having spiritual experiences but did not have a clue what they meant. It was not until teachers from the East arrived in the United States that I was able to get some understanding. The Maharishi was brought by the Beatles after they met him in India at the same time that Sri Swami Satchidananda was brought to New York from Sri Lanka by the artist Peter Max. Swami Satchidananda told the hippies to clean up and do yoga and meditate, to find joy naturally without drugs. He questioned our LSD tripping and told Tim Leary, 'If a pill can make you a saint, then a pill could make you a doctor, an engineer, a lawyer, or schoolteacher, because it is much more difficult to be a saint.'

"I lived in a commune in upstate New York, and we would meditate together. I began to understand that there is an inner self that is free, uncontaminated by the chaos and confusion of past conditioning. Then I met Swami Satyananda, a yogi from India, and he invited me to train with him at his ashram, the Bihar School of Yoga. It seemed like the only way I could resolve my past and find any real meaning to life.

"So from the 'flowers-in-your-hair' hippie life in New York, I went to the yoga ashram in India. To my surprise, when I got there, no one was particularly loving or even very nice. In fact, they were very hard to be with— they were quite cold, bossy, rude, and unfriendly, and I was confronted on every level with discomfort. I really wondered what I was doing there, but I knew that if I could pass this test, if my meditation practice could stabilize my mind so these people could not adversely affect me, then I would be free. It is one thing to sit and be quiet in a cave, but can we be peaceful in the midst of chaos, difficulty, and confusion? The ashram was one of my most important teachers, the training, discipline, and hours of meditation the greatest of gifts.

"It was many years later that I crashed. I had been chasing the light, believing we were the beautiful ones, that everything was wonderful. But I had not yet faced my shadow, where the remnants of my past lay. I was living in England, which was a bigger challenge than I had anticipated and gave rise to an even bigger shift in my mental state. I had to be with just me and, as much as I had years of spiritual training behind me, this was a different level of confrontation. I lost the plot and spiraled into a black hole. There were three things that helped me through this part of my life: my tireless wife, my friend and therapist Maura, and meditation. I retreated into the quietness within and, slowly, slowly, I found myself again."

Growing up in the English countryside might sound idyllic, but for **Deb** it was an emotional roller coaster. Having an angry, sometimes violent father led to a disjointed existence, both at home and away at boarding school:

"We had no traditional family home as we moved constantly, living in numerous places, both before and after my parents' divorce when I was six years old. My father was an irate, emotionally volatile, and absent parent, and there was little affection between us. When I was about five, he had bought a new car, so we went for a ride to get milkshakes to celebrate. On the way back, about a mile or so from home, I threw up all over the backseat. He was so angry he stopped the car and made me get out before driving away and leaving me there on my own. It was a while before my mother was able to come and get me.

"When I was eight, I went to boarding school. By then, my mother was a single parent so it was probably the best place for me to be, but I did not enjoy school or the split life that boarding school imposed. Dormitories are loveless places. There was no stability, no consistency. And I always felt different, like I was the odd one out, preferring to read or write poetry than go partying. It felt like no one really knew or understood me, as if I was locked in this solitary world inside while the real world went on around me. My grandparents provided some sense of steadiness as I would often stay with them during vacations. My grandfather was a lover of words; he wrote the Charles Dickens encyclopedia, and was the editor for Winston Churchill at Cassell's publishing house. He seemed to understand my inner torment, and we would write poetry together, but he died when I was thirteen. I left school at fifteen as education seemed irrelevant. I was looking for something that could not be found in a classroom. At that time, my mother took me to the meditation retreat I mentioned in the previous chapter. It was the only thing that made sense, that put everything in its right place, and that finally gave me a sense of belonging."

Extreme poverty can be a major cause of dysfunction, resulting in a lack of education, anger and violence, hopelessness and worthlessness. But it can also be a spur to finding a deeper meaning to life, as **Deepesh Faucheux** explains:

"I had a very chaotic and insecure childhood because my family was so poor. We lived in a Mexican-American ghetto in Houston, where you could not walk down the street safely. I sought refuge in the Catholic Church. There, I found spectacle, ritual, and this window into history so colorful and substantial that it was like a lighthouse in the storm. It was so completely different from everything else I knew that I spent all my time there. One of the most destructive elements of poverty is the lack of hope; when you are that down, you do not know that there is an up. The church gave me an up; it gave me hope, motivation, the possibility that there was more than just pure survival. Compared to the chaos of my home and my neighborhood, the church was a sanctuary where I could seek refuge. It gave me a whole different way to look at the world, much bigger, more profound. None of the rest of my family was involved, but I loved it. The whole atmosphere of the church, especially going there as an altar boy at 6:30 each morning to serve mass, was very contemplative; there would be all these old people doing their beads. I learned Latin; I learned the Bible inside and out. I went to Catholic school, and after my first year of college, I joined the Order of Priests at the university.

"That first year was beautiful. It was all contemplation and silence. The next year, when they sent us back to the university, I lived in a cloistered

house but I did classes with all the other students. It was a very tumul-
tuous time during the second Vatican counsel with Pope John the 23rd, the
whole reform of the church, and it was very difficult to be in the seminary.
The younger and older priests sitting in the dining room were kicking each
other under the table. They were literally fighting over doctrinal matters,
the old ones competing for the hearts and minds of all the young seminar-
ians, of which I was one. We felt caught in the middle between the old
conservative church and the new upheaval. The civil rights movement was
distracting us and eventually we left *en masse*.

"In retrospect, I now realize that what I was attracted to in those early
days of the church was the meditative state induced by the incense, the
chanting, the ritual, and the spiritual exercises of St. Ignatius practiced in
the monastery. This altered state gave me the courage I needed to go
beyond the limitations imposed by my childhood world."

Experiencing parental violence and emotional turmoil can
either make us equally angry, or it can turn us inward, asking
why and constantly searching for answers. For some, at the
moment they needed it, the right person was there to answer
their seeking. **Jack Kornfield** recalls:

"I had a lot of family pain. My father was violent and abusive, and we were
all frightened of his unpredictable rage and beatings. I also had a deep
sense, as most young people do, that there was something more to the
world than materialism and the superficial level of success in our culture.
When I was a college student, I encountered a wonderful old Chinese professor who would sometimes sit cross-legged on the desk and lecture on
Lao-Tzu and the Buddha and Eastern wisdom. His teachings touched my
heart and gave me a sense that although there is suffering, there could also
be an end to suffering. What a revelation!

"He taught how there is a way to work with the difficulties of life, that
we can transform both our inner life and our relationships in the world.
That inspired me to go to Asia to find a monastery. I joined the Peace Corps
in the 1960s and asked them to send me to a Buddhist country because I
knew I wanted to go into a monastery, perhaps in Nepal or Thailand. I was
fortunate enough to end up in northeast Thailand, near the border of Laos,

in an area that had some of the great old forest monasteries still operating deep in the jungles along the Mekong River Valley. There, I found extraordinary meditation masters and communities of practitioners."

The blatant insincerity of many adults can lead some people to great disillusionment and, therefore, to seek for meaning elsewhere. When the right role model does appear, they will do whatever it takes to emulate them. For example, **James Gimian** remembers:

"As a teenager, I felt there was this huge shortcoming as people seemed to be taking the movie on the screen as reality, whereas I saw that there was an empty quality to it all. I tried everything from intellectual inquiry to drugs to find out what was behind this veil of appearance that I was both intrigued and confused by. I spent most of the time tearing down the authority figures in my life because they didn't carry with them that kind of experiential emptiness about the world, or to put it another way, they didn't walk their talk. The appearance that they presented, the words they spoke, did not hold up to their behavior when they were offstage, so all their words became meaningless and could not convey anything very profound, yet they seemed to believe in them and expected everyone around them to also believe in them.

"When I finally met somebody, who happened to be a meditation teacher, for whom there was no difference between the person I saw in front of me and the person they were offstage, I figured, well, if meditation was the way to be able to be like that, then it was what I had to do in my life."

|||

Drugs and Addiction

The use of hallucinogenic drugs to alter consciousness has been an integral part of many different cultures throughout the history of humankind. They can "open the doors of perception" as Aldous Huxley wrote, beyond the reality we are faced with each day; they can reflect aspects of our mind we had no conscious awareness of and stimulate the desire to know more. But other drugs, such as barbiturates, cocaine, or meth, can lead to our being pulled into a dark place within ourselves and to the slippery road of addiction. The journey out of addiction to these is a tough one, but it can also be a powerful teacher that awakens us to the truth of who we are. As **Debbie Ford** admits:

"I can't get rid of my fear; I am one of the biggest scaredy cats on the planet. How do I love myself when I am scared to death? I embrace the light, but it is not there to deny our human existence. How would we evolve? Can you imagine if we were the Stepford wives all walking around with these plastered smiles? No, we are here because we are suffering; we have pain because something is lacking or missing. Thank goodness for lacking and missing! It makes us open up. It has us expand.

"I got here through a lot of pain and a lot of suffering. I really thought I was all of my stories and dramas and limitations and insecurities and worries and fears. I bottomed out of my life with drug addiction. I used drugs to fill a deep hole inside me, and I was a bad user for about thirteen or fourteen years. I found a lot of ways to abuse, all different kinds of drugs—cocaine, valium, quaaludes. I wasn't a picky drug user; I would use whatever there was, even sugar and Coca-Cola. I also went on the chase for success. I opened my first clothing store when I was just nineteen. I was addicted to money and to wanting more and to fantasy and to men.

"Eventually, I had to find some meaning to my life. I started to ask, 'Who am I? What am I doing here?' I knew that drugs did not work because my life was so out of control. I went through four treatment centers. Finally, it was meditation that allowed me to see that I wasn't my story. I wasn't my pain, I wasn't my suffering, I wasn't my skinny legs, I wasn't my defects. That I was bigger than all of it, that I was connected to this collective soul, this collective heart. I give thanks every day that I was a drug addict. I say thank you to all my addictions. That hole that I felt, that emptiness inside, it made me who I am today."

When we are faced with personal difficulties or loss, we often look for an escape or a way to avoid our pain. Drugs can fill this need. But at the same time as obliterating the pain, they can also disconnect us from our own reality and send us into a downward spiral.

| KRISHNA DAS |

"In 1973, when my teacher Neem Keroli Baba died, I lost it. He was my source of happiness and he was now gone. I was lost for eleven years. I got addicted to cocaine; I was totally strung out; I was like a burnt-out building. I got very self-destructive and harmful for a very long time. In 1984, I began to reconnect with myself and realize it was okay to be alive. I started doing therapy and other things to try to lighten my load a little bit, but it was another ten years before I began to really heal by chanting.

"Chanting is meditation as you are engaged in a concentration practice; if you start thinking about something while you are chanting, you have only one option, which is to let it go and come back to the sound. I started chanting for this very reason. In 1994, I was standing in my room in New York and suddenly I knew that if I did not start chanting with people, putting my ass out there in a public way, I would never be able to access the dark corners of my heart and I would never be able to clean them up. I knew chanting was the only tool I had available. As a result, the front room is now easier to live in."

A combination of a dysfunctional family and drug use can take us into places of continuing rebellion, anger, and denial. It can also take us to a place from which we cannot escape back into destructive old habits—jail.

| NOAH LEVINE |

"I was in jail for maybe the twelfth time; I thought I was probably going to be in prison for a really long time for robbery, drugs, you name it—I had done it. I had all the mental torture about how much worse life was going to get, and all of the suffering from the past—the shame, guilt, and regret, the remorse, anger, vengeance, and resentment—all were playing out in my head. I was seventeen years old, but they didn't put me in prison. They said, 'We are just going to keep you until you are eighteen and then we will let you go. But if you get busted again, we will send you to adult prison.' I was in the juvenile jail for about four months, and then they put me into a kind of group home, like a youth shelter, keeping me off the streets.

"I was already acknowledging how much I hated myself and everyone else, and having to admit the pain of that hate. I had had enough suffering, and I knew that the avoidance, intoxication, the greed, and the hatred had failed me. None of it had worked to find any sense of happiness. As a matter of fact, it had created more suffering on top of the already difficult human experience. I had built-in rationalization and denial and total identification with my ego. But something happened that last time in jail, where I broke through and there was what alcoholics call a *moment of clarity.*

"It came in the form, for the first time in my life, of taking responsibility for my actions. As long as I had been blaming everyone else, feeling like a victim in this punk-rock rebellion mode, and as long I was in denial and blame, I was hopeless. I could not change because I was stuck. But that last time, in 1988, I was looking at my third felony with a suspended seven-year prison sentence, and at that point something started screaming inside me: 'This isn't everyone else's fault! You are the one taking the drugs! You are the one committing the crimes! You are the one doing the same thing over and over and expecting it to be different!'

"With that internal realization came an inkling of possibility, of 'I got myself here, maybe there is something I can do to get myself out of this mental place.' Then my father called and said, 'You are locked up again. Why don't you try meditating?' I had no answer, no reason not to. Getting the meditation instruction gave me a little hope. The immediate result was a relief from the future and the past. One breath at a time. Half a breath at a time. Even that half a breath was a welcome relief.

"I think I used meditation those first couple of years the way a lot of people use prayer, which is the sort of foxhole prayer, only when it gets bad enough. Like, 'Oh God, please get me out of this one. Save me this time, I will be good, I promise.' When I got stressed out, when I got afraid, when I couldn't sleep at night, when my mind got too loud and abusive, *then* I would bring my attention back to the breath. I was never too disciplined about a daily practice until a while later when I realized that my problems went way deeper than having been a drug addict. I was free, and within a couple of years, I had all of the things that I thought would make me happy. I had the motorcycle and the low-rider car and a beautiful girl-friend and the great apartment, and I thought, Now I will be happy! But I was still miserable and my ego was still running the show. And I still did not know how to not steal, I didn't know how to tell the truth, and I didn't know anything about generosity or humility. I was still in that dysfunctional survival mentality.

"The turning point for me was when I got in trouble for doing graffiti spray painting all over the city—$20,000 worth of damage. I almost got sent to prison for that. It led me to a place that finally said, 'The only thing that I have ever done in this life that has ever worked is meditation. It is the only place where I have ever really found relief.' Meditation showed me how confused I had been. It reminded me to just be in the present moment. And it brought a slow transformation as I learnt how to tell the truth, to be generous, to be kind, and to be forgiving. I believe all serious spiritual practice is a revolutionary act. The term *revolutionary* means to revolve, to turn over. It certainly turned me over."

|||

Stress and Illness

We tend to take our physical bodies very much for granted and our physical health even more so. As a result, when something goes wrong, it can be alarming, even frightening. We ask ourselves, "Why is this happening to me?" as if we had been walking around inside a stranger, only to suddenly discover that our body has a mind of its own. Touching our mortality, however, is often the time that transforms us the most, the moment that awakens us to a more meaningful reality. As **Marc Ian Barasch** recounts:

"I was editing the *New Age Journal* and so I was on top of the world. I wasn't just a successful magazine editor; I was a *New Age* editor! I had a lot of traditional ambition and arrogance, and with this job, I felt like I had the world at my feet, that I had arrived somewhere special. When you are in a position of power, you tend to look at people in terms of their use; in the case of an editor, you need someone to give you a good story on time, and if she does then you like her and if not then you don't like her. And then I got cancer. Suddenly, I was no longer in that position and instead I had to accept that I really needed people. But when that happens you are confronted with how much love you have given to others because that is what you get back. I found that a lot of my relationships—ones that I had assumed were based on kindness and compassion—were actually based on air as people ran the other way. When people did come forward, it was like a gem in the dirt, a ruby in the dust.

"I had to learn to love myself in a state that I was not proud of: unemployed, sick, unable to get well quickly, and get back on the train. It was very humiliating to realize that I had hit rock bottom with nothing to fall back on, no resources, nothing. When you fall from a position of pride, how do you keep equanimity and generosity? It gave me a far greater appreciation for the human condition and human suffering. For my own health and sanity, I had to not only create a healthier story and narration, but then I had to give up the narration entirely and just see what life would bring. I did not know if I would ever emerge from the place I was in, so I had to just be where I was, and that became my meditation and my healing. To just be with what was."

Medical doctors tend to be open to the idea of meditation, as they constantly see the results of stress and illness in their patients as well as in themselves, for which they know there is no medical cure.

| JOAN BORYESENKO |

"I came to meditation in medical school when I was probably twenty-two or twenty-two years old. The first entry to it was physiological because, like a drama queen I always feel my emotions very intensely. I had hypertension and some sort of an immune dysfunction, I had bronchitis and migraine headaches and irritable bowel syndrome—a long list of stress-related illnesses—so I was ill pretty much most of the time. The typical egotistical stories that I told myself then are no different from the ones I tell myself now: things like you are a fraud, you open your mouth and nothing will come out, everyone else is here at Harvard because of merit but you are here because of some sort of bizarre error, you do not belong here, soon they will find out unless you are perfect, unless you do everything perfectly, nobody will love you. It is a very hard thing to be a perfectionist because nothing is ever good enough. I think at that time I was also a very angry person; I was either angry at myself or angry at somebody else, blaming them for not loving me enough.

"One day, one of my lab partners looked at me and said, 'You know, you are sick like this because of the power of your own mind. You actually believe what goes through it, and you are always manufacturing really scary stories that your body responds to.' I was aghast. Then he said, 'I found a few years ago when I started to meditate and practice yoga that I didn't buy into the stories the same way anymore. I bet you that if you do the same that your illnesses will diminish.' I tried it and he was right. It totally changed my relationship to the story. I have never stopped since then and now I do believe in myself!"

Where doctors may be open to meditation, scientists tend to be more skeptical of anything that cannot be physically proven. But scientists also get ill, and illness can change opinions quite dramatically.

| SUSAN SMALLEY |

"I was a human geneticist concerned with evolutionary biology and human behavior. I had the experience of being in the world from a very self-centered, even cynical, narrow-minded view as a scientist who really thought that science was the only way of discovering knowledge, to becoming someone who now realizes that, although science is a powerful and important way to discover knowledge, it needs to be balanced by first-person discovery of knowledge or truth. I see the two as really flip sides of the same coin.

"Seven years ago, I would roll my eyes when people talked about meditation and yoga; I did not think they were valuable in any way. But then I had a personal brush with death, with melanoma, which led me to face the very fearful state that I might die. It was mild, but it was still enough to make me question everything I had always believed in, which was that biology will cure all and science is the tool to understand everything. I did not think there was another way of knowing, but it stimulated me to see that maybe I didn't know as much as I thought I did.

"I took a leave of absence from UCLA, and I literally dove into trying everything I could. I started to study my habits. What did I do on a day-to-day basis? I did little things like I stopped wearing a watch, I used a different burner on the stove, lots of things just to become aware of my life patterns. And I took a yoga class—the first one I had ever taken. I started meditating and it became central to everything. I spent about six hours a day meditating and doing yoga while my kids were in school. It was a big break in the conceptual framework of my world and led to a very profound experience that lasted for about a month. It was an experience of what I now refer to as the oneness of the universe, or complete interconnectedness, where I lost all envy, greed, fear—they just disappeared. All I felt was this profound sense of connection and love and kindness.

"I really saw the interdependent nature, the oneness of the universe, and it shifted my worldview. I could no longer understand how anyone could have feelings of hatred or anger toward someone else, because we are all part of the same thing. It was like cutting off your left hand and pretending it wasn't a part of you. I became committed to living my life from the perspective of remembering that we have this very deep connection."

We take our physical body very much for granted until a part of it is suddenly no longer there. This can throw us either into a place of despair or of waking up to our reality, as **Robert Thurman** experienced when he lost an eye:

"Losing my eye made me realize that I was split in half. I was a Harvard playboy with a wealthy wife and a beautiful daughter; I loved the theater and drinking and dancing on tables and going to Mexico; at the same time, I was seriously reading books about awakening and enlightenment. It had been going on like that for years. I was an elite kind of weird protestant, although I wasn't religious. I used to race motorcycles and small sports cars, and I was changing a tire when the rim flipped the tire iron into my eye. I was out for three days, and when I woke up, they had taken my eye out. It was kind of a mess, but it became a great benefit to me. Losing my eye made me realize that everything is impermanent. As my teacher later said, I lost one but gained a thousand more. I gained a thousand eyes into the deep visceral value of impermanence, what we call in Tibet the immediacy of death, meaning that death is right here with us now. And that insight shaped all my subsequent experiences."

In a similar way, **Ken Green** also experienced the loss of a part of his body—his nervous system. This left him paralyzed for more than a year, but it also had a profound impact on his understanding of meditation and led to a deeply spiritual experience:

"My life was going along with the normal ups and downs, and then one day, while climbing a ladder to repair some roof tiles, I fell fourteen feet. I survived, but was badly injured with nine broken ribs, a collapsed lung, a torn phrenic nerve, an injured diaphragm, and a full array of lacerations and damaged muscles. A few months later, I seemed to be on the mend, but my body had been so traumatized I came down with Guillian-Barre Syndrome (GBS), a rare neurological autoimmune disorder that can occur after physical trauma. It usually happens to A types, so it is tailor-made for control freaks like me. The antibodies go on a frenzied attack, stripping the myelin sheath from the motor neurons. My entire peripheral motor nervous system shut down, while the sensory system and all its input signals remained fully intact. The outer world rushed in, but I had no ability to physically respond. I was shut in, unable to move anything except for my eyelids and my penis.

"Within twenty-four hours, I was transformed from a running, jumping, highly active man into a full quadriplegic—from totally functional to totally nonfunctional. It was very scary. I went from being very independent to being hurled into a closed system, a world without exit, where I was completely dependent. I could not breathe, talk, gesture, cry, or scream. If my thumb got crushed when the nurses turned me over, I could feel the pain but I had no way to express it. The simple pleasures of moving, eating, or talking were gone. I was quadriplegic for a year, followed by a very slow, arduous rehab.

"This period in my life was also a genuine time of spiritual awakening. The shock of having all control stripped away became a unique, unexpected, and unconventional opportunity to be in the present moment. I had little choice but to surrender. If I focused on my body as a prison, then it became a tomb; if I allowed myself to develop storylines of self-pity, it became a realm of regrets—and always accompanied by a tsunami of crushing space. But if I let go and let my mind extend out, that very imprisonment immediately became my liberation. My practice was to keep choosing not to get caught in my body, to not be in that limited pain space, but to step out and extend beyond it. Since I could not breathe, I followed my thought out into space. The thought became the breath.

"I was very alone in my body, although wonderful people were caring for me. But by living meditation moment to moment, day to day, loneliness becomes solitude, which is very beautiful and tender. Loneliness is when you are feeling sorry for yourself, which becomes isolation. Solitude is celebrating the richness of the world without expecting any feedback. When I was lying paralyzed in hospital, I could just see out the window. I could see this little sliver of blue sky, but that sliver was my journey to the moon and to the stars, and if I saw a bird fly over it, I became the bird and was able to fly."

|||

Overwhelming Experience

Apart from the harrowing experience of a traumatic childhood, drug addiction, or illness, we can gain the ability to connect to our inner self through unexpected and unlooked-for experiences of awakening, moments that take us out of our normal, rational selves and offer us a glimpse into another dimension of reality.

Not many of us have the experience of seeing earth from above, as astronaut **Edgar Mitchell** did. It was entering the vastness of space that led him to a deep transformation:

"We were coming home after being on the moon. We were flying in the plane of the ecliptic, which is the plane with the earth, the moon, and the sun, but oriented perpendicular to it and floating through space virtually sideways while rotating. The purpose of this was to keep general balance on the spacecraft, but what it caused to happen was that, as we rotated, a 360-degree panorama of the heavens appeared in the spacecraft window every two minutes. As my job had been the landing craft on the moon, I could now sit back and enjoy the view. It was pretty awesome, particularly since the stars and the galaxies and all the heavenly bodies are ten times as bright in space as they are on the highest mountain on earth.

"I became immersed in the vastness of space. Suddenly, I realized that the molecules in my body and the molecules in the body of the spacecraft and in my partners were prototyped and perhaps manufactured in some ancient generation of stars. Instead of just being an intellectual thought, it was very visceral. I realized the connectedness of everything, like the ancient mystics all said, and it was accompanied by this feeling of ecstasy, an overwhelming experience that I had never had before. It was totally blissful.

"When I got back to earth, I started talking with Eastern mystics and holy men, and with spiritual people from all over the world. I studied virtually all the meditation disciplines and techniques and practices that there are. I wanted to know what had happened in that transcendent experience. The only answer I came to was that I was in resonance, a deep quantum resonance with the ground of my being. A theologian would say the ground of our being is God; I would say it is a field of infinite energy and potential and that when we have such experiences we are in quantum resonance with that deep reality. And when we get in resonance with that deep reality, we have this feeling of deep peace and the sense that everything is really okay."

Transformation can also arise from within ourselves, dependent on nothing but our own dreams and emerging insights. **Byron Katie** recalls:

"I fell in love with myself one morning in February of 1986. I had checked myself into a halfway house in Los Angeles after years of suicidal depression.

A week or so later, as I lay on the floor of my attic room (I felt too unworthy to sleep in a bed), a cockroach crawled over my foot and I opened my eyes. For the first time in my life, I was seeing without concepts, without thoughts or an internal story. All my rage, all the thoughts that had been troubling me, my whole world, *the* whole world, was gone. There was no me. It was as if something else had woken up. *It* opened its eyes. *It* was looking through Katie's eyes. And it was crisp, it was bright, it was new, it had never been here before. Everything was unrecognizable. And it was so delighted! Laughter welled up from the depths and just poured out. It breathed and was ecstasy. It was intoxicated with joy, totally greedy for everything. There was nothing separate, nothing unacceptable to it. Everything was its very own self. For the first time I—it—experienced the love of its own life. I—it—was *amazed!*

"These were the first moments after I was born as it—or it as me. There was nothing left of Katie. There was literally not even a shred of memory of her—no past, no future, not even a present. And in that openness, such joy. There is nothing sweeter than this, I felt; there is nothing but this. If you loved yourself more than anything you could imagine, you would give yourself this: a face, a hand, breath. But that is not enough: a wall, a ceiling, a window, a bed, light bulbs. Ooh! And this too! And this too! I felt that if my joy were told, it would blow the roof off the halfway house—off the whole planet. I still feel that way.

"I live in constant meditation, and if a thought should ever show up as anything less than goodness, I know that it would spill over to other people as confusion, and those other people are me. My job is to enlighten myself to that, and to love the spent rose, the sound of the traffic, the litter on the ground, and the litterer who gives me my world. I pick up the litter, do the dishes, sweep the floor, wipe the baby's nose, and question anything that would cost me the awareness of my true nature. There is nothing kinder than this, nothing.

"At forty-three, after ten years of deep depression and despair, my real life began. What I came to see was that my suffering was not a result of not having control; it was a result of arguing with reality. I discovered that when I believed my thoughts I suffered, but that when I didn't believe them I did not suffer, and that this is true for every human being. Freedom is as simple as that. Suffering is optional. I found a joy within me that has never disappeared, not for a single moment. That joy is in everyone, always. When you question your mind for the love of truth, your life always becomes happier and kinder."

The people in this chapter, and the many others throughout the book, found their sanity and freedom by simply sitting in still-ness, which makes meditation the best and cheapest remedy there is for many of our most pervasive ills!

|||

4

|||

The Only Way Out Is Within

For fast-acting relief, try slowing down.
LILY TOMLIN

Imagine you are a caveman out with fellow tribe members on a hunt for food. You have spotted a large bear, and adrenalin is beginning to pump through your body in anticipation of the coming hunt. As you close in on the animal, your heart rate begins to increase, your breaths become shorter, your stomach muscles tighten, and your concentration deepens. The level of adrenalin in your system is rising rapidly as you near the point of attack. The next few moments are crucial in determining whether you fight to the kill or must run for your life.

Now imagine a day when everything suddenly seems too much to cope with. Perhaps your child has kept you awake all night with toothache, you have to be at a business meeting first thing in the morning but you get delayed in congested traffic, the meeting goes on longer than planned, and you have to skip lunch in order to write a report. An angry client arrives, demanding better service, when your mother calls in need of help with her car. In the midst of all this, you may not have noticed that your heart rate was increasing, your breaths were getting shorter, your stomach muscles were tightening, and your anxiety level rising. Adrenalin is pumping through your body, but in this case, there is no bear to fight and nowhere to run.

Although each separate incident may appear benign, if our response to circumstances becomes increasingly stressed to the point at which we lose our equilibrium, then the body will translate this as life threatening and put out the red alert. Becoming fraught with tension and physically distressed, until we are overwhelmed and out of control, is like a steam cooker coming to full pressure. As Simon, a participant in one of our workshops, told us, "I don't get stressed. I wake up stressed." And although we are the only ones who can turn down the heat, unfortunately we often feel powerless to do so.

| PETER RUSSELL |

"When I am working in corporations, I ask how many people get stressed by traffic, and most people say yes, traffic jams definitely make me stressed. Yet sitting in a traffic jam is the least stressful part of driving! We have nothing to do, nobody is demanding anything from us, and it is a moment when we can completely relax. So why do we make it the most stressed part? Is it because we feel out of control? We are going to be late for the meeting, and if we are late, we will be criticized or lose an opportunity, or we are going to be late getting home. It is the voice that wants to be in control of things that is stressing us out, not the traffic jam. So, instead of getting stressed, we can actually use the time to relax and enjoy being stuck in traffic!"

Physical symptoms of the stress response include digestive disorders, such as changes in appetite, irritable bowel syndrome, diarrhea, stomach ulcers, and indigestion; as well as headaches, high blood pressure, palpitations, hyperventilation, insomnia, back ache, hives or eczema, excessive sweating, and nervous reactions such as grinding teeth. At the same time, the hormone cortisol is released, which suppresses the immune system, so immune-deficient illnesses from the common cold to cancer can also be directly or indirectly caused by stress.

If stress increases we become less able to adequately adapt, causing us to overreact, lose a clear perspective on priorities, get muddled or disorganized, become depressed, or rant and rage for no apparent reason. We may have more anxiety and panic, irritability and frustration, debilitating fear and insecurity, rapid mood changes, restlessness and nervousness, addictive behavior, memory loss, or paranoia and confusion. And all of these are just a few of the possible effects.

| JEFF SALZMAN |

"I was the guy who at forty-two years old had all the money I could ever spend. I had the most beautiful husband imaginable. I was living in a beach house in Florida. I had my library of books. I really had nothing to worry about, and so I ended up staring out at the beach with the only thing I had left: the fact that one day I was going to die. I started worrying about dying, and I started worrying about my heart. This is what happens if you are basically neurotic, which I am. I went and got a blood pressure machine. Within three or four weeks, I was taking my blood pressure forty to fifty times a day. I had these big elaborate charts, and I was watching my blood pressure rise. In other words, I developed an obsessive-compulsive disorder, and it continued to spiral for the next four years, to the point where I was in a low level of panic all the time, I was always sweating, I had super-high blood pressure and heart arrhythmias. I tried lots of things, including Prozac, but everything I did made it worse. I was never suicidal, but I was wondering, is this life tenable for me? I could not sleep; I could not concentrate on anything. It was impossible to have a meaningful conversation with anyone because I wasn't really present. I was stressed to the max, but it was entirely my own doing."

Such an experience shows how easily a limited pattern of thinking can become a full-blown neurosis. Not me, we think, I don't get that stressed. Perhaps not, but try this: Imagine you are squeezing some toothpaste out of a tube but you have forgotten to take the cap off. What happens? Deb actually did this in one of her most unaware moments (they do happen!), and the toothpaste soon found another way out—through the bottom of the tube and onto her clothes. Now imagine that the tube of toothpaste is you, under pressure and beginning to experience psychological or emotional distress. But you do not take your cap off, as it were, by recognizing what is happening and making time to relax and deal with your inner concerns. Instead, you just keep squeezing yourself to do more. So what happens to the mental or emotional pressure building up inside you? Eventually it has to find a way out, and if it cannot come out through the top—by being acknowledged, expressed, and resolved—it will find another way of making itself known.

It will find the weakest point, whether through your digestive system, your nerves, immune system, behavior, emotional balance, or sleep patterns. Repressed or ignored, it can become illness, depression, addiction, or anxiety; projected outward, it becomes hostility, aggression, prejudice, or fear. But all of this is within our own personal domain.

| LINDSAY CROUSE |

"They are very pervasive, but we have to find a way to remove ourselves from all those messages of unfulfilled desire coming at us or we do not have a chance to clear our minds. The kind of constant busyness we are a part of is actually a kind of aggression against ourselves, because we have no peace. More importantly, we construct the world by how we think. For instance, when we are in love, we will run out in the rain with our lover, dancing and singing and celebrating, getting entirely wet; whereas most days when we open the door and we see it raining, we use an expletive. It is not the rain's fault; there is no quality in the rain that should make us either happy or unhappy. That is coming from us. So, if the way we are seeing the world is coming from within us, then the world is a reflection of how we are thinking and feeling and acting and speaking. In that case, we need to take time out to deeply consider how we want to behave."

Causes of Stress

Stress affects us all. Research by the Center for Disease Control and the National Institute for Occupational Safety and Health found that up to $300 billion, or $7,500 per employee, is spent each year on stress-related absenteeism or decreased productivity, while most conservative estimates suggest that 70 to 90 percent of illnesses are either affected or caused by stress, with a correspondingly large proportion of visits to doctors. As such, it is a major problem. On top of that, there is no medical cure that can alleviate stress. Prescription drugs cannot lighten our workload or change our life conditions.

Stress is a derivation of the Latin word meaning "to be drawn tight." Studies show that job dissatisfaction, moving, divorce, and financial difficulties are at the top of the list of known stressors, or places that make us tighten up. But as we all respond differently to such circumstances, what may appear as an exciting challenge to one person can be debilitating or overwhelming to another. For instance, a divorce may seem to be a high stressor but for some it can be a welcome relief! The difference lies in our response to the stressor, for although we may have little or no control over the circumstances with which we are dealing, we do have control over our reaction to them. If we respond negatively to stress it can then have further repercussions.

| JOHN GRAY |

"Stress occurs if there is something challenging and we do not know how we are going to get to where we want to go. This means we have a need that we cannot meet so we start to compensate. Then we start creating false needs like, 'If I can't get the love I need in my relationship, then what can I get? Well, I can have ice cream.' People are often desperately seeking money or something out there because they have gone through the stress of not getting what they need emotionally and they make other things important, which is called compensation."

In other words, the cause of stress is not so much the external circumstances, such as having too many demands and not enough time to fill them. Rather, it is about our *perception of the circumstances as being overwhelming* and our *perception of our ability to cope* when we feel stretched beyond what we perceive we are capable of. If we believe we cannot cope, then we will begin to lose ground; if we believe we can cope, then we will be able to ride over any obstacles.

What we believe colors our every thought, word, and action. As cell biologist Bruce Lipton writes in his book, *The Biology of Belief*, "Our responses to environmental stimuli are indeed controlled by perceptions, but not all of our learned perceptions are accurate. Not all snakes are dangerous! Yes, perception 'controls' biology, but . . . these perceptions can be true or false. Therefore, we would be more accurate to refer to these controlling perceptions as beliefs. Beliefs control biology!"

Luckily, we can transform our beliefs and our perceptions. The idea that it is our work, family, or lifestyle that is causing us stress, and that if we were to change these then we would be fine, is seeing the situation from the wrong perspective. Rather, it is the belief that something "out there" is causing us stress that is actually causing the stress. And although changing our circumstances certainly may help, invariably, no matter what we do, it is a change within our belief system and our perception of our capabilities that will make the biggest difference. In turn, this will help develop the relaxation response and begin to normalize everything the stress response has put out of balance.

The Relaxation Response

Most of us think of relaxation as putting our feet up, having a beer, watching a good movie, walking the dog, or perhaps joining a fitness club. Certainly these activities help, but too often they only deal with the more superficial, immediate aspects of stress. They make us feel better for a while, until the next deadline or traffic jam begins to push us over the edge again. To make more lasting changes, we need to loosen and release unconscious levels of stress from where accumulated tension and resistance affect both our behavior and our health.

| TAMI SIMON |

"When I feel stressed, I sit in meditation and ask myself, 'Where in my body am I feeling it?' Often it is in my gut, or some place of holding. I go in and look for that place of tension and say, 'Okay, you don't have to hold onto anything, your chair is supporting you, the earth is supporting you, this context is completely open and free, and you don't have to be clutching.' Then I can literally and physically sink down into the earth. I feel my feet get heavy, I feel my hands open up, I feel my back get heavy and drop, and through that, I start dropping my energy. It is a deep relaxation. I am no longer in my mind, but I am sinking into my body and the ground."

When the relaxation response kicks in, we are able to deal with conflicting situations without the red flag waving, without adrenalin being released, without feelings of fear, anxiety, or hopelessness. This means our physiology remains balanced: Metabolism is not shut down, heart rate does not increase, blood pressure stays normal, breathing remains natural, and nervous system activity is balanced. At the same time, we increase our mental faculties, such as concentration, efficiency, memory, and creativity. Emotionally, this means we have greater tolerance, ease, and generosity, self-confidence, and self-esteem.

In a stressed state, it is easy to lose touch with compassion and kindness by getting overly focused on competition and our own survival; in a relaxed state, we are connecting with a deeper sense of purpose and innate altruism. The power of thought is such that if we think we are getting stressed or overwhelmed, we will be more likely to induce the stress response; in the same way, if we think easeful and relaxing thoughts, we will induce the relaxation response. This makes a significant difference in our communication and relationships. For instance, in a stressed state, we can get irritated or overwhelmed by relatively small events—a child interrupting our conversation or a colleague being late for a meeting—until we become upset or tense. In a relaxed state, we can view such disturbances for what they are without letting them accumulate or increase our irritation. We stay balanced and non-judgmental, more likely to be concerned as to why our colleague is late rather than focusing on the inconvenience.

The more aware we are of our own reactions, perceptions, and behavior, the more we recognize the stress response and can generate the relaxation response. Mindfulness enables us to be attentive when our breathing becomes shorter or there is a tightening of the abdominal muscles, when a headache develops, we get short-tempered, or there is a growing hopelessness or confusion. Such awareness also recognizes where self-perception is limiting our behavior and, therefore, making us more susceptible to prevailing pressures, and how to release this.

| CYNDI LEE |

"I would have these adrenaline rushes as if I were nervous about something—kind of a little low-grade anxiety—and then I would immediately start to get anxious. It would get all blown up in my mind. By meditating with it, I learned to recognize that I was not anxious, I did not need to go into drama queen mental mode, I could just let this be, let it rise, and let it pass."

|||

Practice Meditation:
Reducing Stress

We expend far more energy maintaining a stressed state than we do creating a relaxed one. This practice enables us to release the inner patterns causing stress:

If stress is rising, become aware of reactive thinking patterns. Are your thoughts becoming more annoyed, self-centered, fearful, or helpless?

If you normally react by getting irritated at interruptions until you are shouting, take some deep breaths and silently repeat, "My work is flowing well. Nothing can disturb that flow. I can easily take a few minutes to attend to other issues."

Most importantly, change the voice in your head from "I can't" to "I can." Repeat an affirmation to shift perceptions and belief patterns and to reinforce your strengths, such as "With every breath, I am more relaxed and flowing through my day with ease."

If you are feeling increasingly helpless with a growing sense of inadequacy, turn your thoughts into ones such as: "I am absolutely capable of fulfilling anything that is asked of me; I have all the knowledge that I need to do this already inside me; I am fully resourceful and able to rise to this challenge."

De-stressing

The word *meditation* and the word *medication* have the same prefix derived from the Latin word *medicus*, meaning to care or to cure, indicating that meditation is the most appropriate medicine or antidote for stress. Deep relaxation techniques and breath awareness meditation are vital components in enabling the relaxation response to be activated; a quiet calmness is the most effective and efficient remedy for a busy and overworked mind.

| PONLOP RINPOCHE |

"Usually, when we feel the pressure of life—and life in general is very busy with all kinds of commotion taking place around us—then we can become very tense and close our heart. We go onto autopilot mode, a state of self-protection and self-preservation. When our mind can relax a little and become calm and more spacious, then we see there is nothing to fear. It is like a warrior. The greatest warrior in history is the one who is calm—if he freaked out, then he would easily lose the battle. In the same way, when our mind is stressed and tense, then we think everyone is attacking us or taking advantage of us, and we cannot see anyone or anything objectively or lovingly. Meditation really helps us not to panic or freak out; it brings us back to this calm ground. When we are standing on this calm and peaceful ground, then we can see our emotions and fears clearly, and we can see how to work with them; there is less judgment and labeling."

One of our students, Helen, had a very critical, angry boss, a woman who would walk in each day and immediately begin to find fault with everything Helen did: the way she was dressed, the way her hair was, and so on. Helen was becoming a nervous wreck, feeling inadequate and shameful, as well as developing a real bitterness toward her boss. She wanted to leave, but jobs were scarce in her area. Helen then started to practice meditation and to develop the relaxation response. This gave her greater objectivity and awareness, which led her to a deeper compassion. She began to perceive what an unhappy and sad woman her boss really was beneath her very tough exterior. She watched her boss moving and talking to people and saw the loneliness in her body, heard the defeat in her voice. Each time her boss approached her, Helen would silently repeat, 'May you be happy, may you be well,' while sending her boss thoughts of compassion and care. This lowered her stress response and balanced her reactive feelings. Soon she was no longer absorbing the criticisms and was able to talk to her boss quite fearlessly.

Helen recognized how her stressful reactions were due to her perception of and reaction to her boss, in particular her belief that she herself was at fault. She also saw the reality of this other woman's unhappiness and how all the criticism and anger was due to sadness, not to anything that Helen had personally done. Meditation had grounded her enough that she was no longer giving her power away but was able to stay steady within herself. Where stress creates tension and chaos, de-stressing is about finding a greater equilibrium and stability in both our minds and our lives.

| JOAN BORYSENKO |

"A long time ago, I came across a definition of meditation that it comes from the root meaning 'right balance.' That rang true for me because, personally, my attention is often so fragmented, egocentric, narcissistic, or self-concerned that there isn't a whole lot of inner balance or alignment with what is. Rather, I am stuck in a state of non-balance. Right balance is when my mind is not spinning out endless movies and delusions, or maybe it still is but I am just not so attached to believing them. Meditation is when I can watch stuff go by and the part of me that usually interrupts and says, 'That's a good story, or that son of a bitch, or I'm guilty and awful,' that part sits back and sees it as just one more story but without attachment to it. This gives me the most delicious sense of spaciousness and peace."

Taking time to be quiet teaches us to just be with what is when the stress response is kicking in and adrenalin is beginning to influence our reactions, rather than over-identifying with it or letting the stress change our behavior. Meditation is so obviously effective for stress-based difficulties that a specific training, known as *Warrior Mind Training*, is now being taught at various military bases, according to a report on *Earthlink News*, October 7, 2008:

"The explosion of practice mortars sent Army Spc. Kade Williams into panic attacks, and nightmares plagued his sleep. The ravages of post-traumatic stress had left the veteran of the war in Afghanistan vulnerable, and he was desperate for help. But sitting silently on the floor with his eyes closed. . . . That seemed a bit far-out. Until he tried it. 'I will be the first one to admit that I was wrong,' Williams said. He now attends regular classes and practices alone three mornings a week. He says he feels safe for the first time since he returned from Afghanistan."

This story demonstrates how meditation offers us the spaciousness to just observe and witness, rather than being dominated by reactive and knee-jerk behavior. We can step out of fear and chaos, and into awareness of the bigger picture.

| SYLVIA BOORSTEIN |

"Mindfulness meditation, the practice of moment-to-moment awareness, is where we can clearly assess what is happening, not only out there, but what is my internal response to it? If I can keep my response clear of the confusion that frequently arises when my experience is startling or frightening and I can say, 'Whoa, I just got startled, I just got confused, let me just take a moment here and see if I can see through this confusion,' then I can let my mind rest for a moment and take a quiet look at what is going on. The point of meditation is to stop the storyline. I might be saying, 'Oh, my life is not going the way I wanted, this or that isn't happening, anger is arising, and I feel uncomfortable about the anger,' and then I say to myself, 'It is like this, whatever it is, it is just like this,' and then I can relax about whatever it is. It does not mean that life is without strife or disappointment or worry or even irritation; it means that it is without getting fussed about. It is just what is going on; that is all; it need not be complicated."

The ability to keep our peace and maintain an even-balanced state is one of the great gifts of meditation that we can bring into every situation. In practice, this means recognizing that there are many situations in which we have no control over what happens, no ability to affect the outcome, but no matter what happens it is possible to stay balanced. This applies to our thoughts and feelings, as well as to our behavior and actions. As the German proverb says, "We cannot direct the wind, but we can adjust our sails."

Such equanimity gives us strength and a sense of being unshakable in a world that is constantly making demands and creating challenges. We never know what is going to happen or when—nothing is predictable, permanent, secure, controllable, or dependable. Everything is subject to change in every moment. We can ignore this fact and live with the delusion of permanency and predictability, or we can embrace impermanence and unpredictability with awareness and dignity.

The Only Tool We Need

In addition to the army, meditation is now being used in many stress-management and pain clinics, corporations and businesses, as a way to alleviate both the symptoms and effect of stress. Mindfulness-Based Stress Reduction (MBSR) training is now offered in many hospitals and medical centers and is being researched by teams of scientists and physicians the world over. Since these programs first began, they have gained enormous recognition.

| JON KABAT-ZINN |

"Things are very different now from the way they were in 1979, the year the first clinic opened. Then, for instance, it was inconceivable that twenty-five years in the future the National Institute of Health (NIH) would hold a day-long symposium on its campus in Bethesda, Maryland, entitled *Mindfulness Meditation and Health*. From the perspective of that era, it was so improbable that you could say it was more likely that the Big Bang would stop expanding and begin collapsing back in on itself. And yet it happened in 2004. The NIH is currently spending tens of millions of dollars on research in randomized clinical trials and various clinical applications of mindfulness meditation.

"Over the years, more than 18,000 people have come through the MBSR clinic at the UMass Medical Center, and thousands more have attended other mindfulness-based stress-reduction programs around the country. Whether referred by their physician or not, people come with a huge amount of pain and suffering, both physical and emotional. Through the cultivation of mindfulness, they develop a more functional relationship with that suffering, they turn towards it, open to it, and actually befriend it to a degree rather than insisting that it stop, and in the process, the pain often transforms or even falls away. It is jaw dropping. I never get used to it, even after so many years. I think it is fair to say that the participants in these programs walk out after eight weeks of mindfulness training and continue to cultivate mindfulness in their lives in various ways for years. For the most part, they will tell you that they are more in touch with their own beauty than they may have been since they were children."

III

The MBSR program has, for instance, been studied scientifically to demonstrate that participants have a more robust response to the flu vaccine because they have greater immunity. As we saw earlier, the number of doctor visits increases as stress increases, but they correspondingly decrease with the added ingredient of meditation.

| JOAN BORYSENKO |

"We did one study in an HMO to see if, when a group of people meditate, do the high utilizers of health care then use less care, and the answer was, yes, they do. And that is enormous. If we could keep the population healthy, it would change everything; there would be more money for education and social programs. I ran a mind-body clinic with Herbert Benson, and the rapidity with which stressed people with a high level of physical symptoms were able to let go of those symptoms and feel less anxious, less depressed, and more joyful was truly remarkable. We did follow-up studies and six months later people were still better. The interesting point was that most of them were meditating many times throughout the day—they would take ten minutes, count down from ten to one, breathe deeply and find that place of silence and balance, and then they would go back to their business."

Apart from releasing stress, meditation and deep relaxation can have a dramatic affect on the more serious illnesses that are often the result of a stressful lifestyle. The relaxation response changes and balances our chemistry, which then improves the functioning of our whole body.

| NIRMALA HERIZA |

"I work with my patients regularly to mitigate and micro-manage stress. As a result, certain biochemical functions, such as the release of cortisol, begin to calm down. This has a stabilizing affect on the cardiovascular system, causing the heart rate and blood pressure to also stabilize, reducing the risk of exacerbation of an existing heart condition or preventing one from developing. With all of my heart patients, I begin the process of behavior modification by having them watch their own subjective reactions to disturbing or aggravating situations, as well as learning how to detach from the object of the disturbance. I use meditation on a daily basis with all those who have been diagnosed with acute and chronic disease. For instance, in the treatment of cancer, HIV, and AIDS, there are relaxation mechanisms in the subtle activity of meditation that specifically support white blood cell count, helping to restore and reinforce the immune function."

We tend to presume that if a serious illness occurs, such as heart disease, we will have to make some big lifestyle changes if we want to get better. Combined with a low-fat diet and physical exercise like a daily yoga practice, meditation and deep relaxation are key ingredients that have been proven to actually reverse heart disease.

| DEAN ORNISH |

"People who have had a heart attack sometimes say it was the best thing that ever happened to them, and I say, 'Are you crazy?' They say, 'Well, no, but that is what it took to begin making these changes that have made my life so much more profoundly joyful and meaningful.' Change is hard, but if we are in enough pain, the idea of change becomes more appealing and we will try just about anything. When we make these changes, the pain subsides, and not only the physical pain like angina from heart disease or back pain, but deeper levels of pain that are more difficult to measure but are often more meaningful. When we can focus on something, which is what meditation does, it enhances our inner communication, giving us more personal power and peace of mind.

"When people are stressed out, they may say, 'My fuse is shorter and I explode more easily, but when I meditate on a regular basis, my fuse is longer. The situation does not change, but how I react to it does.' Meditation allows us to experience more of an internal sense of well-being. It dampens our sympathetic nervous system. It enhances our parasympathetic nervous system, so we can relax. Our mind quiets down. Our breathing becomes slower and deeper. Our metabolic rate balances."

Illness and Wellness

Stress can be as physically, psychologically, and emotionally debilitating as illness. But it is easier to see the connection between stress and relaxation and meditation than it is to see how meditation could help someone who is very sick, perhaps dealing with such issues as cancer or AIDS. At such a time, we are often more prone to self-pity, helplessness, and dependency on caregivers and doctors, and less likely to be able to help ourselves. Yet meditation is, without doubt, an effective medicine that not only reduces stress-related physical problems but also moves us out of negative mindsets so that we can accept and be at peace with what is happening.

| JOAN BORYSENKO |

"We started an AIDS clinic at the very beginning of the epidemic, before the HIV virus had even been isolated, and it was truly remarkable to watch people move from a place of feeling they were a passive victim of something that is going to kill them, to a place of inquiry, to asking, 'What can I learn about myself?' I remember one man in particular, Mark, this young twenty-eight-year-old handsome gay guy with a great job and a great life who looked at me and said, 'I never thought I would say this, but I cannot imagine what my life would have been like without AIDS because I would never have come to this level of self-discovery, or this level of inner peace.'"

These words were voiced by our friend Mark Matousek. His memory of that time is one of transforming his worry and fear into a powerful inner strength.

| MARK MATOUSEK |

"Mortality led me to meditation. Addicts talk about being 'scared sober.' I was scared into sitting. Being diagnosed with a then-terminal disease at age twenty-eight, I was forced as a survival mechanism to pursue an inner life. I felt compelled to discover if there was anything metaphysical beyond this booby-trapped bag of bones, a life beyond or alongside the body. By sitting and watching my breath and my thoughts, by learning to sit *through* bad moments, an invisible, metaphysical muscle seemed to strengthen in the stillness. Running from pain or fear made the badness worse, whereas when I stopped in the midst of it all, took my seat and let the feelings burn deeply through me, let the day's particular nightmare play itself out with as little reaction as possible, clarity slowly took the place of hysteria. Sitting was a way to root through the pain, to connect in bad weather to the ground of being, to touch silence. It was a moment of eternity in the midst of clockwork time, a place to empty out, grieve, refill, to remember the face behind the mask, simply by stopping and being still.

"That was twenty-plus years ago. My health crisis passed but the practice stayed. Meditation is on my shoulder, a reminder of beauty, truth, fragility, sorrow; a voice that whispers: 'Remember to love.' If my outer world had not been threatened, I would never have looked for an inner one."

Illness offers us a very clear, step-by-step process that gives us the opportunity to traverse through layers of personal transformation. This process is enhanced when we use meditation as a healing tool.

| JOAN BORYSENKO |

"The crack in the wall initiates a process of change, which can lead to either despair or transformation. Such as the day you get an AIDS diagnosis, that is it, your life is cracked wide open, and the world as you know it ends. This is the first stage of change. The second phase of the process is liminality. You are dwelling at the threshold of something, but you do not know what it is. This has often been described as the stage between no longer and not yet: You cannot get your old life back, but you do not yet know what your next life is going to be. If you talk to sages from different spiritual traditions, most of them will say that it is very important to know that we do not know. Only when we are comfortable with the unknown can we actually recognize life as it emerges freshly in the moment, instead of constantly running our ego agenda.

"In this stage of not knowing, one of three things can happen. Firstly, you can despair and give up, go into depression, or kill yourself slowly through drugs and alcohol. Secondly, you can insulate yourself so that you believe you are essentially unchanged, which is a place of denial. And the third possibility is that by wandering in the wilderness stage, you actually learn to be with what is. You find that place of inner balance and acceptance, and are different as a result.

"The third stage of the process of change is return. We return to society transformed. We may not return as something wonderful to the outside world, but the inner change has happened. Oftentimes people who are wandering in the wilderness realize they have a choice between despair and hope, between remaining static and transforming, and they will choose to meditate at that time to deepen the experience."

This level of deep change affects us all differently, but there is often a common thread of gratitude for the illness. For instance, we saw the actor Michael J. Fox talking about how he coped with having Parkinson's disease and how he was forever grateful for what the illness had taught him. Given the choice, he said, he would not be without it. In a similar way, Matthew Fox recalls a friend of his who had AIDS and who saw it as the greatest of gifts:

| MATTHEW FOX |

"I had a friend who died of AIDS. He was a pro baseball player, heterosexual, very handsome, and he said, 'I was a very rakish guy. I bedded every woman I could. But this AIDS thing is the best thing that ever happened to me because it taught me the real preciousness of life.' He would go around and speak to high schools, warning kids about AIDS and to use condoms, and because he was very athletic, the kids, especially the boys, really listened. He said, 'I know I am dying, but AIDS is the biggest gift of my life.' What an amazing thing to say. He died when he was maybe only twenty-seven years old, but he wasn't the least bit full of self-pity or anything. He was sharing what he had learned, his wisdom about life. It was beautiful to see this kind of spiritual maturity that happened due to this disease. That is how healing happens. It is not escaping death or overcoming a physical disease. Rather, it is about entering into a much fuller and wiser way of living on the earth, even if it is brief."

The much-loved American spiritual teacher Ram Dass had a stroke some years ago. He shared with us how he had always been very independent, and so one of the first lessons he had to learn was about becoming very dependent on others, which was initially very hard but which he came to see as one of many blessings. He also talked about the influence of his teacher in his healing.

| RAM DASS |

"When I had the stroke, I had a picture of my meditation teacher, Neem Keroli Baba, in my hospital room, and I talked to him. I said, 'You always had your eye on me. What have you done, gone out to lunch?' I was thinking how I had his grace on the one hand, and I had the stroke on the other hand, but then I started to put them together. It took about a week before they merged, and that is when the stroke became grace, although it was a fierce grace. I am much more silent now, which is also very graceful! Meditation gives me purchase on the stroke; it teaches me I am not my body but that I am awareness. It frees me from identification with the limitations of the stroke."

Dying of cancer is rarely graceful; more often it is painful and emotionally demanding. When Denise was faced with the final stages of stage-four metastatic cancer, she used her meditation training as a tremendous source of strength during these hardest of times, as recalled by her partner, **Fleet Maull:**

"When Denise was told she had around six months to live, she did not freak out. She just said, 'Okay, what's next?' Meditation is both the stability of the mindfulness awareness practice and the ability to hold one's seat, because it trains you to hold your seat in the face of your life. She did not feel sorry for herself; she did not worry. Meditation had taught her not to run away physically, and not to run away into fantasy and discursiveness, but to sit in the midst of the fire. She was able to be fully present with her heart and mind open to everything."

|||

Healing the Mind and Body

Normally, the more stressed we become, the more our breathing becomes rapid, short, and shallow, and the more we ignore our physical needs. In other words, we get stuck in our heads and become increasingly ungrounded, while stress and tension accumulates and is held in our body. Healing, on either a physical or a psychological level, becomes possible when we start paying attention and get to know these held places.

| MIRABAI BUSH |

"I have learned that strong emotions like anger and jealousy are experienced in the body. I feel them as bodily sensations, as heat or a tightening. Now I know that when those sensations start, that it is time to stop, breathe, pay attention to what is going on. I really have learned to take time and not to act as soon as intense emotions arise. I know that if I act immediately, I might make the right choice, but I could just as easily make the wrong one and do something harmful to others or even to myself."

The mind and body are in continual and intimate communication, the body expressing the denied or repressed parts of the mind through physical disturbances. As we think so we have become; as we have become so we can see how we have been thinking. By meditating with awareness of the body we can begin to unravel the emotional and psychological patterns that have developed, we can hear what the held places are saying, what issues are being ignored, and what is needed to bring a deeper release. As **Christine Evans** describes in *Your Body Speaks Your Mind:*

"I try to just notice myself, without judgment. I notice that I feel sick when my ex-lover rings. I notice that I feel sad when my lower back is massaged. I notice the area between my shoulder blades that aches when I'm tired or feeling tense. I notice that the sick feeling, the retching and vomiting, is about not accepting how I really feel and not believing that I have the right to feel whatever it is."

A positive change begins when we recognize that physical difficulties are the way the body deals with underlying imbalances or traumatized energies, while healing is the resolution of those imbalances. But accepting our vulnerabilities, repressed emotional trauma, and psychological or physical pain is not so easy. Our usual response to such pain is to get it to go away quickly and by whatever means possible. Instead, in the stillness of meditation, we can gently enter into the pain and let it play itself out by letting go of resistance, of layers of self-protection, of ingrained patterns of thinking and behavior, of repressive control over our feelings, of all the ways we have held on and to what we have been holding on to.

| PETER RUSSELL |

"We don't want to feel physical pain; we would rather take painkillers to get rid of it. But pain is a call for attention, an alarm mechanism in the organism, which says, 'Attention please!' We usually say, 'No thanks, I am not going to give you my attention, I am not going to feel that, I will subdue you with chemicals.' I suggest we do the opposite. That we do what the pain is asking and say, 'Okay, here is my attention. What does the discomfort feel like?' When we let our attention go to any particular part of the body, the blood flow increases and brings healing. Just by sitting with it and really allowing it in and being with it, the pain begins to shift and unwind."

Becoming aware of ourselves just as we are leads to a deeper acceptance of ourselves. We cannot accept something we are not aware of and we cannot become aware without paying attention, watching, and listening. In this sense, meditation is a form of medicine and healing—the process of becoming whole. This is not the same as curing, which is the fixing of a particular part. Rather, to heal from any form of pain is to bring all the different aspects of ourselves into a unified whole and to be transformed as a result.

Meditation creates the space for us to see how our mind works, how thoughts and dramas come and go. But instead of getting lost in the story and then feeling bad about it, we can develop greater objectivity. When we no longer need to identify with our story, the diagnosis or prognosis, the details or the dramas, then we are free to expand into our true potential.

| TAMI SIMON |

"This is strong language, but without meditation I might not be alive. I do not know if meditation can save anyone else, but it saved me. I was riddled with a kind of existential longing and despair. I wasn't sure that I belonged on the planet, that I would ever have a place on earth for myself, that I would find a way to fit in as a human, that I would be able to relax. I was desperate and freaked out. When I started meditating, it was the first time I felt any synchronization in my being, any rooting or anchoring, I felt a sense of incredible unlimited joy and possibility. Suddenly I had a reason for my existence and, in a sense, at that moment my life was saved."

|||

Part II

TRANSFORMING FROM THE INSIDE OUT

5

|||

Growing Roses Out of Compost

*Let us not look back in anger or forward in fear, but
around in awareness.*

JAMES THURBER

Soon after his release, Nelson Mandela was asked by Bill
Clinton if he was feeling angry the day he walked away from
twenty-seven years in jail. "Didn't you hate them?" asked
Clinton. "You must have felt some anger?" "Sure I did,"
Mandela replied. "I felt anger and hatred and fear. But I realized that if I kept on hating them then once I got in that car
and got through the gate, I would still be in prison. I let it go
because I wanted to be free."

Such self-acceptance as Mandela displayed is rare.
Normally, we do not accept and release our negative feelings
so easily; we are more likely to repress or disown them. But we
ignore these parts of ourselves at our peril, for when denied
they cause guilt, shame, depression, relationship failure, anger,
sadness, and anxiety. When recognized, such hidden places
contain great resources of strength. Locked in the darkness of
past experiences, conflicts, and traumas is a depth of feeling
and insight. "Our hang-ups, unfortunately or fortunately,

contain our wealth," writes Pema Chödron in *The Wisdom of No Escape*. "Our neurosis and our wisdom are made out of the same material. If you throw out your neurosis, you also throw out your wisdom."

The impetus that brings us to greater self-reflection and awareness is often the result of a wounded sense of self, as seen in some of the personal stories in chapter three. From this place, the urge comes to grow into a sufficient, strong, and healed self, like a weed that it impelled to grow even through concrete in order to reach the light. The obstacles that confront us as we proceed—the dragons in our mind—represent those parts of us that have been pushed away or ignored. To run or hide from them simply increases our resistance and makes us a casualty of our own limitations.

| DENNIS GENPO MERZEL |

"Instead of being a victim of my humanness, I am owning it and consciously choosing to be a human being. And, therefore, when I suffer, when I have anger, jealousy, or self-loathing, I can accept it because these are qualities of a human being."

Can meditation help us to embrace our essential humanness? We have seen how it is the appropriate remedy for stress and illness, but can the same be said of more psychological states of conflict, such as anger or fear? And how do we deal with shadow issues that invariably arise during such a self-reflective practice?

| MICHELLE LEVEY |

"In the unmeditative culture that most of us grow up in, the response to suffering is denial, take a pill, distract yourself somehow, go shopping, drink, watch TV, all the many ways we have of numbing ourselves. Meditation asks that, instead of distracting and avoiding and numbing, we just stop and sit with our inner selves. The seed of healing our psychological stress and mental afflictions is found within, in the same place that suffering is found. Eventually, we have to stop running away from pain and simply be with it."

When we sit in meditation we can begin to remember and reclaim those parts of our being that had become lost in denial or repression. Meditation invites us to openly meet those places we have previously hidden from, no matter how unpleasant, ugly, or unlovable we may think they are. As long as they stay in the dark recesses, they will continue to dominate our behavior. Only by exploring the true nature of these repressed aspects and accepting that they are a part of being alive can we bring real transformation. All this may sound somewhat daunting, but the outcome is one of relief, release, and greater freedom.

| DAVID SHINER |

"Meditation taught me to just be present and feel everything that is there, to feel the pain and not run from it. And it gave me the ability to laugh at it. I am a clown, so I am constantly revealing our deepest weaknesses and pain in order to generate laughter. A clown is, seemingly, searching for his or her place in life: what is the meaning of all this, where do I fit in? It is the existential dilemma of what am I doing here and who am I? That touches the audience on a very deep, primal level, because somewhere inside each person they feel that way too."

|||

HANGING OUT WITH ANGER

Anger is a difficult place to start as none of us really want to admit that we get irritated, bitchy, or lose our temper—we much prefer to think of ourselves as being wonderfully tolerant and serene. But even if we do get mad sometimes, we can still be a nice person—the one does not wipe out the other. The difficulty is when anger does arise it tends to dominate and control our behavior, condemning everything as wrong except itself.

| ED |

"Anger has been a great teacher for me as it has always kicked me in the butt, showing me where my behavior was inappropriate. One evening I was driving home and our neighbor had parked her car blocking the driveway to our house. She had done this many times before, and each time could have caused an accident, as we could not pull off the road. This time I lost it and yelled to her to move her car. This triggered her anger, and she ran toward our car and started trying to hit me. My only wish was that I had not responded the way I had!"

Anger may appear as irritation, frustration, rage, and hatred; repressed anger may become depression or bitterness. The emotional fallout from anger can be huge, and, invariably, we have no control over the repercussions—it has been described as a single match that can burn down an entire forest. It takes over, and in the process leaves little room for awareness, our heart goes out of reach, and we lose connection with both our own feelings and the person we are mad at.

| MAURA SILLS |

"I have done anger; I have harmed people. It has been done to me; I have been harmed. I see people acting out anger and thinking it is okay, but there is no awareness of the affect on the other. I come from a family that was angry; it was the way we related to one another. I believed that if people had trouble with my anger, it was their problem, and I had a right to act the way I wanted. But when we express anger, we are creating more pain and suffering in ourselves and in the world. I am not saying all anger is wrong, but it is what we do with it that can cause so much damage."

Trying to eradicate anger is like trying to box with our own shadow: It doesn't work. Getting rid of it implies either expressing it and probably causing emotional damage, or repressing it, which just suppresses it until it erupts at a later time when it usually causes even more harm. If we keep avoiding it, it will keep running after us. There is, however, a midpoint between expressing anger and repressing it. This is a point at which our feelings can be voiced, but with awareness and acceptance. When we can witness and recognize the many faces of anger before it erupts, slowly we become able to stay present as it arises, keeping our heart open, breathing, watching emotions come up and pass through us. We watch as anger fills our mind and makes such a song and dance, and we just keep breathing and watch as it leaves.

| DEEPESH FAUCHEUX |

"Ducks don't do anger. Ducks fight over a piece of bread and then they just swim away. But people keep processing everything that happens to them. That processing of the story—what so and so did to me, she wronged me, why doesn't he respect me—keeps the energy identified as anger and resentment, instead of seeing it as simply energy. Meditation gives us the ability to notice things arise and not be swept away by them. It creates a gap between having a reaction and noticing a reaction. We get to feel the energy arising simply as energy by disconnecting from the storyline that goes with it."

We do not need to own anger as "my" anger, but simply to see it as anger, something that comes and goes. Identifying with anger makes it become solid, real, justified; by not identifying with it, we see that it is not who we really are, merely a fleeting need of the ego to assert itself. Owning anger makes it stick and stay around longer than it needs to, like a fly caught in flypaper and unable to escape. Naming it for what it is enables us to see its transience. So we got angry, okay! Feeling guilty for getting angry is just adding more suffering to an already painful situation. We name it, see it as the ego in action, honor the passion, and watch its destructive nature dissipate under the spotlight.

| ROBERT THURMAN |

"You are going to be angry when someone knocks your coffee all over you, or when they say you are a dork instead of saying how great you are. You are going to feel this surge of heat from your solar plexus, which is when you can either lash out or take ten deep breaths or leave the room because your emotion is so powerful. If you have meditated on how fruitless and useless and absolutely destructive anger is no matter what, then you may still get angry but you will get angry a little less each time. If I don't meditate, I can easily get frazzled. I was very hot-tempered as a young person, and I am not totally cured, I do not pretend to be a holy person, but I am much freer of it now."

Going Beneath Anger

Anger is a complex emotion, as there are often layers of conflicting feelings hidden beneath it, such as hurt, insecurity, or fear, trying to make themselves heard. The power of rage is such that it can act as a defense mechanism and overshadow these other emotions, causing us to lose touch with ourselves and struggle to articulate what we are really feeling.

| RABBI ZALMAN SCHACHTER-SHALOMI |

"We get to see that underneath anger, there is fear, pain, and sorrow, and we cannot deal with anger unless we also deal with what sustains the anger. We forget how we are hardwired. The reptilian system within us makes sure we are secure and safe. If we do not feel secure, then the dinosaur will rear its head and roar. So under anger is always the question of how safe does the reptilian feel."

Getting angry may really be a cry for attention or for contact, having lost our connectedness with each other; it may be expressing feelings of rejection, grief, loneliness, or a longing to love and be loved. Often anger is really saying "I love you," or "I need you," yet we are hurling abuse at each other instead.

| MATTHEW FOX |

"Beneath anger, we often find grief. This is so important, but our culture is not teaching us how to deal with it. This is why so many young people are angry—because nobody is instructing them on how to feel their grief or steer their grief into something constructive. Grief work is such a very important part of understanding anger."

If we repress or pretend anger is not there, then all these other feelings become repressed and denied as well. Only by recognizing what the real emotion is behind the expression can there be more honest communication. Meditation is very important here because, as anger dissipates, our deeper feelings emerge. As such, meditation not only invites us to witness anger, but also to get to know and make friends with it.

| RAM DASS |

"I still see anger arise, even after thirty years of meditating. But now, when it does, I can say, 'Hello, old friend' and I invite it in for a cup of tea. Meditation has helped me to overcome the more negative places, like anger, because it gives me the chance to bring together my identification with my awareness. That gives me purchase to not identify with these states. For example, I am loving awareness and what I am aware of is anger."

In the quiet spaciousness of self-reflection, we see ourselves more clearly and can embrace ourselves just as we are. Meditation is not a cure-all; it is not going to make all our difficulties go away or suddenly transform our weaknesses into strengths, but it does enable us to rest in an inclusive acceptance of who we are. This does not make us perfect, simply more fully human.

| JUDITH SIMMER-BROWN |

"When I first started meditating, I thought that all the things like anger would go away, but what I have found is that I am the same person with the same habitual tendencies. I am still prone to irritation and anger; I still have a hair-trigger temper. The difference is that I can allow space to feel the feeling, it is very much a part of who I am, but I am not driven to act on it, I am not compelled by it in the same way. I have a much greater sense of resonance to my own pain—a familiarity with my habitual patterns—and to other people and their pain. It has made me a much more patient and kinder person."

Using Anger to Bring Change

Although anger can cause untold damage, this does depend on how we use it. Getting angry at injustice or unfairness can be the defining moment that snaps us out of apathy or fear; it can be the impetus that makes us demand change, whether of ourselves or others. This is using the power of anger for transformation, rather than for destruction.

| KEN GREEN |

"There is nothing wrong with passion or even a little irritation as long as we don't let the neurosis become neurotic or self-serving. I was pissed off at times when I was paralyzed, I was really frustrated, but it became the fire that ignited me to change. The only problem is when the fire starts burning things down. Cooking a meal is wonderful—burning down a forest does not help anyone."

The passion and power fueled by witnessing injustice can move us to heroic or compassionate acts, to fight for justice and basic rightness, for what is appropriate and humane. The energy of anger can stimulate us into letting go of past states or ways of being, into cutting through limiting beliefs and destructive patterns of behavior. It is in moments like this that we can use the power of anger to benefit and inspire others.

| DEEPESH FAUCHEUX |

"Thich Nhat Hanh, a Vietnamese Buddhist monk and meditation teacher, described an incident where he and his group of young monks and volunteers had rebuilt a bombed-out village and called all the people in from the forest to celebrate and come back to live there, but then the Americans came and bombed it again and killed many of the villagers and volunteers. Thich Nhat Hanh was enraged. He put his hands in his face and wept. Later, he wrote a beautiful poem about it called 'For Warmth.' In the poem, he says 'No, I am not crying, I hold my face between my hands to keep my loneliness warm . . . to prevent my soul from leaving me in anger.' When he talked about that poem, he said, 'I needed not to discharge that angry energy. I needed to use that energy to help rebuild my country.' In this sense, anger is energy that can both transform and be transformed."

|||

BEING WITH FEAR

Whereas anger is hot and loud, fear is more subtle and pervasive, possessing different faces and disguises. On the one hand, it is a natural response to physical danger, but fear can also be self-created, such as the fear of failure, of the dark, of being out of control, of being different, or of being lonely. We fear loving because we fear being rejected, fear being generous because we fear that we will not have enough; we fear sharing our thoughts or feelings in case we appear wrong or stupid, and we cannot trust because we are dominated by self-doubt and insecurity. We can find this self-generated fear in its acronym: false evidence appearing real. It appears real, even though it may have no real substance, arising only when the ego is threatened or undermined, which makes us cling to the known and familiar. Such fear creates paranoia, worry, nervous disorders, and apprehension.

| SHANIDA NATARAJA |

"In the majority of cases, the suffering in the world is the consequence of fear: fear of people who think differently from us, fear of change, and ultimately fear of death. This is because the left side of the brain stores a conceptual map of the world; it is our personal worldview that defines our sense of identity and our relationship with others and our environment. Obviously, we need to have this conceptual map in order to operate in the physical world, but if it is too rigid then it limits our experiences as well as our personal development. Anyone who appears to challenge the validity of our view or threaten our sense of identity is disregarded by our ego, and we respond with a lack of tolerance. As modern society places so much emphasis on left-brain attributes, such as striving, achieving, and acquiring, we are usually unaware that it is this lack of tolerance in our left-brain view of the world that is actually the source of our suffering."

The immediate effect of fear is to shut us down, to contract our energy inward and, in particular, to shut off the heart. Just for a moment, let your body take the stance of feeling fearful. What is your posture? Most people hunch their shoulders forward, fold their arms across their chests, or assume a similarly contracted position to shield the heart, fear having triggered the need to be on the defensive. In this self-protective place, the heart goes out of reach and it is impossible to feel love or even friendliness. Try saying "I love you" with real meaning while your arms are firmly folded across your heart.

By recognizing fear when it arises and just being with it, rather than reacting to it, we reduce its power. Attempting to stop or repress fear will create further resistance and tension. If fear is rising, we can use the breath to keep open, breathing consciously into our heart area while naming the fear as fear. Say it softly. Watch what happens to the body as fear tries to take hold. As long as we keep the body open and stay in a place of complete acceptance, it will be very hard for fear to establish itself.

| GAY AND KATHLYN HENDRICKS |
"The only real solution to fear is to let yourself acknowledge it and feel it until it dissipates. Fear is natural. Your body spent hundreds of thousands of years perfecting it. Get good at distinguishing between real threats and

imaginary threats made up in your mind. Go ahead and let yourself feel fear. It is normal; it is human. Breathe with it. Dance with it. Above all, do not tempt the universe by shaking a fist at fear and saying that you will not acknowledge its existence. Doing that puts you on a collision course with the forces of nature, like shaking your fist at thunder and saying you are never going to listen to it again."

As long as we push away, deny, or ignore fear, it will hold us captive or keep us emotionally frozen, unable to move forward. In that place, we become fearful of love, of spontaneity; we are unable to appreciate beauty; instead, we get angry or hide behind self-constructed walls. Fear reinforces separateness and isolation; it creates loneliness and enmity. When we bring the monsters out of the dark and into the light, we see them for what they are. The nature of fear is to hold us back, to keep us in a place of limitation and closed-heartedness. This is transformed when we have the courage to turn around and face it, accept it, get to know it, and surrender our defenses, resistances, and fixed ideas.

| JOSEPH GOLDSTEIN |

"I am very familiar with fear. There have been times in my mediation when fear would arise that was not rational, not connected to any present circumstance. Rather, it was a primal fear that was coming to the surface. In working with it, I learned that a key element of the practice is to totally accept the feeling of fear itself. We may think we are being mindful and aware, but usually it is with the agenda that the fear should go away as it is a very unpleasant emotion. It is very easy to fool ourselves into thinking we are accepting something when we really just want it to be over. It was only when I came to a genuine acceptance—expressed in the thought, if this fear is here for the rest of my life, that is okay—that the knot of fear began to unwind.

"Such a radical acceptance loosened the whole psychological pattern. At that moment, the whole mass of fear that had been locked inside completely washed through. Of course, it is not that fear never arose again; rather, my relationship to it changed and became more accepting. Before this happened, I was creating a whole self-story around fear: 'It's so deep, it goes back so far, I'm going to need thirty years of therapy to unwind this.' After that moment of acceptance, I really saw it just as an arising cloud formation that comes together and then dissolves as the conditions change."

At the same time, while looking at fear and feeling fear and being with fear, we also need to go beneath fear to find its source. What is triggering this desire to withdraw, to contract, to close down? What is making fear so fearful? What else is there, perhaps disguising itself as fear, that makes us want to push it away, unseen and unacknowledged? Can we bring this into the light, see and really feel it for what it is?

| GANGAJI |

"I grew up in the south, so I was profoundly conditioned to be racist. In meditation, my conditioning became more visible, but so did the ability to discover what was behind that conditioning, which I saw was fear. Fear is about survival. When you drop under that and experience the fear with-out trying to change it, just letting it be, then it becomes still. When you open your heart to fear, rather than trying to fight it or deny it or even overcome it, then you find it is just energy. There is a deconstructing that happens quite naturally of our racist and nationalist views, our gender or religious views. Then we are left with what cannot be either deconstructed or constructed.

"As the mind approaches the space in meditation where there is no ego, there is no definition of anything, then there is a moment of truth where the only word is surrender, a willingness to surrender. It is a moment of meeting the death of how we have defined ourselves, defined who I am, who you are, what meditation is, what oneness is, and it is a letting go of everything."

|||

Inviting Fear In

| ED |

"As we walked on the beach, we saw a tall crane at the far end attracting a large crowd of people. Weaving our way through the rows of glistening semi-naked bodies basking on the sand, we got closer and saw, high above us, someone about to bungee-jump. Fascinated, we watched him jump, bounce, and fall again, until coming to rest a few feet above the beach. Not for me, I thought, I could never do that. Yet at the same time, I was being drawn toward the crane and I knew I was going to have to do it, to confront myself in this way.

"The guy in front of me in the line was nervous, so I reassured him that all he needed to do was breathe and he would be fine. He was. He went up and he jumped. Then it was my turn and up I went. Suddenly, my knees started shaking, I could not control them, even though inside I was determined to stay sane and calm—I did not want to lose it! When I stood on the edge of the platform, a large rubber band attached to my ankles, my body simply would not move. There was no inner programming, nothing in my brain that recognized how to cope with this situation. I knew I had to jump, had to challenge myself in this way, but my body and my mind both said no. Every time I wanted to jump, my body stood still. Nothing connected.

"Below me, a few hundred voices started shouting: 'Jump! Jump! Jump!' The minutes ticked by, and it felt like an eternity. And then something inside simply surrendered, let go of resistance, released the fear, and I jumped. And beneath the fear, I discovered an enormous reservoir of sheer joy!"

Remember times you have met fear and moved through it, so many times when fear arose but you kept going? Fear may close the heart, but fearlessness comes out of heartfulness, out of releasing resistance. Fear will stop us from facing our demons and participating fully in life, but fearlessness will give us the courage to jump off a crane into the unknown.

| JOHN MILTON |

"If we think of ourselves in the context of being a flow of human being-ness that has flowed through many generations and families, then we will have seen periods of great difficulty, such as the time of the cave bears or the saber tooth tigers. These memories are carried through our ancestral lineage and many of those ancient fears may arise as a primal fear of the dark, of the unknown, of not being in control. We have to be willing to go through that fear, to embrace it and honor the truth of it, to relax into it. When that happens, when we completely trust what is, then the possibility for a complete surrender into the now is possible. But we have to pass through that gate of fear to develop total trust."

In other words, being fearless does not mean we have to stop or deny the fear; fearlessness is not a state of being without fear. Rather, it is the experience of fully feeling the fear, naming it, getting to know it, taking it by the hand, and even making friends with it.

"There's a world of love and there's a world of fear, and it's standing right in front of you," said the singer Bruce Springsteen to David Hepworth in *Springsteen: The "Q" Interview*. He continued:

"And very often that fear feels a lot realer and certainly more urgent than the feeling of love. The night my son was born, I got close to a feeling of real, pure, unconditional love with all the walls down. All of a sudden, what was happening was so immense that it just stomped all the fear away. But I also understood why you are so frightened. When that world of love comes rushing in, a world of fear comes in with it. To open yourself up to one thing, you've got to embrace the other as well."

Fear closes the heart and resists love, whereas love is an open heart that embraces fear. So now try taking the posture of love. Watch how your body opens and expands, your arms reaching outward, accepting and inviting. Fear may still be there, but love can welcome fear—it can embrace any negativity. Watch how your breathing gets deeper, fuller. Where fear shuts out love, love holds fear tenderly. It is like the sky that contains everything. With your arms stretched wide, try saying, "I am frightened" and really mean it.

Letting fear in and making friends with it does not necessarily come easily; fear is a powerful feeling that demands understanding and patience. Fear comes—we breathe and let go. Fear comes—we see how the mind needs reassurance and tenderness. Fear comes—we replace it with love. When we do this, we are inviting the fearful and anxious parts of ourselves to get to know each other, even to sit down for tea together.

| PETER RUSSELL |

"Normally, we push our emotions away or we hold onto something we don't like. We think of letting go as getting rid of something, we think if we could only push this right away, it won't affect me anymore. But we need to do the opposite, to allow it fully in. To let in what is happening, and emotionally receive the experience. And then we can let it be. That is the meditation: just accepting something as it is without trying to change it. Then the shift and the healing can happen."

As long as we deny or reject fear, anger, jealousy, or any other emotion, then we are not accepting and embracing ourselves as we are. Whether a thought or a feeling is either positive or negative makes no difference; it is still an integral part of our being. To reject one part is to remain in denial of the whole.

| BYRON KATIE |

"The work is not to stop the mind, but to invite the mind—to invite every single thought—to come forward into the light. I see all thoughts as the beloved. Why would you want to get rid of the beloved? Why would you want to medicate the beloved out of existence? I invite every single thought to come to me as if it were my dearest child. The whole world is an effect of mind. Inside and outside always match: When you are frightened, the world seems dangerous; when you love what is, everything in the world becomes the beloved. When mind is not at war with itself, there is no separation."

Meditation encourages us to feel fear and get to know it so that it is no longer the enemy. As we do that, then we begin to see the benefits of fear, the gifts that it brings, the unexpected insights and flashes of understanding that move us into a deeper awareness. No longer denying fear, judging it, getting angry about it, or being frightened by it, there is a place within us that allows all these feelings to come and go, rejoicing in their presence for they awaken us to our reality.

| DAVID SHINER |

"In our culture, we are raised with so much fear. The process of meditation is one of slowly peeling away our resistance so we can enter that fear more deeply; there is a greater vulnerability, as well as an acceptance of the vulnerability. Rather than pushing that away and living within the walls of fear that the mind has created, we can start to accept this tremendous vulnerability and realize it is not going to hurt us, that it is actually a good thing. I can feel more deeply. I can go more deeply into my creativity. I can trust the choices I make. There is gratitude."

|||

Practice Meditation:
Meet and Know Your Fear

Breathing steadily, staying open, name the fear.

Then go underneath or behind or into the center of it to find its source.

There may be sadness, loss, inadequacy, and tenderness there.

Keep going deeper, just watching and releasing.

As you do this, so fear will begin to move through you without stopping, without landing.

You will be able to see it, know it, and keep going beyond it.

THE SHADOW SIDE OF THE MOON

| ED |

"One of my most painful childhood experiences is of my father and I having an argument. He was in the bedroom with the door closed, but by playing outside his door, I had disturbed him. When I was angrily told to be quiet, like any kid I shouted back, 'I didn't ask to be born!' Little did I know this would trigger a huge reaction. My father came flying out of the room and nearly attacked me. Later, I came to understand that he must have felt responsible for making my mother pregnant and, therefore, he felt responsible for her death so soon after my birth. So much power was in both of our shadow minds."

There is a huge amount of energy stored in the shadow, the inner place of repression. As we begin to connect to this, we will feel more complete, as if something lost has finally been found. As we touch into levels of trauma and grief for past mistakes or abuse, places of shame or abandonment, in the touching is a knowing of ourselves in a fuller way. Confronting and healing the shadow brings us to a deeper acceptance of our humanity and our connectedness with all others, especially those who are suffering.

| SEANE CORN |

"When I met my shadow right in front of my face, I knew in my meditation that spirit was saying, 'Honey, if you want to be a healer, you have to heal yourself, you've got to walk right into this fire. This is your shadow, and this is what is keeping you from self-love. You are not going to be of any service to this world unless you go right into it and find out who that little girl in you is.' I have got to love the prostitute in me, I have to love the impoverished within me, the illiterate within me, to love the wounded parts of myself across the board, so that I can hold someone else who is wounded in a real regard. The lightest people I have ever met have had to excavate the darkest parts of their souls. My greatest teachers have been the junkies and the whores who have been able to pull themselves out of those circumstances and have then turned around to pull someone else out.

"Meditation helps me to connect with my shadow, and it is a huge shadow! If I can come to terms with the parts of myself that scare me, then when I meet them, I can bow to them, I can understand them, 'Oh, I get it, you are my teacher. You are here to kick my ass on a psychic level and open my heart to truth.' Even though the shadow energy might be painful and uncomfortable, at the same time my heart will bow and surrender to it because it is there to teach me what I need to know."

If the shadow is not seen or met in this way, then it can erupt into our lives unbidden. Perhaps triggered by anger, stress, or emotional conflict, our behavior becomes out of control and we lose our relationship to reality. This is where meditation is of such great benefit. It not only grounds us in sanity, but provides the spaciousness to watch the unfolding show without getting drawn in to it and without closing our heart.

| ANDREW HARVEY |

"Usually, we do not see our own shadow because we are so scared of acknowledging it that we shut down when it begins to appear. Meditation calms us sufficiently to be able to grasp the way our mind moves into rage, jealousy, violence, sadness, a sense of abandonment, all the stuff that keeps coming up like marsh gas from within. It helps ground us in the peace of our inner being so that we can stand the depths of the revelation of the shadow, so that we can embrace it, totally accept it without being shattered or destroyed by it. Instead, we are more noble, generous, and compassionate because of it."

The Dark Night

Entering into the dark places can occur when we are thrown into what is known as the dark night of the soul, a time of torment and loss of connectedness. Such a time is expressed in all the mystical traditions as an integral part of the spiritual path, an experience of inner confusion and emotional turmoil that leads to a deeper awakening and opening. There is a great purification and healing that takes place when we allow ourselves to surrender to such a dark time. Many of the world's spiritual teachers, saviors, and saints have known this darkness and walked along this path, for there is tremendous wisdom that emerges as we get to know this hidden part of ourselves. Ed's own experience is such an example:

| ED |

"I thought I had done my homework. I had trained with my guru in India and become a swami, a devoted yoga monk, and meditation adept. I had seen the light and believed I understood that I was fully awake. No more ego! No more separate me! But I had yet to return to living in the world. Shortly after I returned to the United States, I was invited to a party. A joint was being passed around. I had not smoked pot in a long time, but I felt so good in my life, so happy, that I thought, why not have a puff—it can't harm me—as I remembered the sadhus ('holy ones') smoking hashish in India. So I took a puff and then another. It reminded me of the divine feelings of love and spirituality; it made me feel Godlike and enlightened. So then I felt the desire to smoke some more. It was so good I thought, okay, why not just smoke now and then—it's no big deal. Before I knew it, my old addiction had been triggered and I began to slip into a familiar delusion.

"On one occasion, I thought I had lost my keys. Immediately, I believed that someone had stolen them, and that the guy who was supplying me with the dope had taken them out of my coat and was going to rob my house. As I became more paranoid, I knew I had to go cold turkey and just stop. But when I did stop, everything that the addiction had been suppressing arose to confront me. Fear took over and I entered the darkest time of my life. After thirty years of going for the light, I was being confronted with a vast darkness, a shadow that was overwhelming. A great abyss opened up, and it was all I could do not to fall into it.

"For weeks, I was lost in a swirling mass of abandonment, terror, and meaninglessness. Fear became my constant companion; I felt helpless. I couldn't find or identify a solid me. I couldn't feel anything physically or emotionally; I was empty and numb. I lost the plot. Where was I? I couldn't even remember what I had just said or follow what someone else was saying. My saving grace was that, due to meditation, I had developed the witness, and so I was able to maintain awareness of what was happening. As long as I did not completely abandon myself, then I knew there was a way through.

"Finally, I called a dear friend who was a therapist, even though I couldn't find the 'me' who needed help. She heard me. She was able to take me to the edge of the abyss and enabled me to stand there and look without jumping in. I began to unravel the knots of confusion and to contact deep, hidden feelings of anger and loss, to find strength in the repressed places, and my power slowly returned. Eventually, I made a breakthrough. As with the end of a hurricane, a calm began to emerge. I was grateful to be alive again, and a deep sense of presence that felt like grace descended. Afterwards, I wrote: 'When the ego cracks, the truth of the true self is revealed; when the heart breaks open, the light can shine through.'"

Such an experience may sound hard to go through, but, as Ed appreciated, he was able to maintain the witness throughout, and this is the great gift meditation gives us: to be able to watch, to be aware, without becoming completely lost. Through awareness, we can make friends with what we find. It does not mean there is an instant healing, but it does enable us to move into a healthier place and find ourselves on a different level.

FINDING WHOLENESS

The healing power of meditation lies in the realization that we can no longer avoid ourselves. When we meditate, we sit with who we are; there is nowhere to run to and nowhere to hide. This is a different approach to anything we may have known before, but it creates the opportunity for a far deeper healing. Whatever is going on within us is there to be seen. But as we are simply witnessing and not engaging, so we are free of the emotional turmoil that usually accompanies such states.

| JOSEPH GOLDSTEIN |

"Through meditation, we can deal with deep-rooted issues, such as anger or fear, in an extremely powerful and pragmatic way. There is a world of difference between being lost in these deeply conditioned patterns and not identifying with them. Fear arises, anger arises, hatred or greed or whatever it is, and normally we become lost in that energy, we get carried away and then act it out. This is the cause of so much pain in the world. Meditation is the middle ground between repression and expression, where awareness is open to the emotion, to the feeling; it is a complete honesty with no suppression at all. We allow the emotion to arise; we see it and are with it in its totality. But because of the power of awareness and non-identification, we are not driven to act on it. We have the space to choose. Do I want to act on it? Is it an unwholesome state that I want to let go of or a wholesome one that is worth acting on? Rather than suppression, meditation creates the space for feelings and emotions to emerge so we can see them very directly for what they are."

Meditation also takes us beyond ourselves and allows us to see a bigger picture, of which we are just a part. The sense of "me" as a separate entity is replaced by an awareness of others and of our essential connectedness. No longer is our story the most important issue, nor suffering something that only we know; what we experience is also experienced by all others.

| NOAH LEVINE |

"When we observe ourselves, we realize that just as I am suffering and wish to be happy, so that same suffering is also felt by other living beings; they share those feelings. When we sit with our own suffering and go deeply into acceptance, when we begin to disidentify from 'my' part of the suffering and just see suffering, then our heart opens to suffering as a universal principle and it reaches out in a healing response to that suffering. We go beyond ourselves to the person next to us or across the planet to those who have the same ache in their hearts or in their bodies.

"The more we observe the nature of mind and reality, then the more we see that fear or anger or grief are completely natural and yet completely impersonal. They are just the normal response of a mind to certain circumstances. They are not Self; they are just what happen when we get into certain situations: Anger arises, fear arises, sadness comes. Meditation enables us to both take it less personally, and, perhaps more importantly, to respond to it more skillfully, to just accept it as it is and to meet it with more care and compassion."

In this way, we are no longer a victim to the desires of the mind, but have a greater capacity for choice. Anger is no longer uncontrollable; fear has less power; we are free to use these emotions if we need to when it is appropriate, but they do not run our lives or determine our behavior. Such emotions may be a part of who we are, but they are not who we are in essence.

| MICHAEL BERNARD BECKWITH |

"As we increasingly wake up, we become skilful in navigating the emotional terrain of anger, fear, worry, doubt—all the ego-dominated perceptions that cause us to think such feelings are real and justified. Emotions of all kinds arise, but we are that which witnesses them. We become aware that we are aware. We realize that we have a body but we are not our body. We witness the thinking mind, but we are not the thoughts that are passing through. Our essence remains the changeless witness to that panorama."

One of the greatest gifts meditation gives us is the realization that nothing stays forever, but that everything is impermanent, including emotions we do not like or want to identify with. When we can sit back from anger or fear or grief and take a breath before emotion takes over, then we can watch it pass, often as quickly as it came, for nothing remains the same, not even those feelings that seem so enormous, important, or overwhelming. Given time, what is vital to us now will soon lose its relevance. Knowing this means that we can let go of the issue with that much more ease.

| JOAN BORYSENKO |

"We come to that paradoxical place when we realize there is no way to control destructive emotions but we can accept them for what they are. Here it is: 'I am full of anger in this moment, I can feel it boiling in my gut, my skin is getting hot, and I see images of wanting to strangle this person.' But in five minutes, that reality will change, so we need not mistake the passing state for who we really are. Rather, we accept that there are going to be times when we get angry and even that we may lose ourselves in that anger, especially if we resist it. But we can just accept; there it is. There is sadness; there it is."

As thoughts come and go, as we watch emotions rise and fall like waves, as physical, emotional, or mental pain is felt and then is gone, we realize that this applies to everything. There is a beautiful sense of rhythm that informs us if we wait long enough even the darkest of times will also pass and that we can trust it to pass. Only when we hold on and cling to suffering does it stay and create more suffering. Knowing this, we can sit with whatever pain may be present, letting it in and letting it be.

| JEFF SALZMAN |

"I think occasionally meditation is calming, but mostly it is about looking at the volcano of energy that is arising in my body and mind. I can sit in meditation and not be moved by the pain; I just let it arise and pass away, not engaging in it. You see everything pass within yourself that you thought was solid and was here to get you, and if you surrender to it, you will die, and you surrender to it anyway and you don't die. Instead, you become more spacious and bigger and more capable, and that gets embodied and can be applied to every situation. Then nothing has the same grip that it once did."

Meditation creates a holding space where times of pain, sadness, anger, fear, hurt, confusion, doubt, or all the other emotions can come and be seen and pass through. Each one of them has a role to play and a reason for being, but we do not need to feel the same way forever. Perhaps there is a lesson to be learned, there can even be a blessing in the pain. As the thirteenth-century Persian poet Jalaluddin Rumi said so eloquently in his poem "The Guest House"*:

> *This being human is a guest house,*
> *every morning a new arrival.*
> *A joy, a depression, a meanness,*
> *some momentary awareness comes*
> *as an unexpected visitor.*
> *Welcome and entertain them all!*
> *Even if they are a crowd of sorrows,*
> *who violently sweep your house*
> *empty of its furniture,*
> *still, treat each guest honorably.*
> *He may be clearing you out*
> *for some new delight.*
> *The dark thought, the shame, the malice,*
> *meet them at the door laughing,*
> *and invite them in.*
> *Be grateful for whatever comes*
> *because each has been sent*
> *as a guide from beyond.*

—*Written by Jalaluddin Rumi and translated by Coleman Barks

If we deny anger, fear, shame, or blame, then they will follow us wherever we go; if we hold on, then it is the ego holding onto the need for some form of recognition. When we can witness without attachment, then pain is acknowledged, and once acknowledged, it no longer requires attention. Making friends with the content of our own minds in this way shows us that behind even the darkest pain and difficulty is the happiness that our Thai monk was constantly telling us was there. All we need is the courage to look.

| JACK KORNFIELD |

"Mindfulness meditation opens our wisdom eyes to see that gain and loss, pleasure and pain, joy and sorrow, birth and death, are all the dance of life itself. It teaches us to be unafraid of these changes and cycles, and to trust the capacity to rest in awareness itself, rather than in the changing experiences. When we trust awareness, when we rest in the one who knows, we come to the place of well-being that is beyond the changing circumstances of the world. And it is this that makes the heart happy and free."

|||

6

| | |

We Belong to Each Other

Do not seek perfection in a changing world.
Instead, perfect your love.
MASTER SENGSTAN

| WILLIAM SPEAR |

"A woman was going to Madison Square Garden to see HH the Dalai Lama, and she needed my arm to lean on. She was very frail and she died three months later from AIDS. But at that time, she was walking very slowly with her arm on mine. We came out of her hotel room and into the hallway, where a maid was standing next to her cart. The maid said, 'Good morning,' and the woman said, 'Good morning,' and smiled as we walked to the elevator. This was a hotel where there was an elevator operator, and as we got in the elevator, he said, 'Good morning.' She said, 'Good morning' to him. We went down to the first floor and out to the front desk—'Good morning,' 'Good morning'—and out to a car waiting for us. The driver opened the door saying, 'Good morning,' and she said, 'Good morning.' We went to the security door at Madison Square Garden, where a big policeman opened the door for us: 'Good morning,' 'Good morning.' We went back to where HH the Dalai Lama was waiting, and there was a man who let us in: 'Good morning,' 'Good morning.' Then we met HH the Dalai Lama, and she said, 'Good morning' to HH the Dalai Lama with exactly the same vibration and purpose and openness as she had every other person. It took my breath away. I realized that she was absolutely present every step of the way. She was going to see HH the Dalai Lama when she came out of the door of her hotel suite, and here he was in the maid, in the elevator operator, and in the man at the front desk. Loving your family can be extended to the ones you exchange greetings with, to the person at the traffic lights or in the grocery store, the dry cleaner, everybody. How do you extend your love and joy to them? You just do it."

We can do this because we are not alone here, each one of us—both directly and indirectly—affect each other. Everyone and everything is dependent on everything else, there is no defining place where we begin or end, independent of each other. Every cell in the body exists in a relationship of co-dependency with every other cell, just as we each exist in a relationship with one another, with the plants, rain, sunshine, and the air we breathe. Something as simple as the page on which these words are written involves every natural element and hundreds of people to make it possible. As Mother Theresa reminds us, "If we have no peace, it is because we have forgotten we belong to each other."

Yet relationships create untold problems! Sitting in solitary bliss with our heart wide open and love pouring out of us toward all beings is relatively easy, but as soon as we come in direct contact with another person, all our good intentions are tested. Our ability to stay open and loving, our selflessness and generosity, all this and more are immediately confronted by someone else's own wants and needs, and by his or her capacity to accept and love us or not. So relationship is not just an integral part of being alive; it is also the most vital and challenging teacher we will ever have!

How can meditation be of any help here? Can it facilitate greater friendliness, acceptance, and appreciation? Can it affect intimacy? Can it enable relationships to not only survive the hard times but even to thrive?

| SAKYONG MIPHAM |

"Most of the time, we are not aware of what we do or say or how we can irritate our partner, we are unaware of what they are feeling, we are not able to really hear them. The mind can become tight, there is less room, and every little thing becomes irritating. In reality, the mind is like the sky, it can hold everything, yet we limit it and make it like a narrow body of water or a canyon. Through meditation, the mind becomes healthier, stronger, bigger, and contains more. The trick is to realize that meditation is not some sort of extracurricular activity, something we do on the side, but is actually the main event."

|||

Everything Is Acceptable

The relationship we have with ourselves (although that makes it sound like there are two of us, when, of course, there is just one, just this) creates the foundation for all of our other relationships. As such, it is essential that we make friends with and accept ourselves as we are, to appreciate everything that we have experienced, everything that has gone into making our unique selves. All the physical lumps and bumps, the psychological and emotional colors, textures, shapes, and patterns—these are testament to our history, to the journey we have taken to reach this place, now. As we saw in the last chapter, if we push away even just one aspect of ourselves, especially the dark corners or hidden monsters, then wholeness is not possible.

"Nothing about ourselves should be unacceptable, every dark, unpleasant, cunning, ugly, and pathological aspect of ourselves," writes William Bloom in *First Steps*. "If we cannot accept it, then we will never be able to transform it. If there are aspects of ourselves that we cannot accept, then our whole process of spiritual exploration and transformation is flawed from the very beginning."

This is not a comfortable place to begin, as many of us believe we are unlovable, unattractive, that we have done or said things that were unacceptable, or that we have to prove ourselves before we can be loved. This belief may have come from our upbringing, what we have been told or taught, or through our own sense of inadequacy. But it is where we have to start if we are to be in an honest relationship with ourselves and, from there, with others and our world.

| KATHLYN HENDRICKS |

"People have a place that they think is unlovable, that something about them is unlovable. We need to bring that unlovableness into meditation, rather than keeping it separate, rather than thinking that once we have meditated for however long then we will get to be lovable. If we can be with our unlovableness *right now*, then it will shift it. If we learn to love ourselves, then our interactions with everyone will be different."

One of the main obstacles to accepting that we are lovable just as we are is that many of us were raised to think that we are fundamentally and intrinsically bad, which can lead to a deep level of inner shame. For example, Ed was often told he would never amount to anything. Such shame is corrosive; it eats away at our sense of worthiness, our self-confidence, and our ability to give or receive love. It is so important we see this and recognize we are not personally to blame, that in essence who we are is not bad, and that there is nothing to feel shameful about. We can be at ease with this label of badness, nurture ourselves, and begin to come out from under its influence.

| DEBBIE FORD |

"Even when I wasn't bad, I felt bad. And for so many years I thought that was just me. Then I found out that 90 percent of the world feels bad. They feel bad at something, or they were bad at some time. We can open our heart to that collective experience and heal the shame. This gives rise to compassion. When we are compassionate, we can hold the human self with all its shame, fear, denial, addictions, and insecurities. Compassion for all the ways we try to get love, keep love, get approval, or try to belong. Every day we can say to ourselves, 'It is okay, I understand. I love you. We allow ourselves to rise above the insanity of our human nature.'"

Accepting our insecure or hidden places is saying, "So this is it, this is what is here, this is where I grow from." Loving ourselves is about being tender and gentle when we fail, having kindness and generosity when mistakes are made. It means picking ourselves up each time we fall and letting go of judgment. Acknowledgment comes first—acknowledging that this is what is, that this is who we are. Then comes self-acceptance, which means we can be ourselves without any embarrassment. Acknowledgment and acceptance are not involved with right or wrong, simply with being with what is.

If we are not at ease with ourselves, then we will invariably find something in others to complain about, something other than ourselves that is to blame for how we are. But when we know our own mind with all of its hidden fears and insecurities, when we see the endless dramas and complexities of the ego, then how can we judge ourselves or be surprised by what anyone else does or says? As a psychotherapist friend once said, "I am not surprised by what anyone says when they come into my office because I know my own mind."

| WILLIAM SPEAR |

"Always, when I meditate, there are obstacles for me to reckon with— judgments, distortions, attachments, my story—all the things that I have going on in my waking hours show up in my meditation. As soon as I see them, I have judgments, just as we all make judgments. They arise out of the chatter of our ego selves and those things that separate us rather than bringing us together, those things that deny access into our own hearts instead of opening the door wider. Meditation is an opportunity for me to practice the non-judgmental attitude I try to live by in my relationships, not only with myself and my loved ones, with clients or people in relief camps, but with my mailman and with the woman at the grocery store and with the next person I look at when I pull up to a red light."

We may have been taught that it is very self-centered, immodest, or selfish to love ourselves, yet how can we truly love others if we cannot love ourselves? How can an open heart discriminate and turn away from itself? This is where meditation can bring great understanding and kindness. Getting to know, make friends with, and appreciate ourselves need not be difficult. Rather, it can be a journey of endless delight as we lighten ourselves of the burdens of shame, blame, and guilt by embracing ourselves with understanding and kindness. Then we can play and even dance with life. Perhaps this song from Ed's early childhood says it best:

> *I love myself, I think I'm grand,*
> *I go to the movies and hold my hand.*
> *I put my arm around my waist,*
> *And when I get fresh, I slap my face!*

Into Me You See

An intimate relationship means that we are willing to let go of our defenses and be seen by another for who we are, including all of our vulnerabilities and weaknesses. And this can be terrifying! Recently, we were asked to counsel a couple experiencing problems. John continually gave irrelevant and meaningless reasons for why he felt the relationship was not working; without realizing it, he was expressing his fear of letting someone else see his own hidden places of conflict. Intimacy means "into me you see," but as much as we may want to share and be intimate, being seen in this way reaches into our dark corners, accumulated doubts, mistrust, places of self-dislike, and inadequacy.

Intimacy can, therefore, cause fear, apprehension, even a shutdown of feelings. Rather than exploring the longed-for togetherness, it can all get too overwhelming, causing us to retreat back into our separate corners, hesitant to reach out again. Being seen so closely can feel as if we are totally exposed, emotionally naked with nowhere to hide. So then we resist and put up an invisible wall in an attempt to protect ourselves from such exposure, or from rejection and hurt. However, as much as this wall may protect us, it also shuts us off from our own heart and feelings.

One of the great benefits of a loving relationship is that it provides a safe space for all of these fears that have never before seen the light of day to be acknowledged, known, and held. In other words, love brings up everything that isn't love. This is especially true as a relationship goes beyond the honeymoon phase and enters into a deepening familiarity. In the midst of all the good stuff, past hurt, insecurity, or self-doubt can emerge, straining a relationship and creating confusion and discord. Yet moments like this are an invitation to embrace ourselves and breathe into the fearful places so that we can come defenseless into a relationship. This does not mean we have to be perfect before we step into intimacy—the monsters don't just pack up and move out overnight—but simply that who we are in this moment is open and willing to share.

| DEB |

"Ed and I thought that we had nothing to hide from each other, but as trust grew it exposed all those corners where we hadn't looked. Pain that had happened years previously was suddenly alive again, creating an emotional roller coaster. My father had a big temper and lost it very easily. Somewhere inside, as I grew up, I unconsciously put my own anger on hold. My first marriage ended when my husband started getting angry. At first, I refused to respond, but one day I could not control myself any longer. The sight of my own anger freaked me out, and that was it, I was gone. When I married Ed, I discovered that I had a whole storeroom of anger locked away inside, but now I was able to face it for the first time. He gave me permission to be angry; he was willing to receive it. I could release it without recrimination."

| ED |

"Growing up without a mother, I always felt no one really knew me. I covered it up by being an extravert. I became one of the most popular kids at school by winning all the dance contests. But I became a monk to protect myself from letting anyone get too close. All that to hide how fearful I was! As Deb and I became intimate, there were many moments when I would feel so exposed, as if I were the least lovable person in the world, and I would wonder how she could possibly care for me. That someone I loved could love me back was immensely reassuring."

Intimacy is not something that can be forced or pulled out of a hat; it comes through the letting go of resistance, through softening and opening to ourselves, and to each other. Instead of trying to make discomfort go away, love asks that we be with the discomfort, the embarrassment, the shame, and that we gently embrace whatever is there.

Knocking Heads

Shortly after we were married, we went to India and spent our honeymoon in ashrams and monasteries. We also had a private meeting with HH the Dalai Lama at his residence in McCleod Ganj, in the foothills of the Himalayas. As **Ed** recalls:

"After some thirty minutes of discussion, I was feeling so moved by this gentle, simple, and loving man that I just wanted to stay there and learn from him. I did not want to leave! I was completely in love with the compassion and wisdom emanating from this delightful being. Finally, I said to him, 'I don't want to leave; I just want to stay here with you!' I thought he would say yes, how wonderful, I recognize your sincerity, but instead he just smiled and said, 'If we were together all the time, we would quarrel!'"

So relax, if HH the Dalai Lama, someone who meditates for a few hours every day, can quarrel, then so can we! Inevitably, there are going to be times when a relationship is troubled, when differences collide and egos clash, when stories and histories intrude, or needs are not met. But the holding on to such disagreements and the ensuing shame, blame, and hostile silence is the real problem. There will always be times of flow and times of discord. Having a disagreement or even getting angry does not make us an angry person; it is not the whole of us. Who we are is still basically good; we needed to make a point and just may have done it in a rather unskillful way.

| ROBERT GASS AND JUDITH ANSARA |

"We can get lost in the story, which usually has fault or blame attached to it—I'm feeling this because this happened or you said that—and so we have learned to just drop the story. Even when we are not in the place that we would like to be, we do not process about how we got there or about how we are going to get out of it; we just stop, because otherwise we can start tearing at each other. Usually, one of us will say, 'Are we having a conversation that is contributing to the greater good?' We get connected first and then talk about what was disconnecting us, rather than tearing at each other from a place of disconnection, thinking that will get us connected."

Invariably, we get upset because we want the other person to be different from how they are. Perhaps one of the hardest things to accept in a relationship is that we cannot change our partner into the person we want them to be. The only thing we can change is our attitude toward them. Instead of seeing what is wrong, focusing on the faults and weaknesses or what is needed for them to reach what we think would be a happier place, we can hold them as they are and be there for them as they discover their own way.

| MARY TAYLOR |

"Before I practiced meditation, I was much more likely to believe the labels I put on things. Sure, I still label things, but I see through them more quickly. I see my spouse for who he is rather than who I imagined him to be, or what I had labeled him as, or my image of who I wanted in a spouse.

Now I can celebrate him for who he is rather than who he is not. No one is ever going to be who you want him to be, not even yourself."

Difficulties in relationship can also show us the many ways our ego-selves try to be right, which can be a cause for great amusement. When we were in India at an ashram—a residential yoga community—we were staying in a simple room and practicing yoga and meditation each day. It sounds idyllic, but we had only been married a few months and issues were accumulating. On one occasion, we were having a big disagreement (we have no recollection what it was about—do we ever remember the cause?) when one of the teachers walked past and heard us. From outside our room, he called out, "So how's the weather?" As we saw our battling egos through his eyes, it reduced us to instant laughter. On another occasion, we were sharing some of our marriage issues with our meditation teacher. He looked at us quite puzzled. "Why not just laugh?" he asked. And he was right. When we see the absurdity of two egos knocking heads and trying to outwit each other, it is very amusing. So often a disagreement is simply about seeing the same thing in two different ways: One sees a white ceiling, the other sees a flat ceiling, but it is the same ceiling.

When a relationship is at its height, it is as if the two separate partners merge into each other and become one. This works wonderfully while there is concord and rapport. But when there is discord, when doubt, selfishness, blame, or fear arises, then we tend to retreat back into our separate selves, communication at a standstill. At these times of difficulty, rather than being merged, the respective egos start to attack each other, to knock heads, in an attempt to find that place of merging again. Shaming or blaming each other simply causes further separation and conflict. Healing comes by recognizing the much deeper desire for unity.

In actuality, those people we have a difficult time with are really our teachers. For without an adversary—or those who trigger strong reactions such as annoyance and anger—we would not have the stimulus to develop loving kindness and compassion. So we should be grateful to them for teaching us acceptance, tolerance, and equanimity; we can actually thank our exasperating partners, relatives, friends, or colleagues for the chance to practice patience. What a gift!

Taking Responsibility

We had a marriage blessing at Samyé Ling, a Buddhist monastery in Scotland. We talked to Akong Rinpoche, the abbot, and asked him what advice he had for people in a relationship. He suggested that if two people disagree or argue, then they should both take time out by themselves to meditate alone and consider what they were doing that might be adding to the situation. So, rather than complaining about what the other person is doing to us, we should look at our own behavior and the effect it is having. In particular, we should explore our own attitudes, motives, and hidden agendas, and how these might be affecting our partner. How am I treating this person? What am I doing to that person to make him behave like this? How can I treat him more kindly? This, Akong explained, takes the emphasis off blaming and shaming, and we get to see where we may also be responsible for the discord; we move from power struggles to ownership.

| LINDSAY CROUCH |

"The time we take in meditation is time we are letting go of the world, of the way we ordinarily think in the world, and just that will help us when in an argument or time of difficulty. We have the strength to hold a little longer with more patience and to consider before we react. Even if we hold for only a couple of minutes more, it is worth it. If my husband and I have an argument or find ourselves really at odds, we both know that we each have responsibility for it, that we cannot just blame the other. We go to different rooms and sit quietly, even if it is just for a few minutes, until we are able to say, 'I am sorry.' The time of being quiet has given us the ability to detach from our bruised egos."

Taking time out gives us the space to let go. Too often we cling to difficulties and make them more than what they are; we replay the irritation in our minds until we become even more bothered. The ego does not want to let go! Yet what a relief when it does and we can return to a place of equanimity. The person on the other side of the argument may not want to let go, but we can work with ourselves and release whatever annoyance is going on.

| SUSAN SMALLEY |

"A fun way of letting go was once visually described to me: Bend your index finger into a hook and think of it as a 'thought' that may grab or anger you, or bother you in some way. Hook your other index finger, and see this as how you relate to that irritating thought. If you hook the fingers together, that is you 'holding on' to something. But then imagine if you just straighten one finger, it does not matter which one. Immediately, all the things or people that you are attached to, that you hold on to, that cause you stress and discomfort can be released, simply by straightening your finger and letting the issue or person go from your mind."

When difficulties or misunderstandings arise, we easily make our partner into the enemy. This is usually due to our own longing to be seen or heard, or to be loved. When we are in a heated quarrel, what we so often really want to say is "I need love." But it is far easier for the other person to be wrong than to admit that we have unmet needs. Only by acknowledging that we are blaming them rather than owning our own feelings can our so-called enemy become our friend again.

| JOHN GRAY |

"When we are hurt, we believe our loved one is the adversary. I see that so much in my own marriage. My feelings would get hurt because I was thinking that my wife was controlling or criticizing or rejecting me. I would always have some reason for the pain, until gradually I saw that the source of my pain was actually the *belief* that she was not loving me. This is the process: firstly, believing that someone is my enemy who is not my enemy. Secondly, the pain continues to grow the more I believe the lie, even though that pain is all self-inflicted. Then I withhold my love. There always seems to be a good reason for doing this, but withholding love from someone who we do love is the greatest pain of all. Whenever we choose to stop loving, it causes a huge source of conflict as our fulfillment in life, our joy in life, is letting that love come through us. I no longer see my wife as my enemy as I have realized that everything she does comes from a place of love. It may be misguided. She may not know what I need. But her intent is to love."

Meditation enables us to see not only how we are responsible for our own feelings, but also that whatever we may be experiencing is a choice we are making in that moment. It is not as a result of what someone else might be saying or doing. When we step back from the heat of conflict and explore why someone makes us feel a certain way, it quickly becomes obvious that it has very little to do with the other person and much more to do with a place inside ourselves.

| JOSEPH GOLDSTEIN |

"There is one basic understanding that helps us in every dimension of relationship: that each one of us is totally responsible for our own emotions. Some time ago, I was in a relationship with someone and as we were having a little argument, she turned to me and said, 'Stop making me feel aversion.' I started to laugh, which, of course, did not help the situation, but nobody *makes* us feel anything. How we feel and how we relate to what we are feeling is completely up to us. Generally, we blame others for how we feel; we think others are responsible for our mind states. If we all took responsibility for our own emotions, then most of our interpersonal relationships would be a lot easier.

"If we have the view that other people are responsible for how we feel, then we are turning over all the power to them. We cannot control what other people do—their minds, their attitudes, or their behavior. But if we understand that how we are feeling is completely up to us, then we can reclaim that power. Then, no matter what anybody else does, it is up to us how we react, how we relate. Nobody can make us feel a certain way."

The Big C: Communication

Taking responsibility is also about being willing to really hear someone. We are often asked what one thing we believe has made our relationship work as long as it has, despite many ups and downs. It is something we both agree on: communication. Without being able to share our feelings, we remain locked in a separate world from each other.

| KRISHNA DAS |
"We define ourselves as separate beings, and if we are separate, then we have to put a wall up around ourselves. We have to protect ourselves and our feelings so that no one else can get to them. Our problems are because this wall does not just protect us, but it also locks us out of our own hearts and so we continue to be isolated and to suffer."

How we talk with each other, how honest we are, how much we are able to share, how much we hold back, how much we are able to express our feelings, how well we are able to hear and receive our partner's feelings, what we think she is feeling, what she thinks we are feeling, what we think has been said or think what was not said, all adds up to the need to communicate honestly and openly. Without it, hidden resentments, secret feelings, and the "I am right but she is wrong" syndrome flourishes. If our feelings are not shared clearly, or if there is any form of deceit or resistance, then this will act like quicksand, pulling the relationship down. Often this means reading between the lines, as it were, for we are not always able to express what we mean.

| GAY HENDRICKS |

"In relationships, there are some real practical skills we have to have, such as speaking honestly and listening openly. In first grade, we spend all our time memorizing the capitals of the world when we could be learning how to communicate with each. To be able to say, 'I feel hurt' or 'I feel angry' or 'I feel scared right now' and how to really hear that, without criticizing or blaming, how to listen with sensitivity. As a man at one of our workshops said, 'I realize I have never really listened to people before; I was just watching their mouths move until it was my turn to speak.'

"In meditation, there is a deep noticing and opening to what is actually going on. It puts us in deeper touch with what our real intention is. In my early relationship with Katie, I caught myself listening with the intent to argue with her, or listening with the desire to prove her wrong. I realized that instead, maybe I could listen to her with the purpose of drawing out her real essence. Once we started to lock into those deeper intentions, life took on a new way of being because at the core there is a resonance that we share. I find that meditation amplifies my direct experience of that resonance. It is the water that gives life to my ability to love."

Within each of us is a very deep longing to connect and to be truly heard. Communication means both giving and receiving, sharing and listening. To listen is to be completely present without any hidden agenda, without advising, blaming, or shaming, without preconceived ideas, without the desire to try to fix anyone or make him better, without comparing his story to our own, or without our own story influencing our opinions. Then we can hear. How hard this can be! But when we are really heard, when the story we live with inside of us is known and received, then there is a great letting go, a release, and it is immensely healing. We are no longer alone in our pain— someone has heard us, someone else knows.

| JACK KORNFIELD |

"While there are many forms of meditation, the essence of these is to reconnect with ourselves and sense our unity with all life. This allows us to live from wisdom and compassion rather than with fear and confusion.

The most important element of meditation is that it gets us to slow down, stop, and pay attention. Then the capacity for deep attention, of kind and compassionate listening, opens a conversation with the heart."

The Shared Journey

Some years ago, we were attending a wedding at Karma Dzong, a Tibetan center in Boulder, Colorado. Chögyam Trungpa, who was conducting the marriage ceremony, said to the aspiring couple, "If you can make friends with one other person, you can make friends with the world."

When we can be honest with another person and allow her to be herself, then we can touch a deeper place together. Anger and hurt arise when we want to protect our tenderness, to shield our sensitivity by covering it with false bravado. Sharing the journey means being willing to feel our feelings, not to hide them behind a façade, but to be bold and honest in our defenselessness.

Being committed to a relationship is a willingness to look at our own issues and how we are affecting or influencing the other person, and, therefore, it is also a commitment to our own growth. Relationship is not just based on how much we love each other but, perhaps more importantly, on how much we are willing to live with each other's neurosis, for that is more often our daily reality. Love does not just fall from the sky, perfect and intact. It has to be reaffirmed and remembered in every moment.

Commitment is also the willingness to stay with the relationship through the tough times. Rather than the fight-or-flight syndrome, where we either argue it out or take off, it is about being present by tending and befriending each other. For instance, we began our marriage with the agreement that only one of us could wobble at any time, so that the other could be there to hold the vulnerability.

| ED |

"Knowing Deb was there when I had to face my demons meant so much; it was my saving grace. Our commitment gives us the strength to accept each other for who we are with all of our different needs, thoughts, and feelings. The mirroring, the confronting, and the communicating are constantly challenging! We try to be honest when we are feeling tested. We look at it, name it, and embrace it. Our relationship is an on-going commitment to making friends with ourselves so that we can be a friend to each other. It is a constant moving with the flow and a releasing of resistance to that flow."

The most rewarding way to enter into relationship together is by meditating together. Meditation is an essential ingredient in a shared journey, not just because it allows us to be together on the same wavelength, but because it gives us the spaciousness to accept and love each others' differences and to see the other just as they are, without any delusions. In that shared silence, the "me versus you" dissolves, and the power struggles and one-upmanship dissolves. There is a dropping away of the superfluous, of the separation and hostility. Meditating together reminds us of our priorities and present-moment reality. We meet in a deeper place, beneath the ego games, where we can connect with who we really are.

| GAY HENDRICKS |

"One thing that makes couples or people quarrel is feeling like they are not in the same space or on the same wavelength, but if we meditate together, then we get on the same wavelength. It is like there may be storms on the surface of the ocean and the boat is getting tossed around, but if we drop down ten or fifteen feet, there is no storm going on, it is calm there. When we come back to the surface, we can see that maybe nothing is really such a big deal. On a very practical level, when we meditate together, we come to that place that is not so critical or quick to find fault.

"If we look at all the hot spots or trouble spots in the world, or all the quarrels between people, it is all about focusing on what is wrong or looking for what needs to get fixed, instead of finding that place that does not need to be fixed. We may be arguing about the concept of water, whether water is this way or that way or two parts hydrogen and so on, when all we need to do is take a drink of water and we will know what water is. When couples have time together, it invariably gets used up with the business of their lives or their relationship. To have sacred time together is really a way of creating harmony and deepening into love."

We do not have to go in search of love, or try to develop it, or pray for it to be shown to us. We have no need to protect it; there need be no concern about being taken advantage of or of being hurt, no fear of losing love or of giving away so much that we have none left. Love could not happen if it was not already an integral part of our being. How can we lose what we truly are? How can we be left with nothing when love is the source of all life? The more we love, the more we are given to love with. We can never lose it; we can only lose sight of it; we can only think we have lost it, but it is always with us.

| DEB |

"The Indian government invited Ed and I to speak at a yoga conference in Pondicherry. Ed was speaking about the beauty and awesome power of the unconditional love that is made manifest in meditation when a man in the audience raised his hand.

" 'Please sir,' he said. 'What is this love that you speak of? Where can I find it? How do I get this love?'

"Ed replied: 'You awake in love, you eat in love, you bathe in love, and you walk in love. Love is your nature; it is who you really are.'

" 'Oh sir,' the man said, 'you have all the right answers!'"

|||

7

|||

The Pearl in the Oyster

Without forgiveness, human society and
existence are impossible.
BISHOP TUTU

We attended a conference focused on gaining insight into men's issues. Brian stood up to describe the abuse that he had received from his father when he was a child. Among other things, his father had threatened him by holding a shotgun to his head. This is serious abuse indeed, and Brian talked about it with anger and bitterness. He said quite emphatically that he would never be able to forgive his father. After Brian had spoken, there were a few minutes of stunned silence. Then a man at the back of the room stood up and simply said, "If you can't forgive, then you can't dance."

What was so eloquently voiced in those few words describes exactly the emotional holding that takes place when there is no forgiveness. Our ability to dance—to move emotionally, to give, to love, to feel alive and free—gets stuck. All the pain, grief, and hurt get held in this immovable or frozen emotional place. We cannot move forward when a part of us is locked in the past, and we cannot be in the present as memories from the past are constantly pulling us away. We become a victim of ourselves.

All around us is the evidence of a lack of forgiveness: broken families, self-hate, guilt and shame leading to depression, countries at war, huge amounts of fear and anger, bitterness, prejudice, self-righteousness and closed-heartedness.

| DEB |

"For a while, I worked in a nursing home, where I saw numerous residents clinging to incidents from the past: words said in anger, distorted memories of how they had been wronged by children who had disagreed with them and left in anger. So much bitterness. They could not let go, even now, so near to dying. They could not heal their differences with their children and come together because over the years the hurt and anger had become solid, fixed, and immovable, as if they were surrounded by prison bars."

When something happens that invokes either guilt and shame at our own behavior or hurt and rage at someone else's—it makes no difference which—then without empathy or forgiveness, the emotion from that incident gets locked inside, held in time, blocking our ability to be happy. We learn to live by ignoring this dark place without realizing how deeply limiting it is, how it holds back our joy and freedom along with the guilt or anger. When the ego is wounded, it points the finger and sees the other person as the cause of the suffering but it does not recognize how, by holding onto hurt feelings, we are simply creating more grief for ourselves.

| GANGAJI |

"One of the hardest stories or definitions to give up is our definition of ourselves as a victim. We have all experienced being hurt by someone, such as our parents or a lover, maybe our teachers. But it is not about denying the hurt; it's actually about opening and meeting the hurt, and then the hurt itself becomes a deepening of our heart. In that moment, it is natural for forgiveness to occur."

The power of forgiveness is far reaching. In South Africa, Bishop Tutu brought understanding, empathy, and forgiveness into action with the Truth and Reconciliation Commission, enabling war criminals to admit their crimes, and in so doing, to be released from their guilt and shame. Nelson Mandela was able to forgive his jailors after being incarcerated for twenty-seven years. In Cambodia, Bhiksu Mahagoshananda strived to bring forgiveness to his country.

| JACK KORNFIELD |

"Mahagoshananda was the great peacemaker of Cambodia, nominated for the Nobel Peace Prize many times. He spent countless years walking across the war zones of Cambodia bringing refugees back to their villages while chanting the verses: 'Hatred never ceases or ends by hatred, but by love alone is healed. This is the ancient and eternal law.' Taking Cambodian farmers and villagers, whose lives had been devastated, step by step in a loving way through the war zone and back to their own villages, brought reconciliation and forgiveness and healing to an enormous part of the Cambodian country."

Forgiveness is particularly compelling when we recognize that who we are is intrinsically no different from the one who needs to be forgiven. Marian Partington, an old friend of Deb, had a sister brutally murdered by serial killers Fred and Rosemary West in England. Marian says on forgivenessproject.com: "I began to go on Buddhist meditation retreats. It was at one of these that I made a vow to try and forgive the Wests. When I came home, I had an overwhelming, involuntary, and profoundly physical experience of murderous rage: it went . . . whoosh! All the way up from my belly to my skull. I wanted to scream, pull my hair out, claw at the ground. So for me, forgiveness began with murderous rage. Until then, I had not thought of myself as a murderous person, but at that moment I was capable of killing. In other words, I was not separate from the Wests."

Thich Nhat Hanh, a much-loved Vietnamese Buddhist monk, often receives letters from Vietnamese people fleeing

Vietnam by boat. On the high seas, these desperate people may be taken over by pirates and robbed of what little they have. In one incident, a twelve-year-old girl was raped by a pirate and was so tormented she threw herself into the sea and drowned. Her distraught parents wrote to Thich Nhat Hanh for advice. In response, after meditating on the incident for a number of days, he said that if he had grown up in the same village as that pirate, with the same circumstances and suffering in life, then he too may have had such a closed heart as to be able to inflict pain on a young girl. He wrote a poem called "Please Call Me by My True Names," where he says:

> *I am the twelve-year-old girl*
> *refugee on a small boat,*
> *who throws herself into the ocean*
> *after being raped by a sea-pirate.*
> *And I am the pirate,*
> *my heart not yet capable*
> *of seeing and loving.*

The above stories of forgiveness are deeply inspiring, yet are we able to do the same thing in our own home? Can we bring forgiveness to our enemies, to those who have hurt us, or even to ourselves?

Forgiving Others

Forgiving other people for the hurt or harm they have done is not easy. We are the ones feeling the pain, however, not them, and the longer we hold on, the more suffering we cause ourselves. How many times have we rerun the tape, gone over the details of who said what to whom, of how it all happened, of hidden motives, of the injustice and blame or the guilt and shame? How many times have we done this, and did it ever help us feel healed, more joyful, or happier? How often do we

have to do this before we see that all of it is going nowhere
other than prolonging our unhappiness?

"The theory behind forgiveness is simple," writes Ken Wilber
in *Grace and Grit*. "If we are going to insist on identifying with
the little self in here, then others are going to bruise it, insult
it, injure it. . . . The ego's first maneuver in dealing with this
resentment is to try to get others to confess to their faults: 'You
hurt me; say you're sorry.' What the ego doesn't try is forgiveness, because that would undermine its very existence."

We are not trying to be simplistic. From a rational point
of view, it can seem impossible to forgive: We are hurt and
want revenge, it is the other person's fault, so why should we
forgive; what we have done appears beyond blame. But if we
want to reach a place of healing and closure within ourselves,
then we have to confront this desire to hold on to the story—to
keep reliving the details or to get revenge—for this not only
causes further suffering but also maintains our separation
from each other, limiting our capacity to trust or to love.

To forgive means to fully acknowledge our feelings: how
angry, upset, abused, betrayed, bitter, or indignant we are;
how unfair life is; how let down or sad we feel, and that it is
absolutely okay to feel this way. We know and feel the pain,
but the desire to no longer continue the suffering is stronger;
we care enough about ourselves to not want to carry the anger
or sadness any longer. We are ready to reclaim our dignity.

Understanding the pain or the motivation behind an act of
betrayal or violence can help emotional turmoil to deepen into
empathy, for if someone causes hurt, it is invariably because
he is hurting himself. Have you ever noticed how, if you are
feeling good, it is almost impossible for you to harm or hurt
anything? You will even take the time to get a spider out of
the bath or to let a fly out of the window. But if you are upset
or feeling very stressed, then you will not think twice about
washing the spider down the drain. In other words, our inner
torment will spill out and harm anyone or anything in its way.

We were at a talk in England where we watched Jo Barry, the daughter of a politician killed by an IRA bomb during a political conference, walk on stage with Pat Magee, the man who planted the bomb. You could have heard a pin drop in the audience, especially when they talked about how they had come to understand each another. As **Jo** says, also on forgivenessproject.com:

"I wanted to meet Pat to put a face to the enemy, and see him as a real human being. Over the past years of getting to know him, I feel I've been recovering some of the humanity I lost when that bomb went off. To say 'I forgive you' is almost condescending—it locks you into an 'us-and-them' scenario, keeping me right and you wrong. That attitude won't change anything. But I can experience empathy, and in that moment there is no judgment. Sometimes when I've met with Pat, I have had such a clear understanding of his life that there is nothing to forgive."

Through standing in another's shoes, we can appreciate her pain, which gives rise to a deeper empathy. This can enable us to accept and release layers of anger, as well as to be non-judgmental when confronted with injustice.

| MARSHALL ROSENBERG |

"I was working in San Francisco with eight fathers who had sexually molested their daughters; I was working with both them and their girls. At one point, one of the men said to his daughter, 'Well you asked for it!' I jumped up and said, 'Time out!' I ran out of the room because I wanted to hit that guy when I saw the look in his daughter's face, a twelve-year-old girl, and her father was saying she asked for it. When I saw the judgment I was making toward this father, I had to go outside and meditate in the hall before I could go back into the room.

"I really wanted him to empathize with his daughter, to see the pain that blaming her was creating. When I went back inside, I said to him, 'I was in a lot of pain when I heard you say that, because I saw her face, and I would really love some understanding on your part of how painful it must be for her to be blamed for this.'

"When we empathize, there's nothing to forgive. We only have to forgive when we think what the other person has done is wrong, bad, inappropriate, or whatever. But when we empathize, we see that the other person is doing the same thing that all human beings do every moment, which is the best they know how. So, when somebody has done something that I really do not like but I empathize with what is going on in him, at that moment there is nothing to forgive.

"When I know I am going to be working with a certain group that I have some rage or prejudice toward, then I know I have got to do some real meditation before I go. I meditate on what is causing me to be angry and have judgmental images of these people, then I try to be conscious of how the kind of thinking that judges people is a tragic distortion of what is alive in me, and that it occurs when needs are not being fulfilled. I translate those messages into a language of life, as when I am connected with life I can't be angry, depressed, blaming, or ashamed. Then I am better able to deal with the situation."

We all contain a measure of dark and light, of good and bad; we all have the potential to hurt each other as much as we have the potential to love. The greed, hatred, and ignorance in another person can cause great damage, but within each being is also the potential for kindness, generosity, and selflessness. It may not have manifested yet, but it is there. In the quiet of meditation, we connect more deeply with this latent potential and can touch on our fundamental equality and basic goodness. The forgiveness meditation in chapter fifteen is a practice that enables us to see the story, let it go, and then go beyond it.

Recognizing Ignorance

| DEB |

"I worked on my relationship with my father for a long time. I was in therapy by the time I was eighteen, went through layer upon layer of rejection issues, need issues, confronting him, talking to him, not talking to him, forgiving him, then not forgiving him. I maintained my relationship with him in the vague hope that one day he would change, that he would actually be able to say something nice, something affirming or loving. I didn't expect him to be able to say I love you, but just something positive, some form of acknowledgement. I was waiting for this day to come, but in the process, I was still being emotionally abused.

"Finally, in my mid-thirties, I came to a point where I no longer needed that affirmation from him. I had touched into a deeper acceptance of myself. And, as the need was released, so I was able to see the hurt and confused man that he really was, someone who had no idea how to give or how to love. I saw that his pain was far greater than mine, even though he was not aware of it. As I separated his pain from my own, I was finally able to see his limitations and ignorance for what they were and to let go. As a result, we have been able to rebuild our relationship."

Forgiveness is not about denying the suffering or ignoring the depth of our feelings. It is not the same as forgetting, which simply puts our feelings in some distant recess from where they usually reemerge and cause further pain at a later date. Nor does forgiveness take away from the gravity of what occurred— a heinous or grievous act is just that; it is not acceptable in itself. It does not justify or make right what happened.

Rather, what we are forgiving is the ignorance that led to such behavior, the ignorance of our essential interconnectedness—that what I do to you I am also doing to myself. Such ignorance means that greed and hatred can dominate our actions. As a Jew, Ed was dumbstruck when his teacher, Swami Satchidananda said, "You even have to forgive Adolph Hitler." But then Satchidananda added, "You don't forgive the act, but you forgive the ignorance that perpetrated it. You forgive the being inside and hope they will learn and change."

When we can bring such understanding to the ignorance and inner pain that perpetuates further pain, while hoping the other person will realize the damage his lack of awareness has caused, then forgiveness and compassion genuinely arise.

| JAMES TWYMAN |

"Two and a half years ago, my wife was murdered by two men in Chicago. We were naturally overwhelmed by the sadness and anger that come from such a tremendous loss. To this day, no one has been caught or arrested for this crime, and so the anger hasn't really had a target. There is no one I can be angry at. Yet very quickly my anger moved to compassion. Not that I don't want justice to be served, not that I don't want these people to be found so that they can face up to what they did, but I began to feel a sense of compassion for what it must have taken for these two men to commit such a violent act. What must they have gone through in order to do it? What sorts of traumas did they have to endure to be so injured, to be so sick, that they could do something like they did to Linda?

"There is still a great deal of anger that I feel and a great deal of healing that I need to do, just in a human way, to move past what happened. But in a larger sense is the realization that allows me to enter into a deep forgiveness for these people and their ignorance. So even though I need to continue to work through my human emotions, I have been able to experience forgiveness on a very real level.

"Violence and prejudice are always caused by the belief that we are separate from one another; the more separate and different we seem, whether it be countries or races or sexes or sexual preferences, the more fertile the ground is for such behavior. When I embrace that part of me that can just as easily be a rapist or murderer, and I accept and love that part of me, then it makes it easier to forgive others. When we realize that we are not different, but that in essence we are the same, then the ground is fertile for respect and inclusion. Ultimately, we realize that the violence I am committing against another is really a violence against myself."

If we think we are separate, independent, and not connected to anyone or anything else, then our actions will be self-centered and self-motivating and the more we will be hurt or will hurt another. By recognizing this truth, we are able to release the boundaries that keep us apart, to honor our shared humanness and make connectedness a reality.

| RAMA VERNON |

"Meditation is one of the few things that enables us to forgive, for without it we cannot see the nature of what it is that needs to be forgiven. When there is true forgiveness, it is healed inside of our being. It is forgiving ourselves for having believed in separation. No matter what that person has projected onto us, no matter what that person has done, when we can see them as ourselves everything drops away that has caused the separation."

|||

Asking for Forgiveness

Knowing that we really only hurt another when we ourselves are hurting, we can see how we have lashed out, caused pain, or hurt someone at those times when the pain in ourselves was unconsciously dominating our feelings and actions. To ask for forgiveness demands courage, humility, and swallowing pride. No one likes to admit they are wrong, but in so doing there is the space for tremendous healing. A single word can make such a difference; saying we are sorry will not change the world, but it will help someone else feel a whole lot better about the world.

| MAURA SILLS |

"I know that we have to forgive, but actually we need to ask for forgiveness as well. The truth is we are going to cause harm and be harmed simply because we are human beings. I do not know if I have helped more than done damage, if I have hurt as much as I have helped in my lifetime. So I ask forgiveness for all that I have done, knowingly and unknowingly, consciously or unconsciously, and in return I truly forgive you for what you may have done, knowingly or unknowingly, that has affected me and taken me away from my better good. We get entangled in all of this suffering and confusion. When we can ask for and give forgiveness, we walk away slightly more humble in what we do and how we are."

In asking for forgiveness, we are also showing how much we care. We enable the hurt one to heal through the admission of our own weakness and failure. Even if we believe we are right and have nothing to ask forgiveness for, some misunderstanding has caused pain and wherever there is pain we can bring healing. Asking for forgiveness also enables the other to see how they may have participated in the conflict. It breaks down the barriers so two can meet as one again. In that moment, does it matter who is right or wrong?

Sometimes it is not possible or appropriate to actually communicate with the other people in order to ask for forgiveness. They may have died, or perhaps they refuse to talk with us, or we don't know where they are. This need not make any difference. We can bring them into our meditation where we can release any held feelings, such as shame, regret, or anger. Then, if we have a chance to see them again, we will feel differently toward them; in turn, this may help them to be healed.

Forgiving Ourselves

| RABBI ZALMAN SCHACHTER-SHALOMI |

"Every night before I go to sleep, I say, 'I forgive everyone, including myself.' I do not want to have a slate full of unforgiven things before I go to sleep. It is like doing your dishes before you go to bed. And then on Sabbath I go over the whole week and forgive everything that has happened, whether I did it or someone else did it."

We usually focus on forgiving someone else: This other person has done this wrong thing to me, and I am hurt, angry, and upset. It is the strongest position to be in as we are the abused or victimized one and the other person is the abuser who has done the dirty deed. However, in a recent workshop, we asked how many people were carrying some personal guilt or shame for something they had done in the past that they could not forgive *themselves* for. At least three-quarters of the people put up their hands. We want healing, and forgiveness, but we can find it very hard to give this to ourselves.

"Forgiving means accepting myself. Gulp! This means giving up an old friend of mine—self-criticism," writes **Treya Wilber** in *Grace and Grit*. She continues:

"When I visualize all the things that prevent me from feeling right about myself then, up there higher than the rest, as a kind of backdrop to all my other problems, is a figure of a scorpion with its tail arched over its back. On the verge of stinging itself. This is my self-criticism, cutting myself down relentlessly, feeling unlovable, the grievances against myself that keep me from seeing the light and the miracles that can only be seen in that light. Hmmm. The big one."

We try to avoid looking inside our dark corners, but accumulated guilt, shame, or self-dislike can become familiar crutches for the ego, affecting our activities and behavior. Guilt for what we have done stays with us long after the event: I am such a bad, hopeless, useless, awful, uncaring, hurtful, unlovable person who never gets it right. We even believe guilt is our atonement, that through it we are somehow redeeming our wrong doing, when in reality all it does is create more suffering. Blame follows guilt: How could I have done such a thing? How can I ever trust myself? How can I ever be trusted by anyone else?

But this is actually like a smokescreen clouding our mind and stopping us from seeing that we are more than the event, that whatever we did is not the whole of us. Without forgetting or repressing what happened, we can put the story down. We can say: "I made a mistake, but I am not the guilt, I am not the mistake, I am not the failure, it happened, but that is not who I am now, and it is not the whole of me."

Forgiving ourselves is an ongoing process: every time we criticize or blame ourselves for being hopeless, useless, wrong, stupid, for all the self-dislike and self-denial, for believing we deserve the bad things that happen, that we must have done something wrong to be so abused, for thinking we should have known better, that it was all our own fault, that we were asking for it, for rejecting ourselves, for abandoning ourselves, for ignoring or denying our own needs and feelings. Whenever we get caught up in such self-negating thinking, we can simply say, "I forgive you." We do not need to create more guilt, shame, or blame—the world has enough already.

| MICHAEL BERNARD BECKWITH |

"Forgiveness is really for yourself, because you are releasing toxins, animosity, and hate out of your own system. I call forgiveness meditation a daily detox, where at the end of the day, you review yourself to see if you are holding onto anything—something someone said to you, someone said about you, something you did that you are not very proud of—and you work with yourself to eliminate that, you detox those particular thought forms so they do not impinge on your connectivity, your creativity, or health.

"Ultimately, forgiveness must be a way of living. It enables us to grow spiritually because we have to go to the depths of our being to forgive when someone has done something terrible to us or to a loved one, or when we have hurt another. We have to go to a place within that is untouched by the world. When we get to that place, it changes our life forever."

Forgiveness in Every Moment

If we do not forgive, it is like carrying heavy baggage that weighs us down so we cannot go forward with it, but we cannot go without it as it contains our history. Or it is like holding on to hot coals but we are the ones getting burned. Letting go of the past, of the story and the details, of the ignorance and the selfishness, we open to the present, to who we are now. We do not need to live in the drama, to keep the story alive, to maintain suffering. We can come back to sanity and goodness and bring that sanity into this very moment.

| JEAN HOUSTON |

"Forgiveness is 'giving forth' in such a way that it releases us from those things that have kept us entrained in fear, hatred, and the great illusion of separation. It is this illusion that we are separate and not part of a dynamic unity of being that has given us the negative ability to regard the other as a stranger. But we can move into co-creative ways of discovering, of seeing in each person the god in hiding with the potential that they can change. Forgiveness releases in ourselves that which has held us back from the ability to love, to engage with all others, all creatures, in a radical sense of love."

Sitting in meditation, we can come to forgiveness and bring compassion to ourselves, making friends with who we are, knowing we cannot change the past but we can change our attitude toward it. As we see beyond our own limitations, beyond the ego, a remarkable thing begins to happen. The boundaries that normally keep us isolated from intimacy, boundaries that have been constructed and maintained over the years to protect us from being hurt, begin to come down, like old walls crumbling and falling. In meditation, we know our deep connection to each other; when there is no separation, there is no need to be protected.

| JACK KORNFIELD |

"There are heart-centered meditations that deliberately cultivate gratitude, compassion, and forgiveness. All of these forms of meditation practice can transform the consciousness with which we move through the world. And when they spread, we can transform a fractured and terribly divided society into one in which people feel respect, dignity, and compassion as their common ground."

In this way, forgiveness is truly revolutionary. It releases the pain of the past so we are free to live in the present. It changes fear and hate into love and acceptance, just as an oyster uses the irritation from a grain of sand to produce the beauty of a pearl. It enables us all to live with kindness and caring.

8

|||

Blossoms Ripening into Sweet Fruit

When we complete the journey to our own heart, we will
find ourselves in the hearts of everyone else.
FATHER THOMAS KEATING

The story goes that, at the time of the Buddha, a group of monks wanted to do a quiet retreat away from the crowds of followers, so the Buddha told them there was a lovely glade in the forest where they could go and he would make sure they would be left undisturbed. The monks found their way to the glade and settled down to meditate. But what they did not know was that the glade was inhabited by a gang of tree spirits who were really upset that these monks should come and make themselves at home in their glade. When tree spirits want to, they can be extremely scary, ugly, very smelly, and unbelievably noisy, ferociously shrieking all over the place. They did everything they could to spook the hermits and make them leave. And it worked. As there was no peace, the monks could not possibly meditate, so they hurriedly went back to the Buddha, begging him to let them go somewhere else. But no. Instead, he taught them a meditation practice of loving kindness, or *metta* in Sanskrit, which develops loving kindness toward everyone, including ourselves and our enemies. And then he sent the monks back to the forest. His famous last words were "This is the only protection you will need."

Thinking the Buddha must be mad, the monks, very reluctantly, went back to the glade, sat down, and began practicing what he had taught them. And it worked! The tree spirits, who at first were not at all pleased to see the monks return, no longer had any effect on them. For all their antics, the meditators just kept sitting there and beaming out loving kindness. Long story short, eventually the spirits were won over by the waves of compassion emanating from the robed ones and, far from than chasing them away, the same nasties that had once been so ferocious now became disciples.

The question is, who are the tree spirits? The story says that they are everything that goes on in our own minds—all the doubts, insecurities, fears, anger, negative thoughts; the list is endless—that keep distracting us. And the point the Buddha was making is that loving kindness has the capacity to overcome all manner of monsters and ghouls and lead us to a true heart opening, proving that love is more powerful than any opposing force. Rather than trying to eliminate negativity, we cultivate the opposite; seeing and knowing pain, we bring kindness.

BEING KIND

Doesn't this sound so nice? Just be kind and loving—how great, what a cool idea, let's make kindness hip. But in practice, it is not always so simple, such as when someone says or does something that is hurtful to us. Can kindness still flow when the ego is upset? There is a story of a monk who meditated for many years on the quality of patience. He was immersed in everything to do with serenity and tolerance. One day, someone walked past him and said, "Eat shit!" The meditating monk immediately replied, "You eat shit!" This only goes to show just how hard it can be to maintain our equilibrium and that even monks can lose it as easily as we can.

Focusing on loving kindness shows us all those places that are bound in the ego and selfishness; it brings us up against our limitations and confronts our boundaries. Where do we meet our edge? Where is our capacity to step over the edge into greater consideration? How genuine is our ability to bring kindheartedness to a difficult situation?

| MARC IAN BARASCH |

"Writing a book about kindness and compassion really helped me to focus myself on others, especially as I am a very selfish person in a lot of ways. I had an interview with a meditation teacher, and I said, 'All I really know is to try to be kind.' And he said, 'I think you've got it!' And I thought, great, I got the gold star. But then he said, 'And now you have to get used to it.' And that made the hair on my neck stand on end. Meaning, it is fine to have this understanding, but how does it saturate your life? That is the core for me: How can I remember to be kind and compassionate, which is essentially how can I have empathy for someone on the spot, even if they are mad at me, even if they are thwarting me, or they are in my way? We have to create a gap between action and reaction, and that is what meditation allows us to do."

|||

Loving Kindness in Action

For loving kindness to become an integral expression of our lives, we have to start by developing it for ourselves. And yet this is the hardest place to begin—how easy it would be if we could just skip this bit and start straight in with loving others! But without a true caring and kindness for ourselves, then our capacity to direct these qualities toward anyone else is limited; if we do not appreciate ourselves, then our love for others will be based on trying to find the love we need, in which case it will not be genuine and unconditional. That is why the loving kindness meditation practice in chapter fifteen begins with developing this quality toward ourselves.

It is extraordinary how difficult it can be to genuinely care for ourselves. It means being tender when we make mistakes and not putting ourselves down, however subtly. Every time, we say something uncalled for, make a fool of ourselves, or feel unworthy—in all those moments, we can bring acceptance, kindness, and friendship; we can embrace ourselves just as we are.

| JOAN BORYSENKO |

"Stop punishing yourself! Put down the whip! So much of the punishment we give to others is a projection of how we actually treat ourselves. So be gentle with yourself!"

As we focus on bringing loving kindness to ourselves, we may uncover a deeper belief that we do not deserve this, do not deserve to be well or to be happy, that we do not believe we are good enough—a sort of built-in self-destruction clause. We have to keep inviting kindness into that self-negation and lack of self-esteem. This is not about brushing over places where we need to take responsibility for our behavior, but about embracing the humanness within us that caused such behavior to begin with.

| DEBBIE FORD |

"Be caring and compassionate to yourself. Ninety-nine percent of the abuse that happens is going on internally. If we want an external change, we have to start inside ourselves. As I teach this to myself, I get softer and kinder with who I am. And as I teach it to my son, his friends learn it from watching him or from being here. Each one of us can get out of denial and be kind to ourselves."

We can repeat specific phrases to encourage the development of this quality, such as "May I be well, may I be happy, may all things go well for me, may I be peaceful." The beauty of these phrases is both in the self-affirmation, and that we can use them all the time, wherever we are. Going to the doctor: May I be well. Going on a date: May I be happy. Going for an interview: May all things go well for me. Feeling stressed: May I be peaceful. And we can apply them to others in our life. Being criticized by your boss: May she be well. Sitting in a crowded train: May all beings be happy. Stuck in a traffic jam: May all beings be peaceful. Someone giving you the finger while you are driving: May he be happy and not cause an accident! Repeating these phrases keeps our heart open.

| JAMES GIMIAN |

"So often we find ourselves at the limits of our ability to be open and compassionate in our day-to-day world, right here, right now. When we can bring our attention and loving kindness to those very ordinary, difficult moments—not run away or cover them over but just be there with them— then we are bringing genuine meditation practice into our life."

Loving Kindness for All

Kindness does not stop with us; we can extend it outward from ourselves, like the ripples on a pond, toward our family, friends, and loved ones. This is relatively natural and effortless. But for loving kindness to be genuine, it cannot just end with the people we know and like; it has to go further, toward those we do not know and even do not like. This includes people we may be having a hard time with, someone with whom communication is difficult, where negative issues have arisen that are pulling the relationship apart, where there is anger, resentment, or dislike.

When we are affected by someone being hostile, dismissive, critical, or hurtful, then it is often because there is a hook in us for that negativity to grab hold of, a place where it can land that triggers all our hidden feelings of unworthiness, insecurity, doubt, even self-hate. However, when we extend kindness toward such a person, as we can in meditation, an extraordinary thing happens: The landing place, or the hook within, begins to dissolve. There is no place for the negativity to take hold.

| DEB |

"Many years ago, I was the administrator for an educational institute in Hawaii, and for some reason, one of the main teachers really had it in for me. No matter what I did, she disagreed or made me wrong. For administrative purposes, I had to be present at her classes and she soon turned all the participants against me. I realized she was triggering childhood memories of being ignored or disregarded, as I would shrink into a small, ineffective place when I was around her. It then emerged that I was going to have to go with her and the class to a remote cabin for a one-week wilderness program. Not my idea of fun! The only option I had was to focus on her during my loving kindness meditation practice, which I did every day.

"By the time we got to the cabin, her attitude had begun to subtly change: She was no longer making me the cause of everything that went wrong. Over the first few days, she changed even more, slowly acknowledging me, and by the end of the week, she was actually including me along with everyone else, once even asking me for my opinion. The interesting thing was that she did not seem to notice that anything was unusual or different. And the whole of the class changed with her. I was astonished to watch it happen. The only thing I had done differently was loving kindness meditation, through which the hook that she had been hanging all her judgment on had seemingly dissolved. She had nowhere to put her negativity; instead, it sort of fell on the floor between us. Eventually, it just slunk away, unable to find a home."

The negative reactions that arise within us during moments of discord or disagreement cause continued suffering and conflict. Extending kindness toward the adversary is, therefore, really extending it toward ourselves, as it releases the inner pain and puts us into a more balanced place. As a Burmese teacher once told author Andrew Harvey, "Out of compassion for myself, let me let go of all these feelings of anger and resentment toward others."

As we focus on the adversary, all manner of divergent feelings may arise about what happened, about who said what to whom, and what someone did or did not do. To get to loving kindness, we have to accept those feelings while also letting go of the story, releasing the details. Who did or who said what is not relevant; what matters is the shared human experience. Hurt and disagreement and anger arise when we forget our essential unity and hang out in separate, isolated places, while knocking heads with each other. By letting go of the story, we are going beyond the ego's affront to the shared space.

We can extend kindness toward people who are upset, angry, or irritable, whether their feelings have anything to do with us or not. In this way, we can stop negativity from affecting us. Whether it is our boss or a bus driver or our partner or teenage children, wishing them well helps us keep our cool.

| ED |

"It was a late Sunday afternoon in the Norfolk countryside in England, and we were driving home after leading a three-day loving kindness meditation retreat. The journey began by driving down a narrow lane and coming right at us was another car, leaving us no room to pass. We drove out of the way as much as we could, but still the other car had to slow down to pass us. The driver was furious and was giving us the finger, even though he was the one in the middle of the road! It would have been so easy to react with, 'Hey, we are driving in our lane, and we are in the right; you are wrong.' But we just smiled and said, 'May he be well, may he drive safely, may he live a long time!'"

From extending kindness toward an adversary, the natural next step is to extend it toward all beings, whoever and wherever they are. Theoretically, this sounds very straightforward, but it can highlight hidden issues of prejudice and resistance. Can we really extend kindness toward terrorists, murderers, or dictators as easily as we can toward caregivers, charity workers, or our loved ones? Can we step beyond personality to the essence of shared beingness? Can we find a place where all beings are equal in our heart?

Prejudice can go very deep. It is only healed when we end the war within and accept those parts of ourselves we find so unacceptable. Then we will have the courage to accept those who are different from us, who have different beliefs, who are a different color, or who live differently. When we can tolerate ourselves, then we can be tolerable toward others and extend kindness to all, equally.

As Mahatma Gandhi said, "We must widen the circle of our love until it embraces the whole village; the village, in turn, must take into its fold the district, the district the province, and so on, until the scope of our love encompasses the whole world."

Inside the Brain

Loving kindness and compassion are such clear outcomes of meditation that they have now become scientifically verifiable. There is an overwhelming amount of research showing how meditation changes the circuits in the part of the brain associated with contentment and happiness and that stimulates the "feel-good" factor, while measured brain wave patterns indicate the immediate and positive effects of meditation. Buddhist monks, with many hours of practice, have had their minds scientifically studied while they were meditating. When asked to focus on compassion, their brains reflected a remarkable generation of clarity and intensified kindness. Similar results have been found in the Shamata Project, a meditation research program that took four years to complete.

| ALAN WALLACE |

"During the Shamatha Project, I led two three-month retreats, designed to observe the effects of meditation. Core teams of scientists and psychologists took saliva and blood samples, monitored behavioral changes, recorded interviews between the participants and psychologists, took EEGs to see how the meditation practice was affecting the brain and physiology, cognitive processes and the quality of attention, and to see whether meditation could enhance the continuity of sustained voluntary concentration, clarity, self-awareness, empathy, and even whether it made them nicer people.

"I met with the participants every day as a group and one on one weekly. I noticed their attention skills definitely enhanced, as they were able to maintain focus for longer periods of time. Their clarity increased, they were working through emotional issues, but interactions became more mellow and kinder as time went on, there was greater empathy, compassion, and kindness, and far greater contentment and happiness."

Not many of us are able to meditate as much as a monk, or even to do a three-month retreat, but data also shows that the mindfulness-based meditation training mentioned in chapter four can produce discernable changes in the brain in a matter of just eight weeks. In other research, it has been found that even two weeks of practice for thirty minutes a day can produce measurable improvements in the feel-good part of the brain. This indicates that we can quite purposefully and systematically develop qualities such as kindness and compassion.

| RICHARD DAVIDSON |

"By taking advantage of the methods that have been featured in neuroscientific research, we can understand the impact that meditation has on the brain. The practices that we have been studying are ones that can be delineated in three major categories: One is focused attention and concentration; another we call open monitoring practices, or ones that cultivate a broader panoramic awareness; and the third are practices designed to cultivate loving kindness and compassion. Concentration practices, like focused attention, engage pre-frontal and parietal regions of the brain, whereas meditation that is explicitly designed to develop compassion and loving kindness recruits parts of the brain that are associated with emotions and emotional regulation, increasing the reactivity of certain kinds of emotional stimuli.

"Neuroplasticity is the study of the brain's capacity to change, grow, and rewire itself. By training the mind, we can actually change the brain to achieve a switching of activity toward greater contentment. The mechanisms associated with happiness are some of the most plastic circuits in the brain that are transformable through direct experience. As the brain is constantly changing, the question becomes, how can we change it for the better?

"I would say there are tremendous possibilities for radical transformation based upon the information that we have, and there is every reason to believe meditation can make a dramatic difference to the expression of destructive emotions. The effect of meditation on the circuitry in the brain clearly underscores the possibility of radical change in a way that could transform anger and fear. There is certainly evidence to show that meditation practices designed to cultivate compassion and loving kindness change the brain in many positive ways."

AWAKENING COMPASSION

We have a newspaper photograph at home of Bishop Tutu, his hands held in prayer position. Underneath it are his words, "Please make it fashionable to be compassionate." That photograph is many years old, but his words are even more relevant today. We can make compassion fashionable, kindness cool, consideration and care hot topics. We have already proven that war does not work, that fighting and killing in the name of religion, to gain domination, or to claim control never has a happy ending. Acceptance, kindness, generosity, and compassion are really the only choices we have in order to transform both ourselves and society.

| MARC IAN BARASCH |

"If you have a culture that has as its tenet what Bishop Tutu always refers to as *ubuntu*, which means, 'I only exist because you exist, my existence is dependent on your existence, my well-being is dependent on your well-being,' then that culture is infinitely different from American culture, which says that 'Obviously, God must love me, because he would not help a sinner to prosper, and if you are not doing well, then there must be something wrong with you.'

"There is a tribe that has a coming of age ritual for seven or eight year olds where they throw a big feast in the tepee. The child will be just about to eat when they hear a whimpering outside and a voice saying 'I am hungry.' The adults will say, 'Somebody is crying' and the child has to give some of his food to the person outside the tepee before they take a bite for themselves."

We do not get such heart-centered qualities as kindness or compassion from outside of ourselves; we cannot find something inside us that is not already there as a part of our true nature. But the ego's need for grasping, gaining, and selfishness easily buries our innate altruism. Each of us are capable of losing our cool, losing perspective, getting caught up in hot emotions and causing harm. Some may manifest their madness in a more overt or destructive way, but we all share the same potential. By knowing our own tendencies, we can more genuinely offer empathy and compassion to others.

| PETER RUSSELL |

"What manifests for each of us personally is different—our history, phobias, anxieties, tension—but deep down, we all work the same way. I can see that what is happening in me is also what is happening to everybody else. This gives me great empathy for other people's stuff, for their struggles, their fears, for the way they behave. Deep down, we are all the same. None of us want to suffer, to be criticized or rejected. We all want to be free from pain; we want to be loved; we just have different ways of going about it. The natural state of mind is that we care, but self-centeredness and self-protection easily overshadow that. When I am not so preoccupied with myself, then compassion arises, spontaneously; I don't have to do anything."

Focusing on our own concerns and problems limits our capacity to be with others; we are too self-engrossed to really acknowledge anyone else's issues. But when we can step beyond ourselves, then the ability to care about another's suffering genuinely and freely arises. This is not just in the big picture of war or poverty, but in all the small stuff in our lives, in our communication and relationships.

| JOSEPH GOLDSTEIN |

"A few years ago, I was working with someone who had a very abrasive personality. It was very hard to be with this person. I found it so difficult that I would just sit there emotionally closed off and defended. When I realized how reactive I was being to this person's energy, something shifted inside me. Instead of instinctively reacting to his behavior, I dropped down a level and saw what was so apparent and obvious: the suffering that was underlying all the unpleasantness. Simply from being willing to see the suffering that was there, in that moment my heart went from being contracted and defensive to feeling real caring. By actually opening to the suffering, instead of protecting myself against it, kindness and compassion became the natural outcome. This is how meditation works. It helps us see that pleasure is not where our deepest happiness lies; it is not in the accumulation of pleasant feelings. It is in the quality of openness itself."

Perhaps no one says it better than HH the Dalai Lama when he recounts how a monk, imprisoned by the Chinese for eighteen years, told him that during his imprisonment there were many moments when he was in great danger. When HH the Dalai Lama asked what he was in danger from, the monk replied that he was in danger of losing his compassion for the Chinese, his captors. This shows how deeply Buddhists regard compassion. For them, it is central to their understanding of the meaning of existence.

| GREGG BRADEN |

"We have taken a number of journeys to the monasteries in the highlands of central China and Tibet. In one monastery, we had the opportunity to have an afternoon audience with the abbot and I asked him, 'In your experience, in your teachings, and in your world view, what is the stuff that holds the universe together? What is it that connects us all?' I asked the translator, and he asked the abbot, and they had this banter going back and forth about how to answer this question. Finally, the translator turned to me and he said one word. That was his answer, one word. I thought it was a mistranslation, that I had heard him wrong, so I asked again. And he came back with the same word.

"He said that the force that holds the stuff in the universe together is compassion. 'Wait a minute,' I said. 'Are you telling me that compassion is a force of nature that exists everywhere in the universe, or are you telling me that it is an experience that we create in our bodies?' The abbot and the translator went back and forth again, and then the translator just said, 'Yes.' He was telling us that we have the capability to create within our own being the very experience that aligns and attunes us with our world. It opens the doors to the truly miraculous experiences of healing and peace, because they are all linked through this field of compassion."

|||

Wise or Idiot Compassion

Opening the heart, developing loving kindness, and feeling compassion toward our fellow humans is one thing. Putting it into action is a different matter. We constantly cause suffering: We hurt ourselves, we hurt each other, we ignore each other's pain and create further pain. We destroy our world so carelessly, giving little thought to the future. How do we prevent ourselves from reacting to people? How do we stay open and loving in the midst of insult or conflict? It is so easy to feel hopeless, to want to walk away from it all. Our caring and compassion are tested and challenged in every moment, every time we are tempted to turn away but chose to stay open instead.

| MICHAEL BERNARD BECKWITH |

"Rev. James Lawson, who was a cohort of Dr. Martin Luther King, shared with me an experience when he and Dr. King were sitting in an auditorium and a man came up and said to Dr. King, 'Are you MLK, Jr.?' and he said 'Yes' and the man spat on him. Dr. King took a handkerchief, took the spittle off of his suit, and handed it back to the man and said, 'I think this belongs to you.' He did not hit the man or cuss the man out; he didn't say how dare you; he had this ability to just be in the moment. Sympathy says I know how you feel, and you actually feel the same. Empathy says I feel for you. Compassion says I understand and I am here to serve to alleviate suffering. It is not trying to feel your pain or feel for you. The compassionate person is standing in awareness and asking the question, how can I serve?"

In the above story, Dr. King displayed a deep awareness of suffering and how to act with appropriate compassion in the situation. Can we do the same? The amount of suffering surrounding us is enormous, and we may feel powerless in the face of it. How many of us can go to Africa to feed the starving or build homes for the homeless? How do we deal with the beggars on the street or the requests for help arriving in our mailbox every few days? How do we decide where we can be of most help?

For compassion to be effective, we need to discover the deeper cause of the suffering and where our actions are going to be of real help and value or where they may actually be supporting an already unhealthy situation. In other words, more than compassion, we also need to see with awareness and discrimination.

This is known as *wise compassion*, action that is inherently skillful, that sees the whole situation and aims to bring release from suffering; its opposite is known as *blind* or *idiot compassion* that does not take into account the whole situation and so, although it looks compassionate, it is inherently unskillful and may actually increase suffering. For instance, offering candy to a starving child is misguided kindness, because they need food, not sugar. Idiot compassion is also seen when we support or condone neurosis, whether in ourselves or someone else. The balance of these two qualities—compassion and wise discernment—is essential in order for us to see where pity is masquerading as kindness.

| DENNIS GENPO MERZEL |

"When there is wise action, or action that comes out of wisdom with compassion then, when we see an injustice or cruelty happening, we are going to respond appropriately. We have the tools to act with motherly compassion, to embrace, to hold, to love another, and we also have the capacity to have a fatherly compassion where we set boundaries and say, 'This is out of order; this is intolerable; this is not acceptable.' When it is time to cut through, it is time to cut through. When it is time to say no, it is time to say no. When it is time to include and to embrace, then that is what we do."

In other words, compassion is both the unconditional, all-encompassing embrace of suffering and the ability to not support ignorance. This means seeing a situation and the cause of the suffering clearly, as well as finding a way to tell the truth so that pain can be resolved and further suffering avoided.

Compassion and Kindness in Difficult Times

| WILLIAM SPEAR |

"Meditation has been a crucial and essential part of my daily life in helping me to do the work I do, whether it is being with people who are dying, or in an area that has just been obliterated by a tsunami or earthquake. I am often asked how I deal with all the dead bodies, the people who have lost their limbs, children who have lost their parents, or the women I have seen who took the lives of their own daughters to prevent them from being raped and horribly abused. The only way it is possible to witness this, other than totally numbing myself out, is to just keep gnawing away at the edges of my own heart, to keep melting over and over again, until I can expand my heart to be big enough to compassionately embrace all that is in front of me.

"If we are in the presence of something that we just cannot bear and we find a way to get into our hearts, then we can begin to soften. When

I find myself holding a child who has just lost everything she has ever known, or playing basketball with guys who have had their legs cut off with chain saws and are tied to a board pushing themselves around on the ground, or talking with those who have just been diagnosed with cancer or HIV, then I try to just be present and compassionate with my heart open, even if it is unbearable. My meditation practice is a practice of constantly opening my heart so that I can be unconditionally present."

When difficult or traumatic times occur, we have the opportunity to really put compassion into practice, to be willing to witness and be with the pain and suffering we see all around us, not to turn away from it or pretend it is not there: the victims of abuse, senseless fighting, the homeless, endless selfishness and greed. Rather than getting caught in the details, the behavior, or the personalities, we can embrace a more inclusive awareness. As Ram Dass says so simply, "True compassionate action comes out of the awareness that we are all inseparable . . . we are all a part of the same thing, your suffering is my suffering."

It also means dealing with our own aggression, seeing the violence within ourselves, the anger, irritation, or moments of closed-heartedness, the fear and insecurity, and bringing mercy and tenderness to those places, to the wounded parts, so the war inside can stop. Compassion is our ability to be with another's pain and suffering, and we can do this because we have seen and accepted our own pain. Being a witness to atrocities and holding those who are in pain as close as we hold ourselves gives rise to ever-deeper levels of empathy.

| ROSHI JOAN HALIFAX |

"I was recently present at Nanjing, China, witnessing something that was like a war crimes trial for survivors of the Japanese who invaded Nanjing in 1937. In a matter of weeks, 300,000 people were massacred at Nanjing, more people than those killed by the atom bombs of Hiroshima and Nagasaki. In addition, thousands of Chinese, from very young children to old women, were raped, many of them in full view of their families. Most of them were killed after being raped, but not all of them, and at this gathering at Nanjing, one of the survivors, an elderly woman, testified about her experience.

"So why is it that I, as an American woman, would put myself there to hear the suffering of such atrocities? It is because I see all wars as my war; I feel that we should bear witness to cruelty no matter how far that cruelty might seem from our own lives, because in reality it is not far at all. Sitting with the deep suffering of Nanjing, sitting with my own response to listening to accounts of survivors and what they went through, and sitting with the deep shame and remorse of the Japanese people who were also a part of this meeting, led to a tremendous upwelling of emotion in me. I met that upwelling with a sense of gratitude and acceptance, as exactly these feelings allow us to engender a deeper experience of compassion.

"Compassion arises out of intimacy, not out of pity. In meditation, we can be present, feeling deeply the suffering of the world, but also not being annihilated by that suffering. We are actually able to bloom in its midst. That is what happened to me when I was in Nanjing. As difficult as it was to be present, to witness such suffering, what bloomed in me was an even more powerful resolve to work with my own mind, my own suffering, and the suffering of others. At no time was pity present in my experience. Pity does not generate compassion, as pity is about an experience of there being a self and another, whereas compassion sees no separation.

"Love and compassion are necessities, not luxuries. Without them, humanity cannot survive. Compassion is inherent to our very nature, and meditation is the matrix for the cultivation of compassion. What happens through meditation is the growing sense of friendship with the whole world. This includes trees, rivers, mountains, animals. We spontaneously and innately feel loving kindness and deep friendship toward all beings and all things."

|||

Compassion Meditation

Normally, we prefer to focus on as much good and to let go of as much bad as possible. However, there is another way that is actually the exact opposite. This is the Tibetan meditation practice known as *tonglen*, or "the practice of receiving and giving." It transforms any notions of selfishness or personal desire and develops true altruism and mercy by bringing compassion into our daily lives.

Tonglen is an expression of great generosity. As we breathe in, we inhale the suffering of others, followed by the immediate transformation of that suffering into compassion and love, which we then exhale or breathe back into the world. This is the art of transforming dirt into gold. We can do this because we can be with suffering, we do not need to hide from it; just as we know suffering, so we also know the power of kindness.

| PEGGY DYLAN |

"We inhale the external pain, the resistance and fear, the great fear at this time in the world. We inhale it and take it in to our heart, where we turn it to joy, to tenderness, to delight, to ease, to healing, to whatever is needed. When it is transformed in our heart, then we just exhale it into the world. We are using the body as a filter for those negative things."

This practice has the remarkable effect of making us stronger. It sounds like it would weaken us to take in pain and suffering, but it does the opposite. It gives us the power to transform any difficult situation or feeling and to respond with love and compassion. Rather than turning away from suffering—feeling too sensitive to be exposed to it, or too weak or fearful to withstand it—we invite it all to come in. We are willing to experience it, taste it, touch it, for the suffering does not land, it does not stay in us, there is no holding. It is instantly transformed. Then what we share, what we give to others, is loving, kind, tender, and uplifting.

| MARC IAN BARASCH |

"How do we go from the discovery that we are basically trapped in this ego state to universal compassion? There is a natural tendency to look after ourselves first, to react against things that seem to threaten us. To get from that sort of automatic response to compassionate action takes something extra and that extra is meditation. It gets us from the insatiable feeling that we are the ego and self to a broader understanding that maybe the ego is not as solid or important as we think it is. It is a deliberate shift from awareness of self to awareness of others."

Every time we see or feel suffering, whether in ourselves or in another, every time we make a mistake or say something stupid and are just about to put ourselves down, every time we think of someone we are having a hard time with, every time we encounter the confusion and difficulty of being human, every time we see someone else struggling, upset, or irritated, we can breathe it all in and breathe out acceptance and tenderheartedness and loving friendship. We can offer this to whoever needs it, including ourselves. Just a few breaths of tonglen will bring armfuls of compassion into any situation. Compassion is the natural response that arises, unbidden, taking us into the hearts of others.

| JON KABAT-ZINN |

"In all of the Asian languages, the word for mind and the word for heart is the same word. If you see the mind and heart are the same, then compassion is built right into it. Mindful attention is itself affectionate. It's open, spacious, curious, and in the seeing of the interconnectedness, then compassion arises naturally as there is no separation. Wisdom is the knowing of no separation, and compassion is the feeling of no separation."

|||

OPENING OUR HEARTS

When kindness and compassion are the focus of our meditation, then the changes we experience are both subtle and transformative. We have greater perception to see things just as they are without our need to interfere and, therefore, we are less judgmental; there is an ability to simply be present and available and an openness to the shared human condition. These qualities are like the blossoms on a tree, the flowers that transform into sweet fruits. They indicate the growing awareness of ourselves in relation to others. We are stepping out of an ego-centered way of seeing the world and opening to receiving whatever is there.

| TAMI SIMON |

"I believe the most important fruit of meditation is the opening of our hearts. If meditation is working, that is what it is doing. Almost every control habit I had in my life and every contraction in my body was a defense against opening my heart. What I discovered was that I could open and be okay, that I do not have to defend myself. I think I was actually afraid of feeling, I thought I would be overwhelmed, but I found that I can be overwhelmed by feelings and it's fine, I'm fine, I don't have to defend against grief or depression. My heart can open and it is not going to destroy me to feel it."

In the old Tibetan teachings, it is said that we do not really become a full human being until we open our heart to embrace all others. Until then, we are like human animals, concerned only with ourselves and our survival and uninterested in the survival of anyone else. Although our own survival is obviously still important after we become more heart-centered, it is matched by our engagement with the welfare of all. As we move further away from the ego's self-involved version of reality, we move into a place of awareness and caring and, in particular, into a fully inclusive loving kindness and compassion.

| RICHARD FREEMAN |

"If we take any being, whether it is our mother or father or a bug or a politician, and we put them outside of our heart, then we distort our own energy; we might get a little tension in the jaw or a slightly shallow breath. We confuse the act or behavior with the being, which is a fundamental ignorance. Someone's mind, their feelings, their physical form is not really who they are. We can put them out of our life, certainly, but not out of our heart as this leaves us disconnected. No matter how much we huff and puff or twist and turn or sit and stare, until that being is back in our heart we are essentially wasting our time. Once they are back, we automatically feel that connection with all beings. We need to have all sentient beings in our heart as we are connected to each one."

Loving others is actually the most self-interested thing we can do, for we gain far more from loving and caring and helping than we do from looking out for ourselves. It gives us an unmatched joy, a delight in being. When the open arms and heart of love replace the closed arms and heart of fear, then delight and happiness replace dread and isolation.

| ROBERT THURMAN |

"When we discover inner happiness, it wells up out of our being. We realize that our basic nature is happiness. We realize this through meditation, through the deepening of awareness, that thinking of others is really much more selfish than thinking of ourselves. This is what is called being a *wise selfish,* rather than being a *stupid selfish* by always thinking or worrying about ourselves and then being dissatisfied because nothing is good enough. When we focus on others, then we forget about dissatisfaction and, presto, we become more content. All the great traditions, whether Muslim, Jewish, Hindu, Christian, or Buddhist, all teach that when we get out of the little self and we embrace others as ourselves and we focus on their happiness, then we have a much bigger pool of happiness. If there is going to be some critical moment when there is a mass awakening, it will only happen because each individual person awakens her or his own heart."

||||

Part III

|||

TRANSFORMING US
TRANSFORMS
THE WORLD

9

| | |

Off the Cushion and into Life

There are many things we cannot take responsibility for in this world, but the one thing we can be responsible for is a quality of presence in this moment.
CHRISTINA FELDMAN

| CHLOE GOODCHILD |

"I was in Northern Ireland because I had been asked to create a musical bridge between the opposing forces of Protestants and Catholics in order to create an atmosphere of listening. We were part of an extensive peace program, and this was the moment when HH the Dalai Lama was going to walk the peace walk, which basically divides the Protestant and Catholic communities. It was drizzling with rain as we stood in a car park by this enormous peace wall. The paramilitary had agreed to a ceasefire and were standing within about fifteen yards of us with raised guns, backing off the crowds, while letting the victims of war in wheelchairs come to the front. We were there to chant the mantra to Tara, the sacred and beneficent hill that was the ancient seat of the high kings of Ireland and that protects the land and the people. Tara is also the great Goddess of Compassion in Buddhism.

"The plan was to open the peace gate in the peace wall, but one of the security guards had told me that what often happens when they open the gate is that the children from the opposing sides start throwing stones at each other. He said to me, 'And they may start throwing stones at you, but we've got a whole security system that will get you out of here in about twenty minutes. Is that okay?'

"HH the Dalai Lama had started walking down the street lined with a hundred thousand people. I was told it would be about twenty minutes before he reached us, as he kept stopping to talk to people, so we just kept singing. The wonderful thing about the delay was that it gave both the paramilitary and the people waiting a chance to really listen to the chant, to the recurring melody line that was praising their sacred hill. I will never forget the look of joyful listening on their faces. As they joined in the chant, the sky cleared, the sun came out, the peace gate was opened and HH the Dalai Lama walked through. The children who normally throw stones at each other were just standing there singing; both sides were singing the Tara mantra. It was totally awesome."

Such a moment of harmony in a war-torn county is a wonderful example of how meditation, in this case a shared chant, takes us beyond differences to a place of unity. In Parts One and Two, we looked at the many ways meditation affects us individually, from dealing with stress, illness, and the more repressed aspects of the mind, to generating qualities of kindness, compassion, and forgiveness. However, the bigger question is, if this is how meditation affects us, then what happens when we take meditation "off the cushion" and bring it into other aspects of our lives? Can we apply it to our environment, politics, or work? Is it true meditation if we do not use the benefits of the practice to extend ourselves outward to others?

| MICHAEL BERNARD BECKWITH |

"It becomes impossible to live for yourself, to live life on the 'me plan.' That is the point of meditation—to get out of the narrow confines of self. It becomes impossible to close your eyes to a world filled with your brothers and sisters on the planet who are suffering. We cannot ignore world hunger and AIDS, wars, hate crimes, bigotry, racism, sexism—we cannot pretend they are not there; we cannot remain aloof to the suffering of others. The point is what we do when we leave our meditation cushion, our church pew, our synagogue, mosque, or temple. Where are we sharing our time, energy and financial resources to make a difference? Meditation sensitizes the heart and tenderizes the mind so that, as you recognize the suffering in the world, you become the compassion that has arisen within you."

Putting meditation into action does not necessarily mean we have to become world movers and shakers, for it is equally important in the smaller details of our lives, such as smiling or holding a door for someone. What is most important is the nature of the action as well as the motivation of the one doing the action.

| MARIANNE WILLIAMSON |

"We are heir to a thought system that says that 'we do what we do, and it is the action itself that determines the result.' However, Gandhi's principle that 'the end is inherent in the means' implies that who we are when we take an action is what determines the result. In other words, I know that the issue is not just what I say; it is who I am when I say it. It is not just what I do; it is who I am as I am doing it. When we come from meditation, then all of our activity is different because we are a different person taking the action. We have just burned off our craziness, hysteria, and layers of anger, nervousness, defensiveness, and fear. The more we meditate, the more we live in a space of our truer self and relate to other people in the space of their truer self, whether we are talking to a president of the United States or some battered woman living in her car."

We put meditation into action simply because we have no choice. When we see beyond our own ego-needs and become aware of our connectedness with all beings, reaching out beyond ourselves becomes a natural and spontaneous expression of who we are. Rather than grasping at what we can get for ourselves, our first response is the care of others. This is not the same as being a martyr or ignoring our own needs. We care for ourselves equally, but we are not obsessed with putting ourselves first.

| JUDITH ANSARA |

"My meditation practice has evolved over the years so that it is not separate from any other part of my life. It is not separate from my reaching out
to touch another, from getting my guests some tea, from working with a
client, from being kind to someone in a grocery line. It is the fabric of my
life rather than something I do. It is the awareness of breath, of sensation,
and the intention to leave a trail of beauty behind me. When I go to the
grocery store, how can I leave a trail of beauty behind me? When I am
working with a client, how can I do that? It is taking meditation off the
cushion so that everywhere we go we leave a trail of beauty."

|||

Being Present

There are several qualities that can be developed to enhance
and deepen our expression of meditation in the world, but the
most immediate and important is that of simply being present.
The ability to be fully present and engaged enables us to receive
every situation exactly as it is, without preconceptions or judgments—to embrace difficulties, deep sadness, upset feelings, or
injustice while staying aware, present, and available.

| MAURA SILLS |

"A monk who used to come to the institute was asked how we can measure spiritual progress, and he said it was by our capacity to be effective,
which he saw as listening and being present. When the capacity to be
effective is diminished or lost, then I think we have lost our humanity. For
me, the intention of meditation is to be here, to really just be here with
whatever is happening, as opposed to being someplace else where there
is no problem."

Meditation is being present: watching the breath, chanting
the scriptures or a mantra, walking mindfully—all are ways
of bringing the distracted mind into just this moment. And we

can bring that same presence into our daily lives. It may not be possible to maintain it all the time; there are endless external distractions, let alone the demands of the ego and on-going internal chatter. But we do not have to let such distractions rule. As we cultivate mindfulness, we naturally see the on-going movie in our minds and are less likely to be caught up in the storyline. Each time we are pulled into dramas and self-centeredness, we can stop, bring our attention back to the present, and rest in that awareness.

| SYLVIA BOORSTEIN |

"I don't make a difference between meditating and having my life. People ask me what percentage of the day do you practice mindfulness meditation, or what percentage do you practice loving kindness meditation, and I like to say 100 percent of the day I am doing both of them. But that is actually not true because I get distracted; I am not checking on myself every second. I would like to have it as an aspiration—that all day every day I am paying attention to whether my mind has slid off into self-serving confusion and suffering, or that I am connected to the world in some healthy way that keeps me lively and happy. I think of meditation as a full-time practice so that it is not separate from my daily life: If I drive my car and go to the market and teach a class and I pay attention and I know what is going on, then mindfulness is happening. I am mindful of the presence or absence of my capacity to care. In this moment, am I bringing attention to whatever I am doing? Is my mind generating good thoughts about other people? Formal periods of mediation simply point me in the direction of how I want to live during the whole day."

|||

Skillful Action

From this place of awareness, we are able to discern between actions that are skillful or unskillful, of where we are being either a help or a hindrance. Skillful action brings out the best in each situation and encourages generosity and kindness, while unskillful actions maintain and reinforce separation; they are basically harmful and self-centered. Wise compassion is skillful, whereas idiot compassion is unskillful, for even though we may be giving and wanting to help, our actions are actually unhelpful in the long run.

| JAMES GIMIAN |

"The key to working skillfully in the world is, first of all, to see things clearly, to see things as they are. But the obscurations, confusions, distortions, and projections of the mind that prevent us from seeing clearly are very tricky. They are also very entertaining, and seductive. It takes an extraordinary set of skills to disarm that whole mechanism, which is what the practice of meditation is all about. Meditation is not some external, learned technique, even though we practice it in that way, but it is a state of mind that arises very naturally, allowing us to see and act clearly."

The opportunities for skillful behavior are present in every moment, from dealing with someone complaining to making sure your kids get an equal amount of attention, from running a business meeting to having to negotiate a peace treaty. Discerning what action is most skillful is usually fairly obvious. For instance, it is generally more helpful to give food to someone who is begging than to give money that may then be spent on something less nourishing, such as drugs; likewise, helping someone in need is fine until he is on his feet, but not if he then becomes dependent and unwilling to help himself. Skillful action encourages us to take responsibility for ourselves, rather than pointing fingers and creating shame or guilt.

| TARA GUBER |

"In the old days, if we did something naughty, we used to get sent to sit in the corner with a dunce cap or we would get whacked by a paddle or sent to the principal's office, all of which created shame and guilt and made us feel we were not good enough. So when we are teaching yoga to kids in school, we have what we call *time in*. When someone gets out of hand in a classroom, we say, 'Take time in, take time in to take time out, and when you are ready, open your eyes and come back into the group.' This helps the kids take responsibility for themselves."

But there are also times when finding the most appropriate and skillful action is not so easy, particularly if it involves engaging with different cultures or traditions, which can make us confront our own basic assumptions. This is exemplified by the experience **Thanissara** had in South Africa. She told us her story in our book, *Voices from the Heart*. It is an experience that we can also apply to those times when our doubts, prejudices, and places of resistance defy our good intentions:

"Many of the black population in rural South Africa have no means of easy transport, so it is common to pass people trying to flag down a ride," explained Thanissara. "This has been made more difficult for this poor rural population as there is an alarming increase in hijackings, so car owners rarely stop. However, on our local dirt road, we are known to pick up those trying to get into town.

"Early on I would open the front door of the car and invite the person to sit next to me and, with limited Zulu, try to engage in simple conversation. But this created a high level of tension due to eroding a boundary, which would normally dictate that a black person sit in the back and that you, as a white, were not expected to interact. So I was left wondering if I should avoid the whole discomfort zone and open the back door, thereby keeping us somewhat unthreatened in our separateness, or try to change these profoundly conditioned relationships by engaging with the discomfort.

"In essence, the challenge is to consider, as an economically more empowered person, how does my life affect those around me, what can I do to help, and perhaps most importantly, where and when does my heart close in defensiveness? There is no way of always getting it right, but it is important to meet the discomfort in a way that allows a balanced responsiveness to emerge from behind the judgments and fear."

Harmlessness

Out of skillful action arises harmlessness. This sounds so simple, but harmlessness, or *ahimsa* in Sanskrit, actually requires a complete shift in attitude. In a world where selfishness and self-interest are the norm, it takes great courage not to react with greed or anger, which can and do cause harm. As Mahatma Gandhi said, "I object to violence because when it appears to do good, the good is only temporary; the evil it does is permanent." Two wrongs do not make a right; to meet anger with more anger does not bring peace.

Gandhi changed the course of history in India by showing how non-violence is more powerful than violence, bringing an end to British domination as he inspired millions of others to follow his lead. Both Nobel Peace Prize winners, HH the Dalai Lama and Aung San Suu Kyi, are long-term meditation practitioners and activists devoted to peacefully reclaiming the freedom of their countries. While HH the Dalai Lama is known for bringing attention to the plight of the Tibetan people and his pacifist attitude toward the Chinese, it is less well known that he rises at four a.m. each day to meditate for at least two hours. Suu Kyi has been held under house arrest for many years for her non-violent approach to the plight of the Burmese people, and she also meditates for a number of hours each day. On-going protests by the monks in Miramar (previously called Burma) are an example of this non-violent desire for peace.

Nelson Mandela, Bishop Tutu, and Martin Luther King, Jr., have all stood out as being fearlessly dedicated to non-violence, often in the face of tremendous opposition, as have numerous other lesser-known figures who, motivated by their meditation, faith, and belief in ahimsa, have added their voices and sometimes even their lives. Quakers, for instance, who have contemplation at the core of their religious practice, have a deeply held belief in non-violence, which determines their main tenant: "To walk across the earth meeting that of God in every man."

| DEB |

"I remember being carried on my father's shoulders during the first Alder-maston March, the ban-the-bomb march that started in 1958 in England and took place each year thereafter. We lived in a Quaker village, and many of the villagers were walking with us. It was the beginning of a life-long involvement with anti-war rallies. I felt I had a duty to do this, to raise my voice in protest over future violence. One year in the early eighties, a group of us traveled about three hundred miles to join the annual march in London. We drove all night and were exhausted the next day when we had to stand or walk for the many hours it took for the thousands of protesters to cross London. In front of us was a group of quite elderly people who had also traveled that far overnight. Like myself, they were Quakers, but their dedication to the cause outshone my own as, despite their age and weariness, they joyfully sang peace songs the length of the city."

Simply through the intent to cause less pain, and by recognizing the fundamental equality of all beings, each of us can bring greater dignity to our world, so that harm is replaced with harmlessness and disrespect with respect. But the journey to manifesting such an ideal is not always a smooth one, as HH the Dalai Lama has experienced in Tibet with many outbursts of violence against the Chinese, and as **Patch Adams** experienced as he was growing up:

"My father died from war wounds when I was sixteen. We moved back to the United States in 1961, and I went to an all-white school in the south. I was beaten up every day for my last two years in high school because I took a stand against prejudice, and then I had three hospitalizations because I wanted to kill myself—I did not want to live in a world of violence and injustice. In the last hospitalization, I decided instead to live intentionally. I chose to serve humanity, which I have done every second since the age of eighteen. I chose to never have another bad day, to put joy in the public space. I chose to operate from a formula based on the intention to be joy, to work for peace and justice, and I have lived that every second for the last forty-five years."

Ahimsa asserts that causing harm never creates peace, whether between people and countries or within our own lives, but that an attitude of harmlessness will. Yet none of us can get through life without causing harm, whether by ignoring someone's feelings, by using more of the earth's resources than we need, or by buying products made by underage and underpaid workers. What do we do when ants or cockroaches invade the kitchen or slugs eat away at the vegetable garden, yet we do not want to harm them? And how often do we do things that are hurtful or harmful to ourselves?

How many times a day, consciously or otherwise, do we put ourselves down, reaffirm our hopelessness, dislike our appearance, or see ourselves as incompetent or unworthy? How much resentment, guilt, or shame are we holding on to, thus perpetuating negativity?

Sitting in quiet reflection, meditation, or prayer has an immediately calming and peaceful effect. When we get off the cushion, that peace stays with us, highlighting any tendency to act with violence or aggression and making such behavior far less likely. It becomes even more improbable as we deepen in awareness of our fundamental interconnectedness, for then violence toward another would be the same as causing harm to ourselves. "By developing a sense of respect for others and a concern for their welfare," says HH the Dalai Lama, "we reduce our own selfishness, which is the source of all problems, and enhance our sense of kindness, which is a natural source of goodness."

Sharing and Serving

Our meditation is naturally extended through generosity, sharing, and serving: the antidotes to selfishness, greed, and desire. A bumper sticker from the Findhorn Foundation in Scotland says it best: "Practice random kindness and senseless acts of beauty."

| ED |

"We were giving a talk at a bookstore in California and had arrived early so as to avoid the rush-hour traffic. As Deb talked with the bookshop owner, I chatted to a customer in the store, a man who was training to be a Zen priest. Then Deb and I left to get something to eat at a Chinese restaurant across the road. As we were eating, the man I had been talking to came in, nodded, and walked to the back of the restaurant. A few minutes later he came back. As he passed our table he stopped and simply said, 'Your dinner is paid for.' Then he left. We were speechless at such a kind and generous act."

In a similar way, tai chi teacher Arthur Rosenfield was in the drive-thru line at Starbucks. The man in line behind him was getting impatient and angry, leaning on his horn and shouting insults at both Arthur and the Starbucks workers. Beginning to get angry himself, Arthur chose to keep his cool and change the negativity into something positive. He paid for the man's coffee and drove away. When he got home at the end of the day, he discovered that he had created a chain of giving that had not only continued all that day but had been highlighted on NBC News and within twenty-four hours had spread around the world on the Internet.

Spiritual teachers from all traditions teach that the path of service or generosity is the most important of all as it is the one that asks us to be the least self-centered. Through caring for others, we are able to step beyond ourselves and release any sense of separation. It takes us out of selfishness and neediness, and in the process we see our own self-centeredness in greater perspective.

| DEB |

"HH the Dalai Lama was giving teachings in Dharamsala, India. It was crowded and cold and very uncomfortable sitting on bamboo mats on the concrete floor. I was longing to go back to our hotel room, to meditate in the solace of my own company. Then, as if he had read my mind, I heard him start talking about the dangers of solitary peace. He spoke of how tempting it can be to want to be on our own, but how easily this can disengage us from the reality around us. That it is vital to be in communication, engaged in giving, sharing, and caring for each other, and that the giving of ourselves is the greatest act of generosity. I stayed put!"

Through giving and sharing, we soon learn that when we give we do not lose anything; we do not have any less. Rather, we gain so much. As the slogan on a friend's tee shirt says: "Giving is the new getting." Or, as one of our teachers, Sri Swami Satchidananda taught: "Who is the most selfish person? It is the one who is most selfless! Why? Because by being selfless, you will always retain your happiness. A selfish person can never be happy. So, to be happier, be more selfless! Look at the apple tree: It gives thousands of fruits. What's more, if you throw a stone at an apple tree, it offers even more fruit. Throw a stone at a person and you know what you will get!"

We may feel we have little to offer, but whether it is a few pennies or a whole bankroll, a cup of tea or a banquet is irrelevant—it is the act of giving itself that is important. As Gandhi said, "Almost anything we do will seem insignificant, but it is very important that we do it."

On a morning walk through the lanes near our house, we came across a backyard filled with used bicycles. We wondered why there were so many. Finally, we met the owner and learned that he was collecting all these used bikes, happily taking his spare time to repair them, and then donating them to an Indian reservation. His goal was that everyone at the reservation, young and old, should have a bike of their own. His joy in doing this was palpable.

Generosity is not about giving just for the sake of giving. As with compassion, we need to see with wise discrimination what is needed, what would help most, and how we can be of best assistance, rather than, for instance, just donating money and presuming we have done a good deed. Generosity can also raise fears about not having enough, so we need to watch if resentment creeps in, or if we feel as if we are always giving but no one is giving to us. True generosity is giving without expectation; there is no desire that something will be received in return, no need to be repaid in any form. Giving without any thought of getting is the most powerful act of generosity, as it is unconditional, unattached, and free to land wherever it will.

I slept and dreamt that life was joy
I awoke and saw that life was service
I acted and behold, service was joy.
— RABINDRANATH TAGORE

TAKING MEDITATION INTO THE WORLD

Meditation in action arises as a natural expression of our inner wakefulness and can take many different forms. We see it in the way we deal with demanding relationships, such as with teenage children, a needy parent, or a sick partner. We see it as our capacity to let go of conflicts or forgive mistakes. We see it in how we treat the physical world around us. And we see it in our desire to reach out to others—perhaps through feeding the hungry, clearing polluted waterways, or working for political change—as we genuinely respond to the needs of the people and the world around us.

| JACK KORNFIELD |

"Meditation has two sides. You sit to quiet the mind and open the heart and to remember who you really are in this great mystery. Having reconnected with the great heart of wisdom and compassion, which is the in-breath, then you get up and you sweep the garden of the world, which is the out-breath. You naturally express the energy of care and compassion, of wisdom and tending, because the world is no longer separate from you. When I ask a class of 400 to 500 meditators how many are involved in direct service work, such as teaching English to immigrants, working in the emergency room at the hospital, being a voluntary preschool teacher, or working in the San Quentin prison garden project, more than half the hands go up."

The following examples show some of the ways meditation can be taken off the cushion and into the world. Each was born through the desire to make a difference.

Off the Cushion and into Politics

As everything is constantly changing, so everything has the potential to change for the better, including the one thing that is often thought of as unchangeable: politics. In its purest and broadest context, politics is the process of working toward a better world; national governance has a great influence in shaping the lives of people, while individual politicians have the responsibility to think clearly and act compassionately for the benefit of all, holding the interest of the people above their own. That, in essence, is no different from the aspirations of someone who meditates, and it is seen in such political leaders as Mahatma Gandhi, Aung San Suu Kyi, and HH the Dalai Lama.

As the original intent of politics is one of betterment for all, can meditation make a difference? We were very moved by our friend Mark Gerzon, who has worked with bipartisan groups and led retreats within government. The depth of his insight explores how meditation and politics can not only co-exist but can actually validate and enhance each other by creating a container for mutual growth and understanding.

| MARK GERZON |

"I use politics as a general term for engagement in the struggles of the world, for justice, for equality, for decency. Meditation is about nonat-tachment, and politics is about attachment. Meditation is about getting distance from your identity and becoming unattached to all the 'I am's,' while politics is about being very involved with all the 'I am's': I am in the bricklayers' union, I am a mother of four, I am a father with disabilities, I am in the more than $100,000 tax bracket. We are supposed to go to politics with our personal interests, to be there as a citizen and advocate for our attachments. And then we are supposed to lump our attachments into categories called left or right, Democrat or Republican, liberal or conservative. We are supposed to vote about them and even to fight about them. Now contrast that with meditation, which is to watch identities and attachments pass by like clouds in the sky so we become more spacious and unattached.

"How does a person who meditates engage in politics? How does a person who is politically engaged meditate? To me, this is like saying how does a person who loves to be engaged in life sleep? And how does a person who sleeps wake up and live life? I could not live an engaged life if I did not sleep, while sleeping would be of no value if I did not wake up and engage in the world. I am not saying one of those is equal to meditation or politics, but I am saying the relationship is there. I see meditation as absolutely necessary leavening yeast for politics. And I see engagement in the world as leavening yeast for meditation. There a dynamic tension between the two. My spiritual breakthroughs have happened because of engagement in the world that has deepened my meditation, and my meditation has changed and been informed by my engagement in the world.

"The first thing meditation did for me was to make me aware of how much I get in my own way. This knowledge gives me a lot more humility and compassion toward other people who get in their own way. It has taught me that my mind gets attached to 'partisan' pieces of the truth of my life, just as politicians do. That makes me a more compassionate observer in politics because the people I deal with are having those problems too. A meditative act is to look directly and openly at the whole, without looking up or down at someone.

"In situations where there are adversaries, there is usually a low level of trust. Creating a higher trust container or environment for adversaries has a meditative impact, because the part that the adversaries have disowned can now enter the room. The same happens in meditation. If we recognize that we have disowned parts of ourselves, then we can integrate that disowned part into our awareness. Carl Jung called this 'making the unconscious conscious.' So, in adversary situations, over here on my right is one person who hates this other person on my left. These two are, in fact, agents for each other's consciousness raising if—repeat *if*—we can create enough trust and space for them to listen to each other. If we define meditation as bringing into awareness the disintegrated, disowned, or disconnected parts of ourselves, then we can create containers for meditative experiences in the real world.

"It is not surprising to me that many people in the field of negotiation and mediation have some sort of spiritual practice, because we have to ground and deepen ourselves. Otherwise, we are just technicians negotiating compromises, and that is not what the world needs right now. The world does not need compromises; it needs synergies. Being present and asking questions from a place of presence are the key steps to transforming the level of consciousness."

|||

Off the Cushion and into the Street

Taking meditation off the cushion means meeting challenging situations such as homelessness with presence, skillfulness, equanimity, and compassion. In today's economy, many people are experiencing financial hardship and can find themselves on the street through no fault of their own. Yet how many of us acknowledge street people as fellow human beings with needs no different from ours, simply without the means to fulfill them? Instead, how often do we avert our eyes when we pass them by and pretend they do not exist?

In an attempt to find out what it would take to see homeless people as being no different from ourselves, Rev. James Morton, the dean of St. John the Divine Cathedral in New York, began an experiment.

| GROVER GAUNTT |

"He designed what he called the plunge: an act of diving into unknown waters and getting completely whacked and disorientated so you can orientate yourself in a new way. And he applied this to the street by sending his ministers out without any money, no place to live, no identification, just like the people they were serving. The first thing they did, quite naturally, was to go to the churches and ask for help, but, of course, very few would help them. So the initial moment of awakening for them was to realize that even the church was no help."

From here developed the idea of street retreats: living on the street for a few days as a spiritual practice, intended to encourage people to bring their commitment to their practice into the very midst of society's neediest, and by doing so to seek a place of inclusivity.

| BERNIE GLASSMAN |

"The homelessness that exists in our society is due to treating people as throwaways, and it will only end when we stop seeing them as garbage. When I started working with the homeless, I wanted to experience, as much as I could, what it was like to look at the world from their eyes. I saw homelessness as another aspect of myself but one that I did not have much insight on, so I decided to go into the streets to try and get that clarity, incorporating meditation into the experience.

"Street retreats are where we live and practice meditation on the streets, begging and sleeping rough just as any homeless person would. We meet for meditation periods together and then disperse to do what we have to in order to survive, such as finding food to eat and boxes to sleep on. I wanted to show that meditation is not just sitting on a cushion but reaches out to every aspect of life. It is a way of bringing us into a state of not-knowing, and when that happens, the experience of oneness arises. But at the same time we had the experience of not existing. When you are homeless and begging, people walk past you, you are completely ignored, you simply do not exist. When you have been so ignored, it is impossible to do that to another person. You can no longer look away from anybody or anything."

| ELLEN BURSTYN |

"I did the street retreat because I was so afraid of it. I could physically feel how much fear I had about being away from my comfort zone, my bed, and especially not having any identity. I had a lot of pride around my financial independence so the whole idea of begging was terrifying. The first time I did it, I had to a cross a street to a restaurant with tables outside. Two women were eating there and I decided to approach them. As I walked toward them, I felt like I was crossing over some line that I had consciously never known was there. I was purposefully stepping through my ego to experience what was on the other side. I approached the women and simply asked, 'Excuse me, but I need a dollar for the subway. Could either of you spare a dollar?' The woman closest to me reached into her pocket and handed me a dollar without taking her eyes off her companion's face. I said 'Thank you' and walked away. I felt a strange pride that I had really accomplished something, but then enormous sadness as I realized that neither of the women had looked at me. I had got what I needed, but I had been disregarded, I had not been seen."

| GROVER GAUNTT |

"Just a day can seem like forever as it is so intense. Suddenly, you do not have the money to get home, buy a cup of tea, make a phone call, or do anything. Fear rises as you are without any identity, any way of saying you are who you are. How do you relate to this world now? You have to find a place to sleep; you have to beg for food. And you watch people move their eyes to avoid seeing you. How can they ignore this, I thought, while sitting in the UN Plaza and watching people turn aside. What are they afraid of? Are they scared they will see themselves? I know I am guilty of the same thing, that I am one of those who turns my head, but who am I protecting?

"When we don't have the experience of something, then we tend to negate or categorize it. Homeless people get categorized as being alcoholics, drug addicts, there to rip you off, or just plain crazy. But every homeless person has a story and a history, just like we do. Before I first took the plunge, I was fearful of confrontation, but I learned that confrontation is just disguised fear. For instance, why do homeless people sleep during the day? Because it is safer. At night, they have to be on the move as they are more defenseless. Yet we move them or harass them for sleeping during the day and wonder why they get upset.

"I rarely pass a homeless person now without saying a few words and acknowledging him as a human being. If you see someone begging, look at him and realize that is me, it is me who is asking. There is no separation. Taking the plunge into the unknown is an expansion into a different way of seeing, an acceptance of all states of being beyond one's own limitations."

Doing anything outside of our experience is a plunge, especially stepping into places that we resist or are fearful of. The added ingredient of meditation to the street retreats was to deepen the experience of inclusivity, that we are all a part of each other, whether we are homeless or not. Such retreats, now held in many cities across the country, confront our fear and in so doing embrace our shared humanity.

Off the Cushion and into Jail

When we are in particularly difficult situations, meditation can become our ally, our closest friend and support, for it connects us to a deep source of inner strength and peace. It can also lead us to sharing with others in ways we would never have thought possible. Taking meditation off the cushion in this context means taking it into places and to people notoriously known for their lack of quiet or interest in meditation.

| FLEET MAULL |

"I was in a jail in southern Missouri that was just bedlam all the time, with people screaming, yelling, fighting, drunks coming in all night. Prisoners were allowed to have their own radios and televisions, so there would be full-blast noise all day and night. My mind was going nuts; it was just constantly racing back and forth. I could not sleep, so I practiced: I sat and mediated on the upper bunk. I would just sit there amid all the chaos and noise. One night, when I had been meditating for about two hours, my mind suddenly became completely clear and quiet. I wasn't totally free of thought; I am not talking about an enlightenment experience, but an experience of profound stability of awareness, so my mind was not moving. I had had this experience before in meditation but never in this kind of environment. It immediately informed me that I could completely handle this prison experience; it was the revelation that okay, I can do this. I knew I was probably going to be in prison for anything from twenty to forty years, I was on my way to a serious penitentiary, and I was having nightmares about being raped, but when I had that experience of mental stability, I knew I could do it. Something in me knew I would survive.

"Within another two months, I was sent to a federal prison. Soon after I got there, I started a meditation group in the chapel that met twice a week. It showed me how I could help out in that world. I led that group for years and hundreds of inmates came to mediation practice. Out of that group, we started the first hospice program in a federal prison to help those who were dying. It was a natural progression, a way to put our meditation to use. I got sent to a prison hospital in Springfield Missouri that had about 600 medical patients, 400 psychiatric patients, and about 300 regular inmates like myself who were there to help out around the place. The hospice program created very deep relationships between the ones dying and the ones taking care of them. We were prisoners together in this very caring and intimate place."

Our own experience of teaching meditation in jail showed us the difficulties prisoners are up against. We had all sorts of convicts in our classes, from burglars to murderers, but when we looked in their eyes we just saw broken spirits. Through meditation, they slowly began to realize that, rather than looking outside for freedom, they could find it within themselves. Until we find that freedom, we are, as Bo Lozoff of the Prison Ashram Project says, all doing time, whether we are in jail or not.

There are now numerous meditation programs throughout the prison system helping many thousands of prisoners to find peace within such a confined situation. For example, in one prison in Alabama, ten-day silent meditation retreats are regularly held, giving the prisoners a profound opportunity to heal their inner wounding. There are also many teachers devoting their time to helping those in jail.

| MARSHALL ROSENBERG |

"I work a lot in prisons, and the people there have done some stuff that I really do not like, like sexually molesting children. So I usually ask each one of them what need of theirs was being met when they did that? And I usually get back, 'Huh?' because nobody has ever asked them that question before. So I will say, 'I'd like to know what need you were trying to meet when you were doing that.' Then they'll usually answer something like, 'I do it because I'm a pervert.' And I say, 'Now you are telling me what you think you are. I am asking you what needs of yours are getting met?' And they say, 'What the hell are you talking about?' And I say, 'I believe you are doing this for the same reason that I do everything. I think you are doing it because it is the best way you know of meeting some need you have. That is what I do every moment—the best I know to meet my needs. And I am confident that if we can get clear about what needs of yours are being met by doing that, I bet we can find other ways of getting those needs met that don't create so much pain for you and others.' After doing this work, one prisoner walked me out to the gate. As I was leaving, he said, 'You are the first speaker we ever had that wasn't plastic!' I loved that."

|||

IO

|||

We Are Not Alone Here

*A monk asks, "Is there anything more miraculous than
the wonders of nature?" The master replies, "Yes, your
awareness of the wonders of nature."*
ANGELUS SILESIUS

In the Buddhist teachings, there is a description of a huge net
reaching in all directions with a multifaceted mirror-like jewel
at each of the many knots, every jewel reflecting all the others.
It is called the Jeweled Net of Indra and represents our interconnectedness: See one and you see all within it. No one can be
separated from or is independent of any other; take one away
and the net becomes unusable. In other words, we are interrelated, interdependent, inseparable, and interconnected all at
the same time, part of an integrated whole, not separate from
the trees, elephants, owls, our neighbors, the people in South
Africa or a river in India.

| JACK KORNFIELD |

"I think of the statement by General Omar Bradley, the chairman of the
Joint Chiefs of Staff in the 1950s, when he said we are a nation of nuclear
giants and ethical infants. Our inner development has not caught up to

our technological and scientific development. It is very clear that we are all interconnected—in modern ecology, physics, and neuroscience with mirror neurons—there is no doubt of that. We mistreat one another because we think of ourselves as separate beings; feeling separated from others gives rise to fear, confusion, self-protection, grasping, anger, and aggression. These are all born out of ignorance and out of forgetting our interdependence in the web of life."

If a butterfly becomes extinct in Australia, it affects the eco-system of the whole world, because a third of our food supply depends on insect pollination. If we pull on a single thread in nature, we will find that it is attached to the rest of the world. Caring for each other and the planet is, therefore, inseparable from caring for ourselves; we are both dependent on and a part of the earth and the woods and the children playing in the street, and they are a part of us. But living with this awareness takes some consideration, for our consensus reality is one of separation and isolation.

| JANE FONDA |

"There are practical reasons for dividing everything up. It makes things easier to manage and to solve, especially technical matters: the us and them, the either-or, the man versus nature, mine and yours. Life is simpler to deal with. But we have applied this fragmenting mindset to all of life so that it has become our reality, which has led to further fragmentation and chaos and planetary destruction. The challenge is to figure out how to deal with our day-to-day life, while at the same time changing our mindset so that we see reality as the unbroken wholeness of the totality of existence, an undivided, flowing movement without borders."

The belief that we are separate and unconnected from one another or from the world around us is the root cause of many of the problems we face, whether environmental or social, personal or global. When we put ourselves and our own needs over and above the needs of others, we do so at a tremendous cost, for it not only isolates us from each other, but also from our connectedness, which is fundamental to our happiness. Until we see this delusion for what it is and awake to an awareness of otherness, we will continue to self-destruct.

| BERNIE GLASSMAN |

"Imagine that each of my two hands has the notion that it is an individual object and not connected to anything else. Left hand calls itself Sally, and right hand calls itself Harry. Then Sally gets cut. Harry has read many things about the oneness of life, but he believes that Sally is separate and thinks, I cannot do anything about Sally being cut, I am not a doctor, and I don't have a first-aid kit. And anyway, I do not want to get my new clothes stained. Harry walks away, and Sally bleeds to death. But that means Harry also bleeds to death, as Harry and Sally happen to be very attached to each other. This is what happens when the experience of oneness is not there.

"Now imagine Sally and Harry both meditate and, while recognizing the separateness of Sally and Harry, they also recognize their oneness with Bernie. When Sally gets cut, Harry does the best thing possible to help her because he knows that to help her is also helping both him and Bernie. This is not a thinking process; it is the direct experience of the oneness of life. The appreciation of this is huge."

The illusion of separateness has so influenced our behavior and attitudes toward each other that it is only when we become more self-reflective that our awareness grows beyond such a limited view to encompass the whole. We become very conscious of the interconnected relationship of our jewel to all the other jewels, as well as of the intrinsic inclusivity of the net that contains them all.

| AJAHN SUMEDHO |

"We are not isolated entities; we do affect each other. The more we experience this in meditation, the more we recognize how our own relationship to society need not be one of just being critical or putting up with or ignoring it, but of using our abilities, intelligence, and talents to serve each other. If I feel a sense of 'me' as a self-centered isolated being, then I will just think of my own immediate pleasure or needs and I have no relation-ship or sensitivity to anything else. But as I open to the truth of our con-nectedness, then I have a respect for all life; I no longer see others as just there for my own selfish exploitation."

On a relative level, of course, we have our own thoughts and feelings, but they cannot be separated from what we were taught by our parents and teachers or from our experiences of pain and joy in our relationships—just as it is impossible to separate our body from the food we eat or the farmer who grew the food or the earth and the rain. There is actually no part of our being that is a separate or independent entity from everyone we have met and everything we have done or from every part of the world around us.

| TIM FREKE |

"We think that we are separate from each other and we are not. We think we are separate from the whole of life, and we are not. This belief makes us act as though we are only one part. But when we are awake to the fact that we are not just the part but really the whole, then we act to benefit the whole. Tim is an integral part of the whole, and everyone and every-thing are also an integral part of the whole and, therefore, one with Tim. Separateness is the conceptual story we tell to make sense of life, the story of who we are, and when we get sucked into it we are not conscious of our deeper being. This is when we cause suffering to each other and our world. Waking up is the recognition that there is no other, that every person or situation is not separate from our essential nature."

Where separation divides and causes conflict, awareness of our interconnectedness means we see the other as our-selves. The jewels in Indra's net are independent jewels and each reflects a different aspect of the whole, yet they are so interrelated that they cannot exist without each other or the entire net. At the same time, every jewel within the net is found reflected within each one.

| BERNIE GLASSMAN |

"Take care of the person next to you. It might be your spouse, your child, your parents, or it might be a stranger. It doesn't have to be big, it doesn't matter who it is, and it doesn't matter if they have nothing to give you; you just do it because it is there to be done. Meditation leads us to the experience of oneness. In that state, we automatically take care of everything we see because it is ourselves; it is not separate from us. We are walking down the street, and we see a person slip; it is not somebody else—we slipped. That is the bottom line for me: Once you take care of the delusion of separateness, then everything else is taken care of."

|||

Affecting Our World

Everything we think, say, and do has an immediate effect on everyone and everything else. This means that our thoughts and actions can lead to chaos and destruction as easily as they can lead to healing and friendship. It also means that we have enormous resources available to us at all times. "Do not make the mistake of thinking you are a powerless individual in a vast world," writes Tai Situpa in *The Way Ahead*. "Know that you are armed with three great powers. You have the power of the body—the source of all action; the power of speech—the source of all expression; and the power of the mind—the source of all thought."

Our *actions*, obviously, have the most direct impact on others. The destructive results of the belief that we are not connected and that, therefore, what we do has no bearing on others, is seen throughout our natural world. While we were in southern Egypt, we hiked far up a dry riverbed into silence and beauty and rubbish: piles of polystyrene and plastic dumped in the middle of nowhere. On an island in Greece, we found large bags of garbage washed ashore that had been tipped into the Mediterranean by passing boats; on the beach in Thailand, we watched local hotel owners burying their garbage in the sand. While in the exotic paradise of Sri Lanka, Deb was happily swimming in the beautiful Unawatuna Bay when human feces floated past her. Apart from polluting the land and water, such garbage and raw sewage is devastating to the surrounding plant, animal, and sea life. Every action we take, even the smallest and simplest of everyday choices, has a consequence.

| MARC IAN BARASCH |

"Nothing exists by itself; everything exists only in relationship. This leads to the realization that life is not just about my own pursuit of happiness or search for comfort, but the ego is always wanting gratification and this can lead to all sorts of problems. For instance, as we do not like to scrub and scrape our cooking pots and pans, we invented Teflon and nonstick pans. But now toxic perchlor fluoride from Teflon manufacturing can be found in the umbilical cord blood of 98 percent of newborns. Everything exists in relationship. Maybe it is better to apply elbow grease to pots, even though it does not make us so blissfully happy!"

We can only misuse the world when we believe that we are independent from it or are in some way superior to it. Yet no action is independent of its effects. We see this particularly in our immediate environment where every creature, insect, tide, or weather pattern has its own unique role to play as an integrated part of the greater whole. Nothing is without a purpose. If we do not understand this, then we easily abuse it.

| MARK MAWRENCE |

"Environmentalism and ecology are teaching us how everything is connected. The environment wastes nothing. It disposes of hundreds of billions of tons of fallen leaves and decaying materials, recycling them in an elegant and beautiful system. Whereas we, in this modern world, waste everything. We excrete hundreds of billions of tons of toxins into the environment, causing the impact that we are all familiar with. Eskimos in Alaska are breathing lead from fumes emitted in Los Angeles. Farming cycles in Hawaii and Central America are impacted by smog created in China. Once we establish that connectedness between us all, whether we live in Boise, Idaho, or Tokyo, we see how everything we do impacts each other."

Our neighborhood is our shared home, and our environment is our shared garden. Picking up rubbish is not just an act of kindness to our eyes, but also so we do not clog our rivers or seas; fighting to save the rainforests is not just so the trees can survive, but also that we may breathe more easily.

| ED |

"I was walking down a fancy shopping street in London. A teenage girl had finished drinking a can of soda and threw it on the ground. I picked it up and handed it back to her, asking 'Would you throw this on the floor in your home?' She looked at me like I was crazy."

Just as ignorance creates ignorant actions, so skillful awareness can generate a more positive outcome. Meditation is one of the most skillful of all actions. Although sometimes labeled as being a self-absorbed, if not selfish, activity, it not only changes our own behavior by increasing our awareness, but in turn we then influence and can change the world around us.

| TAMI SIMON |

"The effect of meditation is a rewiring of priorities. These are the priorities of our relationship with the earth and other people and how our heart is doing on any given day. The earth is what we are, what are bodies are; we are the same as the soil and the trees. The people we live with, who we wake up next to, who we sit across the dinning room table from, the people we work with every day—these are the relationships that should be our priority. When those things become our priority, we will make all kinds of different decisions as a global world."

The impact of our *words* is less obvious than that of our actions, but they are just as effective. Words are heard and felt; they reverberate throughout our system, affecting those who hear them and causing either joy or conflict. They can start wars or mend hearts. As such, they should not be used lightly, but with consideration of their influence.

| JOSEPH GOLDSTEIN |

"We need to understand our own minds. We need to see our own patterns and expressions. In a way it is so obvious. If we are full of judgment or anger or fear, we are just contributing to the problem. And if we let judgment go and become more loving and accepting and compassionate in ourselves, then that is what we give to the world."

Thoughts may be subtler, but when used purposefully, they are equally powerful. From our thoughts are born our words and our actions; they influence our behavior and beliefs, who we care for and who we dismiss. They also influence the unseen and unknown as we send our thought waves and energy out into the universe. It is our responsibility, therefore, to ensure that these thoughts are positive and creative ones.

| GREGG BRADEN |

"My first year in the Southwest desert was in the middle of one of the worst droughts in hundreds of years. A neighbor asked me if I would like to come with him to pray for rain. I had some expectations and judgments about this, but I agreed. I thought I was going to see some hooping and hollering and dancing, but none of that happened. We went to a stone circle high in the desert. My friend stepped inside the circle with his bare feet, closed his eyes for about a minute, and then he said, 'I'm hungry; do you want to get a bite to eat?' I said, 'Sure, but I thought you were going to pray for rain?' He said, 'No, if I were going to pray for rain, rain could never happen because the moment we ask for something we have just acknowledged that it does not exist right now and we may be enforcing the very thing we would like to change.' So I said, 'If you did not pray for rain, then what did you do?' And he replied, 'I felt the feeling as though it is already raining. I felt the feeling of what it feels like to stand with my naked feet in the mud of our pueblo village because it is raining. I smelled what it smells like when the rain falls on the earthen walls in the pueblo.'

"We went to get a bite to eat, and by the time I got home, big black clouds were overhead. It rained all that night; it rained all the next morning, and the next afternoon. It rained and rained, and the ground was so dry, it could not soak it up, and it began to flood, and roads were washed out, and cattle were stranded, and crops were destroyed. I called my friend and I asked him, 'What happened? This is a mess!' He said, 'That is the part of the prayer that the ancestors could never figure out. They could get the rain going, but they did not know how to tell it how much!'"

|||

Experiencing Our World

To know that we are all interconnected and a part of each other is not always enough; we also need to experience this in a living, vibrant way. One way to do this is by being outside. So many of us have lost touch with nature, yet just taking time to sit in a city park can reconnect us to the life with which we share our world. If we meditate on our shared connectedness, and we do this outside, we will move from the confines of the ego-self into the wholeness that surrounds us. And when we let nature communicate with us, we discover there is much we can learn.

| JOHN MILTON |

"The process of meditating in nature allows us to become very quiet and still. We begin to actually have the experience of not being defined just as an individual being, separate from the rest of life, but as a being that is totally interwoven and interconnected with all life. Such meditation is appropriate for these times as we are so out of touch with the rest of life, which has led us to the point where our relationship with the planet itself is threatened. I think it is more that *we* are in peril, rather than nature. Our own capacity to really experience the deep joy that comes from being a part of all life is the most endangered thing that we face.

"If we only do our meditation practice in buildings, in human-constructed places, then we do not have that primordial connection to nature that is so needed. The vision quest that is found in many different traditions is probably one of the oldest spiritual practices on the planet. This is the process of going alone into nature for a period of time to embrace the great mystery in solitude, to have a deeper experience of the truth beyond our built-up world. When we do vision quests or sacred path solos, we focus on meditating with each perception, with sight, smell, taste, and touch: We see what is all around us, we smell the richness of the earth, we reach out to touch our world. By meditating with these perceptual fields, we have an experience of communion with the great mystery, with the sky and the trees and the earth beneath our feet."

In this same way, the Native American people, as with many other native peoples around the world, live in harmony with and are intimately connected to the earth. Because their lives are so much a part of their environment, they have a natural reverence for it and have integrated a deep awareness of how nature works into the way in which they live.

| JOSEPH MARSHALL |

"Interestingly enough, in my native language of Lakota, there is no word for wilderness; Native Americans do not separate themselves from the world the way many English speakers do. We are all a part of the entire system, of the whole environment. There are words to indicate 'where man is not,' but that is not the same as wilderness words. We speak from that sense of connectivity, and it is one of the things that we always acknowledge when we go into a sweat lodge or to some kind of a healing ceremony. We are also realists. An environment behaves in certain ways in order to success-fully survive, and we have to know and deeply respect this as much as possible so we can work with rather than against it. It is not apart from us, and we are not apart from it."

The awareness of nature is also an awareness of the sacred and of the necessity of bringing the sacred into every part of our lives. We rarely talk about things being sacred—our daily life seems far too mundane in comparison, and so the subject is normally relegated to the more unreachable aspects of religion.

Yet the sacred can be found in every moment; it simply needs our awareness and recognition.

| SARASVATI BURHMAN |

"Clearly our history of political and economic support for capitalism has played a major role in our present environmental problems. But there is individual responsibility too, and here I do not just mean our failure as individuals to recycle, carpool, or monitor our water consumption. We live in these bodies that are expressions of nature, yet we fail to comprehend the sacredness of all life. We treat other living beings as little more than commodities for our consumption. Once I asked a Hindu villager why the cow was sacred in Indian culture. He replied that the bull plows the fields and the dung is used as fuel for fires. The cow gives milk, yogurt, and butter for food and medicines. How could something that gives so much not be sacred? Then he asked me, 'How can we return such generosity by killing?'

"In ancient Celtic spirituality, trees were regarded as sacred beings. They are like the cows of the plant world, providing so much that is necessary for other life forms on our planet, not the least of which is the oxygen we breathe. Their fruits and nuts provide food without requiring any violence on our part. Is it right to so mindlessly destroy them as we do? A person who meditates for a period of time in a forest begins to feel the same universal consciousness emanating from all living beings. Such an experience of the sacred changes the way we relate to each other and to other species."

|||

Appreciating Our World

To recognize the sacred is to appreciate all things as they are, to see the beauty inherent in everything from a doorknob to a moonlit river, from the preciousness of life to the magnificence of its unfolding. There is an old Tibetan story about a blind turtle that lives in the ocean and comes to the surface only once every thousand years. A gold ring floats in the ocean. The story goes that the chance that the blind turtle will put its head into the ring when it comes up for air is as rare as it is for a human to take birth. This story is told in order to emphasize how precious our life really is.

In meditation, as we watch thoughts move through our mind, or watch aches and pains come and go, we are witnessing how all things are temporary and insubstantial. This awareness can generate tremendous gratitude for what is here now, just as it is. Yet it is easy to forget to appreciate what we have and to put our happiness on hold. We make gratitude something we will come to some time in the future: When things are better, when our children get married, when the weather changes, when we have more money, then we will be grateful. So much time is wasted waiting to be happy, when all we need to do is experience the magnificence of what we already have.

For instance, take a moment right now to appreciate the chair you are sitting on as you read this. Consider what went into the making of this chair: the wood, cotton, wool, or other fibers, the trees and plants that were used, the earth that grew the trees and plants, the sun and rain, the animals that were involved and maybe gave their lives, the people who prepared the materials, the factory where the chair was made, the designer and carpenter and seamstress, the shop that sold it—all this just so you could be sitting here now. You can include the building you are in or the clothes you are wearing and all the elements involved in their making.

Or think of your body and all the different organs, functions, and systems that sustain your life, such as your heart, digestion, or immune system. Or think of the food that nourishes you and where it came from and all the people and plants and weather and transport that were needed to get that food on your table. It is so huge; there is no beginning place. There is just an endless stream of connectedness that has come together to enable you to be here right now, in this moment, reading this, sitting on a chair. And we think we have nothing to feel grateful for or worth appreciating?

| ED |

"We were in Australia on our honeymoon, and I wanted to show Deb what a great body surfer I was. So I strode into the waves and swam out beyond the breakers, ready to surf back. But I didn't know about Australia or about this particular stretch of beach. Suddenly, I was being pulled out by a strong undertow. No matter how hard I struggled, I was going nowhere. I was being swept out until, finally, by swimming diagonally to one side, I managed to inch my way to the shore. Deb, of course, knew nothing of my struggles. She just saw this bedraggled show-off limping back along the beach. But the gratitude, the appreciation, the joy of being alive was far greater than my battered ego. Everything was suddenly so vivid and precious; the sand beneath my feet felt like gold dust."

We can develop an attitude of gratitude by making a list of things to remember to appreciate. We can do this hourly, daily, or weekly, finding different things to appreciate each time. Anything can go on that list: pets, people, grapefruit, flannel sheets, clean water, sunshine. . . . Then say, "Thank you!" Say it out loud, and again. We can never have enough gratitude; let it fill every moment, every thought, and every feeling.

Fixing Our World

Appreciating nature, honoring the world around us, and recognizing the sacredness of all life are essential for our survival, but we also have to act. Given all the environmental difficulties we are facing, such as pollution, climate change, and the loss of biodiversity, we may not have too much time to make the changes that are needed.

| MARIANNE WILLIAMSON |

"We are like the *Titanic* headed for an iceberg. If we continue with the behavioral patterns that now dominate our relationship to the earth and its resources, it is said that we only have fifty years before the planet will be overrun with something like 200 million environmental refugees, and if you have this kind of a situation on the planet, then human suffering will be immeasurable. Our job is to move from probabilities to possibilities, and the only way we can do this is if enough of us, within our own minds and our own hearts and our own lives, reach a state of consciousness that moves us out of the time-and-space continuum as we now experience it. We are at the eleventh hour, and somehow we have to expand this hour, and that can happen when we meditate."

As we recognize what we have done to our planet and we see the work that needs to be done to put it right, we may feel either overwhelmed and incapable or desperate to try and fix it all at once. But, as the saying goes, "We can only do it one person at a time." Taking time to meditate may seem irrelevant when we are confronted with the need for so much action; it is easy to think that meditation has nothing to do with saving the world, that it is just something we do for ourselves. Yet the combination of action and meditation is essential.

| ED BEGLEY, JR. |

"There is so much work to do that we say, 'Oh, the whales are dying, we can't leave the dolphins, and look the rivers are so polluted, we have got to do something, come on—let's move, I can't sleep tonight, I have got to drink some coffee and get up for that rally tomorrow, we have to save the environment, it's so terrible.' Although we are not going to solve all the problems by just sitting on the side of a hill or by spinning a prayer wheel, we also have to be still and centered so we can act with clarity. In other words, in order to do this work, we need to have an inner resource we can always come back to. If we do not have quiet time, we will get too burnt out to be able to clean up the rivers or save the whales. We have to sit still and recharge. We have to be in the moment as it is happening, and we cannot do that if we do not have mediation as a resource."

Beyond being an essential resource, meditation also provides the spaciousness necessary to find new and creative answers to difficult problems. Searching for solutions can be an endless occupation, but times of quiet reflection will feed our inspiration and insight, making our choices of action more sustainable and balanced.

| MARK MAWRENCE |

"I was asked by the mayor to serve on the board of directors of the Bay Street district, a non-profit corporation that manages the entire downtown area. We had an enormous crisis as homeless people were flocking here due to all the foot traffic. The pedestrians made for lots of easy targets along the sea front, and the promenade was almost shut down because we were getting hundreds of complaining letters a week, there were articles in the newspapers about all the homeless people with panhandlers accosting citizens, driving away diners, scaring children, and on and on. The mayor asked me if I could fix the problem. He said, 'Please, could you do something, Mark? You're an out-of-the-box thinker. Please do something.'

"I held hearings. I listened to the homeless groups, I listened to neighborhood groups, and I listened to the police and city agency workers. Basically, everybody ended up screaming at each other. The activists would say if the homeless want to urinate on themselves and die in a shop doorway, it is their right and no one should ever stand in between them and their right to do that. Then the opponents would say let's rent buses, put a nice buffet on the buses, lure the homeless onto the buses, and drive them out of town. We had this very typical split: tolerance versus toughness.

"The mayor wanted a report and I had no idea what to do, so I decided to do my second most favorite form of meditation next to sitting: I went surfing. I experience surfing as a very powerful meditation as I am not only fully present and aware of every moment, but I also enter into the sound of the sea, become one with the waves and go beyond thinking. In those thoughtless moments, creativity often stirs with solutions to any difficulties I am dealing with.

"I sat on my board and let all of the screaming go out of my mind. I did not think about the problem; I was there to rest my thinking and just be silent. I was floating quietly, letting the waves lull my mind, when two dolphins jumped out of the water right in front of me. It was awesome! And it was as if the dolphins jumped into my mind, which was completely open and receptive. In that moment, I immediately knew what to do.

"Long story short, I raised about $350,000 to forge life-size bronze dolphin sculptures. Where the blowhole should be is a little coin slot to put money. Everyone is encouraged to give to the dolphins, rather than giving to the homeless. The money the dolphins collect feeds the hungry, it clothes the homeless, it puts people up, it pays for shelters for abused women, it does job training, and it gives medical treatment to the needy. All the homeless charities are now supported by the dolphins."

|||

Shaping Motivation

We watched as an eager young television reporter from CNN asked HH the Dalai Lama what was the first thing he thought of when he awoke in the morning. We thought that this most revered teacher would say something deeply profound or insightful, something along the lines of vowing to save the world from its own ignorance. Instead, he simply replied, "Shaping motivation." He said that we all, including himself, have to be vigilant so that our intentions are focused in the right direction. He said that shaping his motivation constantly reminds him to extend loving kindness and compassion to all others. Such motivation extends us beyond ourselves so that we are not limited by a lack of confidence or self-esteem.

| MICHAEL BERNARD BECKWITH |

"As we clarify and deepen in awareness, then the contents of our emotions, and the beliefs and actions they engender, have less effect on our life. We begin to pause before we take action. We ask ourselves about our motivation, our intention, and if what we are about to do is in the highest service of ourselves or another. As spiritual beings having a human incarnation, we have the capacity to think independently of circumstance and experience. We can be aware of our emotional content and not allow it to dictate our actions. We can actually observe fear, doubt, worry, or anger, and not act on them."

It is easy to underestimate ourselves or to think that one person really does not make a difference. But even small gestures or acts can have a very big impact—consider how much of an effect a single mosquito can have! Each one of us has something special and unique to offer, and even more so when we are in touch with our essential interrelatedness. We can each act to leave the world a better place than we found it.

| JON KABAT-ZINN |

"The world needs all its flowers. Sometimes we may think, Well, I am not a flower, I am not beautiful, and I don't have any qualities that might be useful. What a hubris that is, to think the world has singled you out to be useless and unbeautiful! It is very important to ask, 'What can I do that would contribute even in the tiniest way to greater levels of well-being and sanity and kindness on the planet?' Even the act of taking your seat for meditation is a radical act of love that extends way beyond your small self.

"Individually and collectively, we are not paying appropriate attention to our experience as human beings. The consequences of this are potentially disastrous for the world. We are ignoring certain aspects of reality in favor of others, and it creates huge amounts of suffering. The cause of that is really a certain kind of conditioning that is driven by small-mindedness or an identification with who we think we are, as opposed to a much bigger direct experience of the unboundedness of human nature."

Motivation guides our behavior and determines whether our intent is arising out of selfishness or selflessness. Is our motivation one of kindness, forgiveness, or letting go? Or is it one of judgment, blame, or grasping? Are we making someone else seem wrong in order for us to appear right? Are we ignoring or dismissing someone? Or are we genuinely concerned, genuinely feeling consideration, respect, and care? If we take each situation into our meditation, then we can ask, 'What is the deeper intention of my behavior? What is my real motivation?' We need to question our actions, words, and thoughts in this way so that we can answer the call of the world.

| ANDREW HARVEY |

"Meditation is an essential part of the solution to the really immense crisis that we are in, because this crisis demands of us that we are able to see the extent of the damage that we have done to ourselves and to the earth and start working with fully motivated wills and hearts in the world. None of that can be done without meditation. But meditation must also have a vision of action with a passionate commitment to service, to really do something about the issues that are now afflicting our future. Meditation without vision would be absolutely empty, while action without the knowledge, wisdom, passion, and love gained from meditation is useless. We need the clarity of meditation to awake our motivation."

Letting go of insecurities and self-doubt so that we can be available and open to what is needed in the moment is a quality that we can bring not only to our meditation but to our communication with the world. The only limits to what we can do are the ones we impose on ourselves.

| JEAN HOUSTON |

"Meditation gives us access to the vastness of the universe. Our challenge is to take this understanding and reinvent our civilization, including agriculture, education, and economics, with an intelligent self-organizing living universe. Instead of degrading the universe's life systems, we must now learn to join all beings together in a mutually enhancing manner. Meditation gives us the awareness to do this as consciousness becoming self-conscious."

|||

Practice Meditation:
Communing with Nature

| FROM JOHN MILTON |

"Amazing and powerful experiences can arise by simply sitting, open and receptive, with your back against a tree. Better yet, stand firmly rooted and

embrace the tree, like an old friend not seen for a long time. As you sense into the tree, you may experience the impression of being held by a loving embrace. Once you have established your relationship with this tree, you may begin to feel a deep communion together that makes it easy for you to trust and to let go of the contractions and tensions you have been holding.

"A tree is extremely centered in its being and is well grounded and rooted. It is at one with the sky above and the earth below. Just as the tree crown lifts to the heavens, feel your spirit opening into the vastness and spaciousness of the sky. At the same time, feel yourself completely rooted and deeply connected with the earth.

"A tree is totally centered in its place. You can find that same kind of center in yourself, wherever you are, if you simply remember what it feels like when you lean into a tree.

"Trust the process of completely letting go and surrendering to what other plants, animals, and rocks have to give you. This may sound like something special, but in truth, anyone can experience this. All you need to do is sit quietly and open yourself and be present for what is given, with no expectations. Relax into the experience.

"In the Native American way, Great Spirit is seen flowing through all the beings of Nature, including you. Birds, plants, stones, mammals, mountains— all are seen as your relatives. For this reason, most Native American prayers include giving thanks to all Creation in this profoundly ecological phrase: "I give thanks to all my relations."

|||

II

| | |

Silence in the Boardroom

*"The most powerful force in business isn't greed, fear, or
even the raw energy of unbridled competition. The most
powerful force in business is love. It is what will help your
company grow and become stronger. It is what will propel
your career forward. It is what will give you a sense of
meaning and satisfaction in your work."*

TIM SANDERS, SENIOR MANAGEMENT, YAHOO!

FAST COMPANY MAGAZINE.

We received a phone call, and the voice on the other end
simply asked, "Do you teach meditation?" Ed answered that
we did. The voice then said, "We would like to have you come
to Thailand to teach our CEOs." The year before, it had been
golf; this year, the VP wanted to try meditation. So we went to
teach these highly stressed top-management bosses the simple
art of being silent. By the end of the week, we had no idea if
they had understood what we were teaching, but on the last
day, when they were free to do whatever they wanted, one of
them requested a meditation session. To our amazement, they
all showed up. After that, the VP signed us to work with management for a year and we became his personal coach.

As stress levels increase, stress-reduction programs are
becoming more common throughout the business world.
Although they tend to focus on time management and simple
relaxation practices, more and more we see yoga and meditation classes being offered in the workplace. Google has offered

both, as have Yahoo!, Rodale Publishers, Morgan Stanley, and Pricewaterhouse Coopers, to name but a few. As Oliver Ryan wrote in *Fortune* magazine, on July 20, 2008:

"The crowd of Harvard Business School alums who gathered at their reunion to hear networking-expert Keith Ferrazzi speak . . . might have expected to pick up strategies on how to work a room, remember people's names, or identify mentors. . . . Instead, Ferrazzi let his fellow alums in on a little secret . . . meditation. Exercise and prayer work too," he said, "but meditation has been so effective that he now spends ten days every year at a silent meditation retreat. In other words, the man whose latest book is *Never Eat Alone* credits much of his success to alone time."

It is easy to see why meditation is having such an impact. Stress creates workplace fatigue, absenteeism, mistakes, a lack of productivity, burnout and breakdown, while meditation has the opposite effect. It helps decrease the amount of stress experienced while clearing the mind, increasing concentration and confidence, and helping to achieve greater perspective to solve problems. It promotes thoughtfulness, which leads to better, more careful decisions. It improves listening skills, which develops enhanced interpersonal communication, and it clarifies purpose and vision.

| JOEL AND MICHELLE LEVEY |

"It might be about getting good business results, but what people also find is that, as they start to become more mindful, their health improves and the quality of their relationship with their significant others or their kids or their coworkers improves. We have seen relationship building between people with better learning skills to deal with difficult conversations or situations, such as conflict resolution. Leaders become more mindful and able to listen, to hear different ideas. Their people feel heard and valued. We have seen absentee levels go way down around stress-related illnesses."

With results like these, corporations now see classes in stress release as both beneficial to the employee's health and as a way to inspire and stimulate creativity. In a stressed state, it is natural to only focus on self-survival and competitiveness; in a relaxed state, we are connecting with a deeper sense of purpose and innate altruism.

| BONNIE REISS |

"I think that whether we are in high-stress work, in politics or business, the discipline of meditation is vital. I served as senior advisor to Governor Schwarzenegger, and it was eighteen-to-nineteen-hour days, seven days a week, working on every kind of imaginable issue needed for running a state that is the sixth-largest economy in the world. Whenever I felt a particularly stressful moment in the office, I would stop and just take a breath or I would take some time to walk outside to Capitol Park. I'd go by a tree or sit on a bench and do a five-minute meditation. In those circumstances, even starting or ending the day with meditation was not enough because I would find myself getting off balance and needing to have a quiet moment in the midst of it all, to take that five-or-ten-minute break in order to come back to myself. When I can be silent and away from people, and I can connect to that inner space, then I get a greater sense of equilibrium and calm. I can think more clearly and make clearer decisions.

"There is no shortage of really intelligent people running a state or a country, working in the senate, or working in government offices. And yet just bringing intelligence to bear on decision making does not, as evidenced by what we see with so much poverty, prejudice, and environmental degradation, necessarily ensure that our state or our country go in the right direction. It is equally as important to bring the sensitive heart of compassion to decision making. Ultimately, more world changes would be achieved by every individual bringing a more loving and forgiving heart to whatever they do."

Yet, the opportunity to just be quiet or self-reflective is, without doubt, the main ingredient lacking in the lives of many businesspeople, normally so filled with activity and demands that stillness or agenda-free time simply does not occur. As a result, the first-time experience of simply being quiet and present can be overwhelming.

| JON KABAT-ZINN |

"I was once teaching a business workshop in Chicago in a big hotel. It was billed as a two-hour workshop on practical applications of mindfulness in business. As I entered the room, people were sitting around dressed in suits, reading the *Wall Street Journal*, cups of coffee in hand. I casually said, by way of an opening: 'Why don't we just take a moment and sit quietly with no agenda?' I didn't give them any instructions; we just sat quietly for about ten or fifteen minutes. I noticed that during this time, a few people began crying. When it was over, I asked them about it. One of the executives said, 'You know—we never do anything without an agenda.' The others agreed. It was a real eye-opener for them, just to sit and be still. It is a reclaiming of what I call the domain of being. Usually, we are so driven by all the doing that, after a while, we forget who is doing the doing and why, and even what the doing actually is."

|||

Finding the Right Approach

Many businesspeople think of meditation as being a bit weird and wacky; they feel embarrassed if people know they are doing it, and yet at the same time, there is a real yearning for something to help them relax and feel more easeful. When we first began working with corporations, we found that their unfamiliarity with the whole idea of meditation demanded that we take a new approach. As mentioned earlier, one of our first jobs was in Thailand at the semi-annual four-day meeting of fourteen CEOs from an international corporation. They all came from different countries, and so we not only had to have an understanding of their cultures, but we also had to find a language that everyone could relate to. In place of meditation, we used the term *silent space*. This was instantly understandable and made the sessions of meditation practice far more accessible. We began each meeting with a few minutes of silence and held longer sessions twice a day. Many of them commented to us that sitting in silence this way was the first time they had ever been in the present moment, in the here and now, without thoughts crowding in to fill the quiet.

| MARK GERZON |

"I have never used meditation *per se* inside companies. What I do is create spaces where people can hold the whole. Before a group that is dealing with a tough issue tells me what is going on, I ask that each one of them take a few minutes to focus on what they want to share or whatever the question is. Some of them might make notes, but they are all sitting in silence. If I called it meditation, they would say, 'Who do you think you are?' The ones who liked it would feel closer to me, and the ones who did not like it would feel alienated. And I would have just defeated the purpose of us being together. So I think of it as intentional silence."

Starting a meeting with a few minutes of silence is a very powerful yet simple way to bring people together that any business can implement, without having to call it meditation. In this way, no one thinks they are being asked to do something weird, yet all come together in a shared space.

| TAMI SIMON |

"We have a minute of silence at the beginning of all of our meetings; even at a meeting between just three people, we take a minute first. Most people are moving from meeting to meeting or this conversation from this email, and when we get rushed, we run over people, we do not listen very well, we make bad decisions, and we are only half present. To just sit down for a minute clears the mind and brings us all into the present moment so that everyone is on the same page before the meeting begins. I tell them that they do not have to think of this as meditation or prayer; they can just think of it as a minute of silence to clear their minds."

Using words such as *mindfulness* or *mindful aware-ness practice*, instead of meditation, also works, as they are instantly descriptive of what is being asked of the participants. Developing awareness or mindfulness of other people and their behavior, and of the greater situation, enables us to then pay that same attention to our own minds, just as we do in meditation.

| JOEL AND MICHELLE LEVEY |

"We were working with the head of manufacturing during a group exercise when the mindfulness card came up. He looked at it and said, 'Mindfulness—who needs this crap?' and he tossed it away. I said, 'Okay, you are director of manufacturing. Do you care about the quality of what goes out your door? Do you care about how many mistakes people make? Do you care about efficiency? Do you care about how well time and resources are used? Do you care about the quality of attention that people bring to doing the work that they do?' I went through this whole list and then basically said, 'Because that is what mindfulness is. It is paying attention. It is being able to manage, and you can only manage what you are aware of.' He picked the mindfulness card back up and said, 'I think I want that!'

"A while later, the general manager left to go to a competitor, and for six months, all the divisional managers had to run the division by themselves. They were so fragmented and polarized that we were called in to help them come together as a team. Two days later, they had a meeting, and the quality manager and the head of manufacturing get up to tell people the values they were going to use to make decisions as they took the division forward. They both talked about the importance of mindfulness."

|||

Disconnection

Ninety-five percent of the executives we have worked with are very talented at what they do in business, but are not nearly as emotionally adept, so their relationships are often in turmoil. In the process of climbing the corporate ladder, it is easy to lose touch with this part of ourselves. And it is not just emotional integrity, but a deeper spiritual connection that is missing as well. This split between our professional and personal selves can lead to the creation of masks and role playing, along with a profound lack of fulfillment. More importantly, it limits the amount of inner resources being brought to the job. It is a high price to pay for corporate accomplishment.

| MICHAEL CARROLL |

"Business leaders are tremendously confident, they are brilliant men and women, the brightest of the brightest, they are competent, studying strategy planning, execution, and have all kinds of knowledge. At work, we spend a tremendous amount of time trying to achieve things, we are always trying to hit the number, do the project, plan the deal, get our MBA, get promoted, build a business, acquire a business. But the problem is, in all this effort to try to get somewhere we overlook how to be somewhere. And in the process of trying to become someone else, someone richer, more successful, more admired, or more powerful, we overlook how to be who we are already. This speeding past the experience of who we are and where we are creates a tremendous blind spot. It makes us unskillful; we neglect ourselves and our health, as well as many of the relationships that are actually needed in order to be successful.

"I spoke with a doctor who was part of a medical affairs team at a pharmaceutical company. He said, 'You know, leadership to me is very simple. My job is to get my team from point A to point B as quickly, efficiently, successfully, and profitably as possible. That is my job.' I replied: 'There is only one small but actually critical difference between us. I also want to get from point A to point B as efficiently, quickly, and as profitably as possible. However, when I arrive at point B, I want our collective sanity to be intact. What happens when you rush to point B is that you neglect your world in the process.' In the rushing, be it personal or business, we are actually creating the very toxicity that we are trying to avoid. Meditation is the key ingredient to this as it trains our minds to appreciate both ourselves and our world.

"Fear affects organizations because people are afraid to be themselves. Uncertainty is seen as an enemy; nobody at work can appear to be doubtful or uncertain, especially if they are in charge. When you ask the average person what their life is like, they will tell you that they are more depressed, more anxious, and more hesitant about their lives than they were ten years ago. Depression is on the rise. Anxiety disorders are on the rise. Suicide rates are on the rise. We are trying to secure our lives rather than live them. If we can embrace our lives and stop being afraid of them, then we can take our seats with a level of confidence and ease."

In any business environment, there is an ingrained push to succeed, and to succeed quickly. The corporate ego is a big one. There is a strong sense of "me first" and of the compulsion to be territorial. It causes a sense of isolation and loneliness—no one is sure who they can trust or who will try to beat them on the race to the top of the ladder. Many of the problems we see arising out of the corporate world are due to the speed at which decisions are made or actions taken, which often leaves important parts of our psyche out of the picture.

| MICHAEL CARROLL |

"We have to reconcile the two worlds of compassion and kindness with business. I have fired more than 3,000 people, I have orchestrated large lay-offs, acquisitions, and all that kind of stuff, and every single time I have done this, I made sure that management saw how to treat people with respect, preserving their dignity, communicating in ways that made them feel they were not being taken for granted, by trying to look after the health and well-being for them and their family. These are things that, if management does not think about properly, if they are not guided to take the notion of well-being seriously, then they will speed past it and create harm.

"At one sales meeting I led, there were maybe two hundred people. The theme of the meeting was being a warrior, so I spoke about how we think warriors are about punching and kicking, but actually warriors have this ability to be at ease and comfortable with their own physical and emotional presence, which comes from a sense of vulnerability. And in order to train the mind that way, you have to be able to still the mind through meditation."

We are not suggesting that it is necessary to get everyone in a business to meditate; that would be wonderful, but it would also be both arrogant and impossible. However, when we personally meditate, then we can connect with our deeper emotional and spiritual selves so that they are brought together in such a way that each can be appreciated and nourished. We become who we really are—our authentic self—and this is the person we take to work. Meditation means we become more balanced in our approach to difficulties and able to inspire others.

| CONSTANCE KELLOUGH |

"We think we cannot make a living and make a life at the same time, so most people go to work grudgingly to make a living and feel that the only time they can really let loose and be themselves is when they are away from the workplace. When I was a management consultant, I saw this all the time and thought how sad it was that we could not bring our 'beingness' and our presence into the workplace. Maybe one day soon, the importance of stillness will be so evident to employers that they will happily sanction stillness breaks during the workday to encourage their employees in cultivating this practice. It is from inner stillness that all new and creative ideas flow and that we make clear, conscious decisions. It is from inner stillness that we become more efficient in what we do because we are in the present moment and we are not impeded by the fears and frustrations of ego. It does not mean we are not in the real world and are not making real decisions based on solid business acumen; it is just that our decisions are coming from presence, from awareness. There are times when we have to be very firm, but it is not fear-based. It perplexes me that people say, 'How can you carry on business if you come from the consciousness of unity, which is love based?' And I say, 'How can you carry on business without it?'"

|||

Ethical Questions

Teaching meditation to corporate employees is a rewarding and dynamic arena in which to work. However, as meditation opens us to the interconnectedness of all life, there are times when we are confronted with ethical choices. Do we discriminate against those companies whose products we morally disagree with? Do we limit our services only to those acting with ethics we do approve? Or are all companies and employees equally in need?

| MIRABAI BUSH |

"We had an opportunity to work in Monsanto as a friend had just become the CEO. He did not know much about meditation at the time, but he had read about Zen and thought it might add an interesting dimension to leadership development. He really wanted to provide ways for his staff to think big and to think differently. We started with a three-day silent meditation retreat for the top seventeen Monsanto executives at the Fetzer Institute, and then for four years, we taught meditation in the workplace and at off-site retreats in Chicago and St. Louis. The response was incredibly positive—people reported profound changes in both their personal and professional lives. But we were constantly challenged by our own community and colleagues.

"Just a few years earlier, I had worked with the SEVA Foundation in the mountains of Guatemala, helping the Mayan people recover their soil and their sustainable agricultural processes. They had suffered terribly because of the chemicals that had been introduced into their soils by companies like Monsanto. I still carried great pain about that. So I understood the negative responses to Monsanto as they were introducing genetically modified foods. Some thought we should not teach there at all, that we would just be teaching people to 'do bad things better' by reducing their stress and increasing their ability to pay attention. I had huge questions myself.

"But inside Monsanto we discovered that they had studied population statistics and believed they could help feed the world for the twenty-first century, that it was 'good science.' We decided that it was not our job to challenge their products but to give them a method to see more clearly, to be more willing to look again at their justifications, and to enter into dialog with counter opinions.

"We created an environment of no judgment. As they learned basic mindfulness meditation practices, they began to look more carefully at what was going on inside themselves, at both their thoughts and emotions, and to be able to let go of the story that they had been told or that they were telling themselves. We always included a loving kindness meditation, and we would direct it from ourselves toward all species with the understanding that unless you have that love and care for yourself, then it is difficult to love and care for others. At the first retreat, I opened my eyes during this practice and saw tears running down almost every person's face. I realized, in a stunning moment of awareness of my own judgments that, of course, corporations are made up of people who, like all of us, have feelings and want to think they are doing the right thing.

"The real work of meditation in the workplace is not just to reduce stress; it is to challenge our firmly held beliefs and to look at the true nature of things. Our work is based on the belief that the potential for positive change comes from within us. If we give people tools to heighten awareness of their inner states, then they are more apt to come up with new ways of creating a better world."

|||

The Best Trickle-Down Effect

On one occasion, when we were hired by a multinational corporation to teach meditation to its senior management, it was because the executive vice-president was a meditator and he wanted his management to have the same experience—in other words, when the boss meditates, the whole company benefits. But what difference does a meditating boss make to the way his business is run, to making a profit, or to survival in the world of competition?

| JAMES GIMIAN |
"When making decisions that influence the direction of our business, I try to keep in mind the diverse talents, skills, and interests of the twenty-five people who work there. I feel that my job is to choose options and initiatives that will bring out the best in everyone, so that the staff will be inspired to apply their highest abilities and passion to the job at hand.

When I hit an obstacle at work, when my efforts are stymied, I find that it is often because my mind has become too small, I am stuck in my habitual way of seeing things and so I miss the bigger possibilities. When that happens, I tend to see it as my own limitation rather than as a problem in the external world. This is a direct result of meditation. In the practice of sitting meditation, I can experience a space beyond habitual thought, a glimpse of being able to see beyond limited thought patterns in daily life. This gives rise to solutions that my habitual mind could never see."

Innovation is a natural outcome of meditation, as is the ability to activate one's vision. Some twenty years ago, we recorded a chanting album at the Sounds True studio. In those days, the business was located in a small couple of rooms above a food shop in Boulder, Colorado. Founder Tami Simon was making a name for the company by recording spiritual speakers at national conferences, duplicating the tapes, and selling them by way of mail order. Sounds True now has its own purpose-built building with sixty employees and specializes in music as well as spiritual teachings on CD, and more recently, books. They are the publishers of Deb's book, *Your Body Speaks Your Mind*, and the CD pack of the same name. One of the first things we noticed when we walked into the building was the meditation room opposite the dining room, available for anyone to sit quietly at any time. It is there because the boss is a devoted meditator.

| TAMI SIMON |

"Probably only a quarter of the people here would actually identify themselves as meditators, while another half do yoga or run or whatever, and a quarter people have no relationship to meditation all. The one thing that permeates our whole culture is that people feel they have the freedom to be themselves. They can wear what they want, they can speak their minds, they are free to have families that are important, and they can leave in the middle of the day for a doctor's appointment and not have to make up some ridiculous story about where they are going. They are allowed to be whole people, with whole lives. And I think that this is the most important product of my spiritual life, that I can encourage people to be genuine, to be who they are.

"We started as a company publishing meditation teachings. Early on, we asked, how can the process of our work be congruent with the products of our work? It is one thing to publish this kind of information for individuals, but we wanted to make sure the processes we used every day were as inspired as the materials we were publishing. We asked, 'How can we do that?' What do those same principles discovered through the ages mean for organizational life? The ancient meditation teachers were not living in a capitalist society, so they did not have to answer this question in the way that we have to answer it today, so we had to be creative and solve this for ourselves.

"So I asked, how about being honest and transparent about what is happening in the company in terms of financial information? How about sharing the rewards with everybody who works here? How about looking at the business as a mini-ecosystem that is interacting with the larger ecosystem of the earth? Is the business fair to its authors or its vendors? Unlike most businesses trying to squeeze as much money as possible out of their relationship with their vendor or manufacturer, we were asking, what is a fair exchange? I do not actually want to squeeze a good deal out of anybody because that other party is me. At the same time, I do not want us to have the lower hand either; I just want to do what is fair.

"Most businesses have as their core purpose to go out and make money. This is a ridiculous concept to me; it is absurd. The reason a business exists, in my view, is to be a service to society and to create a flow of exchange such that it can be sustainable. Businesses should focus on solving the world's problems and doing so effectively so that there is a flow of commerce that sustains the gifts that we are bringing to the world. That is it. And how much you grow, who cares? Is it for some individual stockholder or peoples' personal gain? That is not a good reason. The only good reason to make more money is so there are more social problems we can solve. But do we do this at the expense of the health of our families or our workplace community? No. All we have are the means, the journey, and the process, so the means and ends have to be completely aligned.

"My meditation practice has increased my natural intuitive capacity, and I trust in my own authenticity, so I will not make a decision that does not feel intuitively right. Although a lot of things happen that are difficult, I have learned not to necessarily act right away, but to say, 'Let me reflect on that, which is my own code language for let me meditate on it.' I take some time and really sit with the issue and wait until something feels like it is clear. If I have to fire someone, I take the time to really calm myself down and look at it from as many perspectives as possible, to feel what is really authentically true for me, and how I can express this in a way that will be the most respectful and kind to the other person. And then I can speak from my own authentic experience. Sometimes it is hard, sometimes it is scary, but that is what I mean by authentic."

|||

Right Livelihood

Steve Demos borrowed $500 and started making tofu in his kitchen and selling it to local whole-food stores. Thirty years later, he sold White Wave for $295 million. Throughout those years, he never wavered from his belief that he could make money without harming anyone or anything he encountered in the process.

| STEVE DEMOS |

"I come from a family where my father was a very hardworking, honest entrepreneur who initiated profit sharing way back when the words were not even known. So I was a product of the era, but I had this great inner conflict. I flunked my draft physical and immediately headed for India, where I ended up disillusioned and in even greater conflict. I had business DNA in my body, but everything around me was telling me that business was bad, unethical, that it took advantage of others and of the environment. We were in India for the same reasons that everyone else was: We were seeking. We hung out at the ashrams, meditating with teachers. I found meditation really resonated with me, and I became very compelled and committed to it.

"And then I heard of the concept of right livelihood: right living, right effort, right everything. Bells and lights started going off inside me. The epiphany or insight was that capitalism itself was neutral and did not have to be the pariah of society; it could actually be a positive force for social change. It became very clear that if I was going to be at rest with my own DNA, then I was going to have to embark on a mission to prove to myself that right livelihood could work in business. It was a complete coming together of both business and spiritual ideals.

"I see right livelihood as nothing more than a working philosophy for the moral boundaries of living. My goal is to take the teachings and insights that I get from sitting on the cushion and basically apply them to a business model in a very narrow interpretation of what the term *right liveli-hood* actually means. The basis that I live by is 'Good for me, good for you, good for everybody who touches it.' I do not sell bombs or exploitive stuff. I do not sell harmful things, or frivolous things. I do not supply people with harmful services or anything that would go contrary to their well-being. I do not exploit the planet. I give back because 'good for anybody who touches it' does not mean that they have to purchase the product but is anybody who is in contact with the actual business: the community I live in, the customers I supply, the vendors I use, my employees, my investors. Any sentient being who touches the product and the stream of commerce coming from it has to be positively benefited from that contact.

"I came back from my time meditating in India with a very specific mission: I was going to prove that you could create enormous quantities of wealth within the context of right livelihood without putting any negative impact on the society, the product, or the people. Investment in White Wave was initially returned somewhere around seventy-five times or more. We made twenty-one millionaires; we retired fifteen or more people. We gave back to the employees $15 to $18 million in after-sale bonuses. I was the largest individual stockholder, and the company sold for about $300 million, and they gave us another $30 million to stay on. In other words, I proved you can make money and live by right livelihood at the same time.

"Meditation is my foundation. That is all it is. If you strip away the dirt, you get to the roots. I would say that meditation has had a life-altering effect on me. It did not make the road smooth. We were faced with the same choices that every other small business is faced with: cutting corners, doing things the right way, or just trying to outrun the devil and make a living. But we were not there just to make a living; we were there to demonstrate that right livelihood makes a very big difference. Meditation was an entry gate for me, and then it was a re-enforcer. It sets the stage that permits me to demonstrate the value system."

|||

Practice Meditation: Meditating at Work

| FROM TAMI SIMON |

"Meditating in the workplace requires that we learn to meditate 'on the spot,' in the midst of challenging circumstances and difficult conversations. Three techniques I have found useful for interrupting discursive thinking and introducing a quality of spaciousness at work—or in any situation—are attending to physical sensations, bringing attention to the back of the body, and beginning meetings with silence. When we use these and other practices to bring meditative awareness to the workplace, what we are doing is creating space for our own feelings, space for other people, and space for brilliance and originality to shine through. Of course, the more we practice meditating in a formal setting, or create space for ourselves in a relaxed way outside of the work setting, the more depth and precision we can bring to meditating on the spot in the pressure-filled environment of the workplace."

Attending to Sensations

"If your mind is agitated, your body is tense; if your body is tense, your mind is agitated. By letting go of physical tension in the body, you create space in your mind to listen to others and act creatively.

"In the midst of a meeting, a phone conversation, or any interaction in which you feel yourself becoming impatient or agitated, bring your attention to the part of your body that is holding the tension. You can do this on the spot by internally scanning your body from your toes to the top of your head, zeroing in on any part that seems tight, clenched, or contracted. Perhaps you will discover that your lower belly is in a knot or your shoulders are up by your ears. Maybe your hands feel like they are gripping something or the bottoms of

your feet are recoiling from the ground. When you discover an area of physical tension, use your in-breath to connect with that sensation. Then, on the out-breath, simply release, relax, and let go. You can actually 'ride the out-breath' and let it carry your physical and mental holding out into space. "

Bringing Attention to the Back of the Body

"Different physical and energetic postures carry different modes of being. If you want to exert and express yourself and move forward into action, you can bring your energy into the front of your body. If you want to make space for other people, listen deeply, and avail yourself of new creative ideas, just lean back slightly and bring your attention to the back of the body. Have you ever been in a meeting in which everyone was interrupting one another and it felt as if no one was really being heard? If even one person in the group brings their attention to the back of their body, a quality of space and receptivity is introduced that can change the tone and course of the meeting. "

Begin Meetings with Silence

"Often a busy day can feel like being on a non-stop train with one action item following the next without a break. Creating moments of silence, moments of getting off the train, interrupts the tendency for habitual reactivity and drops you into the depth of your being.

"A simple way to introduce silence into the workplace is to begin meetings with a few moments of being quiet together, what I like to call 'taking a good minute.' People use this shared silence in different ways—to breathe and relax, to appreciate a few moments during the day that are calm and spacious, to let go of previous work concerns, or to connect in a silent, energetic way with everyone else at the meeting. When 'a good minute' is introduced at the beginning of a meeting, it is a way of saying that you value each person's renewal and want people to bring their full presence to the task at hand. "

|||

I2

||||

Contemplative Activism

We must come to see that peace is not merely a distant goal
we seek, but it is a means by which we arrive at that goal.
We must pursue peaceful ends through peaceful means.

DR. MARTIN LUTHER KING, JR.

| RUSSELL BISHOP |

"The year is 1971. I am at UC Berkeley, the protest is going on at the People's Park, and the context is to go on strike, shut it down, power to the people. I get hit in the chest with a tear-gas canister that I pick up to throw back at the cops. As I do this, I find myself outside my body looking back at myself, and I see this long-haired, bearded hippie screaming, 'Why don't you blank idiots love us?' And then I am right back in my body, suddenly realizing how the purpose was love but the strategy was yell, scream, and throw things. I walked off the strike line as this wave of awareness washed over me. How could I make a difference in the world with peace and acceptance as the means?"

Activism is dedicated to fighting injustice and bringing about social change, but is angry activism really effective? Is activism different if it arises out of a contemplative and compassionate response rather than an angry reaction? How is our motivation and behavior influenced when there is the awareness that we are not separate but that each is a reflection of the other? Does meditation make any real difference when we are faced with such extremes as acute poverty or machine guns?

Transforming Anger

| SEANE CORN |

"Back in the eighties, I was an activist for a bunch of different organizations, but I was a horrible activist because all I did was project my rage. I was the one with a soapbox and megaphone telling everyone how to live their lives. But it didn't serve anything. What I realize now is how the world changes by embracing, not by pushing away. Rage pushes away; it is a threatening energy that alienates. So, as an activist today, I invite by stepping in and being as honest as I possibly can."

Anger may be an initial motivation for protest, but it does not often bring about the changes that are desired. Rather, it invariably creates more negativity. Anger is exclusive and calls for further exclusivity, rather than being inclusive and, therefore, working toward wholeness. Meditation is essential, for it not only brings us to the awareness of our interconnectedness, but also to the realization of the fruitlessness of anger and the benefit of working compassionately. Then activism informs us of when and how best to use it, rather than being used by it.

| RAMA VERNON |

"We can create change through anger, but we cannot create transformation through anger. The change will always revert back to something else. Meditation creates clarity of mind, and when we have clear thinking, our actions are more focused and we have greater power. If our minds are scattered, then whatever actions we take will only cause confusion. There may be moments when we need to use anger, but it is not the same thing as being angry. I have used anger with the KGB, as it was the right thing to do at the time, but I was responding with anger, not reacting. If we react with anger, it can actually fuel a situation and we become part of the problem instead of the solution."

Pacifism or harmlessness does not mean that we are weak and helpless or that we can easily be taken advantage of. It means that the same issues that cause anger can, instead, generate compassion. And although anger may sometimes be used for specific reasons, compassion can be used without hesitation in every situation. This is especially important for those people actively engaged in working for social change.

| ROBERT GASS AND JUDITH ANSARA |

"Social activists are people committed to making a better world. When you can demonstrate to them that there are certain attitudes and behaviors that will actually create more results for justice and are more collaborative, less angry, more partnership oriented, and you show that this works quite dramatically, then they are already there. Meditation is an integral part of this process as it loosens the boundaries. People get to clarify what they serve, to increase their self-awareness so that they can see what works and what is an obstacle. This means loosening the grip of the small sense of me-ness. For some, it becomes a sense of we-ness with their brothers and sisters; they extend it that way. To others, it is to a larger sense of purpose with the communities that they serve, rather than just serving themselves."

The fire of fury may stimulate our motivation, but it cannot keep us going for long; when we are ruled by anger, we are soon depleted. Exhaustion is the inevitable downside. Compassion, on the other hand, is a constant source of energy and sustenance. The more we give, the more we get to give with. There is no time where we run out of compassion.

| JOSEPH GOLDSTEIN |

"I taught retreats for environmental and social activists. One of the major issues for people who are engaged in such action, often in the front lines of conflict, is energy burn-out. This is because the work is often fueled by anger at conditions of inequity and injustice, but anger is unsustainable. It is a motivation that literally burns us up. Compassion is a much more sustainable energy. It can motivate a lifetime of active social engagement."

We usually think of activism as being *against* something, whether it be war, torture, or dictatorial government, whereas activism based on contemplation is being *for* something, such as fairness, freedom, and peace. This gives us a whole new perspective, not just of activism, but also of the deeper causes of injustice and violence and, more specifically, of our normally angry or even aggressive response to such behavior. Being *for* something shifts us from maintaining the negative to supporting the positive.

| RABIA ROBERTS |

"In my youth, I was fueled by anger. Then I worked with Martin Luther King in the civil rights movement for three years. What I learned from King was the beginning of nonviolent activism, and that we are not here to defeat or hurt anyone, but to reveal the injustice that exists in the situation and see if we can come to a greater healing. The anger abates, and the sense of having to be against something instead of for something changes dramatically. Without guns, our most effective tool is to be willing to stand up collectively in the face of violence and to call forth the witness of the larger world to the injustice that is happening.

"Meditation practice turns the telescope around so you can see how you invent a self and a story. You become familiar with how thoughts and emotions drive you. Once that happens, the ego-self loosens its grasp. You are not so compulsive any more or so reactive. You respond to what is going on, but you no longer react against anything. You also begin to understand equanimity, how to keep your balance when emotions or disturbing thoughts arise. It is meeting the angry person with a sense of 'I am listening to what you are saying, but I do not understand it with all that anger.' That is what made both Gandhi and King brilliant, as well as respected even by those who hated them.

"Like activism, meditation wants to reveal the reality behind the illusion. You see through the stories. You begin to realize soldiers are not necessarily heroes but are victims. In the nonviolent worldview, there is no blame; you can hold someone accountable but there is no blame for what is happening. If you are full of aggression and agitation, all you are doing is adding that negativity to the mix. That is why war cannot bring peace."

|||

No Choice

The impulse to help others, to stand up against injustice, to make a difference in the lives of those who are unable to help themselves, and to do this in such a way that it does not create further harm, is an integral part of the contemplative life. For Ed, going from the world of drugs and discos in New York City to India, where he became a swami, a yoga adept living in an ashram, and where he watched his teacher giving whatever was needed to the poorest of the poor, connected him to the heart of service. For Deb, being raised as a Quaker deeply influenced her desire to participate in nonviolent activities. For Kiri, it was due to her Buddhist childhood, where she was taught to meditate when she was just a child and to always think of others first.

| KIRI WESTBY |

"I was six when I received my first formal meditation instruction. At school, we meditated every day for fifteen minutes both before class started and at the end of the day. When I was young, my mother would read the obituaries to us from the newspaper. She would say, 'These people died today, Kiri. We could die at any point. So let us do something great with our day. Let's help somebody today.' When you are raised in this way, it is natural that you then want to create a life in which you are doing whatever you can for other people.

"I wanted to do something that would not negatively affect anyone else. The summer I left school, a friend and I took off traveling, and eight months later, we were in Cambodia. For seven or eight hours, we rode in the back of a pickup truck with seventeen other Cambodians, bags of rice, and chickens right through the middle of the whole bombed-out area where the Khmer Rouge were still very active, and then we took this slow boat for another twelve hours up the Mekong river. I saw my first refugee camp and my first Red Cross camp, and I knew this was for me. I had no problem being there; there was no fear. I just knew that helping in this way was my path; the impulse to be of be of assistance gave me no choice.

"I went to Nepal where I helped to run a shelter for trafficked girls on the border with India. The girls had either escaped, or there might have been a police raid in the brothels in Delhi or Bombay and we would go and get them. Some were eight years old or younger. Some were twenty years old and had been in the brothel for years, forced to live in cages. Ninety-seven percent of them were HIV positive. The most intense suffering you can imagine is an eight-year-old girl who has been raped continuously for longer than she can remember and who jumped out of a two-story building and broke her leg in order to get to the shelter, only to learn that it was her family who sold her to the brothel and so she has nowhere to go. And yet we could still find moments of happiness and laughter together.

"I needed to meditate before I could even leave my room in the morning. It gave me the strength to recognize that suffering is the human experience that we all have in one form or another, and not to feel over-whelmed by it, not to lose my balance. Without that meditation, without that space each morning, I would have been too filled with the suffering; I would have been paralyzed by it. My mom once told me that once you have learned to meditate, it is like an invisible tool that you always have with you on your belt. It was without doubt the most useful tool I had.

"I worked with Urgent Action Fund for five years, traveling into war zones and listening to stories of what was happening to women and girls. Every morning I would sit in meditation as it enabled me not to react to all the aggression I was surrounded by. In the Congo, I had to cross the border that was just a tree log with fifteen-year-old boys sitting on it holding semi-automatic weapons. I would very calmly say, 'I am just here to speak with some of the girls.' Often I would have money duct-taped to my stomach or in a pouch—cash for the women so that they could start an orphanage or take care of the kids—and I would have to convince these boy-soldiers that I did not have anything on me. I could not meet them with even an ounce of aggression or they would shoot me without hesitation. I got very good at dealing with boys with guns!

"More than anything else, meditation released me from anger. I could feel anger come up, but I knew that my way of surviving and working in this context was to let it go, to know that these boys were not the enemy but were just as much a victim of this whole machine of war, forced into the army at such a young age. Really there was no enemy; it was just a whole environment of people who had been used and abused. I would constantly remind myself of their human qualities so I could start the day without any aggression."

|||

Seeing Self in Others

Meditation and contemplative practices change us. They open our hearts, letting in the pain of the world around us; they show us the reality of suffering and how we are an integral part of that suffering. If one person is in need, we are all in need. For Seane, this awareness got her off her yoga mat.

| SEANE CORN |

"First yoga changed my body; then meditation changed my attitude. Then I realized that whether my practice was fifteen minutes or four hours was irrelevant because it was not about how yoga can change me, but how I, through this practice, can begin to change the world. What I really felt was how dare I not step into the world and hold that space?

"I first started by working with child prostitutes in Los Angeles. I did not know how my life was going to change when I entered the shelter, but I met my shadow there. I hated those girls—and it wasn't just girls, it was young boys too—they were so arrogant and defiant as they were so wounded. They were also like a mirror in which I saw the part of myself that had been abused, and how I had not dealt with my own defiance, arrogance, or wounding. They really did not accept me at first. Are you kidding? This big-mouthed, floppy-headed white girl from New Jersey bouncing in to tell them how to do yoga? They slaughtered me! It was the most humiliating experience I had ever had because I went in trying to fix them. I did not go in there recognizing that I am them. They took one look at me and were totally unimpressed. No way I wanted to go back. I sat in my car and cried and cried. The next time I went, I was way more humble as I had recognized that we were there to serve each other.

"I have to love the prostitute in myself, I have to love the impoverished and illiterate within me, I have to love the wounded parts of myself so that I can hold someone else in a real regard. Those girls rejected me for weeks—it was like pulling teeth. Then one day, I will never forget it, I walked into the shelter and there was this little Goth girl who had OCD and used to cut herself with razor blades. When she saw me, she jumped up, ran to me, and threw her arms around me. I was overwhelmed. Then, one by one, the other girls got up and hugged me. After that, I had to come to the shelter ten minutes early to do the hug thing and I had to leave ten minutes late to make time for the hug thing. Because once we connected, all they wanted was appropriate touch, to have a moment of connection that was safe.

"My shadow was right in front of me. I knew in my meditation that spirit was saying, 'Honey, you want to be a healer, you got to heal yourself, you got to walk right into this fire. This is your shadow; this is the thing that is keeping you from self-love. You are not going be of any service to this world unless you go right into it and find out who that little girl in you is.' I met her, and I healed her through these young kids.

"The next challenge was going into the field and meeting the children in third-world countries. I worked with Youth AIDS in the largest slum of all of Southeast Asia, particularly in the brothels there, working not just with the prostitutes but also with their clients and their children. And it wasn't just teaching them about HIV/AIDS but helping to empower them to make better choices. You cannot ask them not to be prostitutes: When you have poverty, you get desperation; you get desperate, you get prostitution. It is just the way that it goes. Teaching prostitutes about safe sex practices is really hard as they get $1 for sex with a condom but $2 without it. If they use a condom, they run the risk of being raped, abused, or losing business. So we try to get all the women to stand together and then we teach the men about HIV and AIDS. There was a porn house in the slum. I had to climb a ladder to get to it and force myself through this hole at the top into a pitch-black room filled with men. We interrupted their porn film and put on our own film about sexually transmitted diseases, and afterward we put their film back on and left.

"Being there was so challenging. It is one thing to sit at home and think how everything happens for a reason, but when I was dealing with a fifteen-year-old prostitute who was dying of AIDS, then my own shit came up. Like, this is unjust, unfair, and so very wrong. I had to do a lot of praying and meditating to be able to keep walking into that place without judgment or anger.

"Mediation was a critical part of being able to go into the field each day as there were times that really triggered my rage. For instance, I was walking through this slum, a labyrinth of filth built on a garbage dump, and I heard a laugh behind me. I turned around, and there was a little girl. I have no idea how old she was, but she was severely mentally and physically disabled. My partner's daughter is also mentally and physically disabled and so I had an intensely personal connection to this girl. I knew that in the United States, because of the privileges and the medical care that we have, my partner's daughter has been able to not only survive but actually have a life. I looked at this little girl in the slum, and I knew that if she was not already being prostituted, she soon would be. That was one of those moments that sucked the life force out of me. The rage flared up, but I knew that I would be no good for anybody if I came into this situation with judgment and anger. So I had to go home and cry, I had to feel, I had to know my anger. I had to get it out of my system and remember the bigger picture: that we are all here to learn what love is and often the process is in learning what love is not.

"I work with an orphanage in Cambodia. The man who runs this organization, Scott, used to be the president of Fox International. He started doing yoga and came on a retreat, and in the middle of a yoga pose, he had this cathartic breakdown. Afterward, he said, 'I hate my life, I hate what I do, there is no purpose or meaning in my life. I think I need to quit.' And I thought, Sure, maybe he'll go home and write a big check to a charity—which would be great—but my guess is he'll probably just get on with his life and maybe meditate a bit more than before. I was wrong. He quit Fox. He sold the mansion, the boat, the Porsche, and now he lives full-time in a small apartment in Cambodia. He just opened his fifth orphanage and has three hundred children. He has no money, but he is totally committed to serving the children.

"Scott took me to this eleven-acre garbage dump in the middle of Panam Pen. Kids as young as three work the dump, picking plastic and metal to sell for 30 cents. Only 25 percent of the kids survive. They get run over by the trucks, they fall into sinkholes, they get hepatitis from the needles or the glass they step on, they get taken away to be prostitutes. Scott goes in to get these kids and puts them into orphanages that feed and educate them. Others just get dropped off at the door of the orphanage. Some have families, so he negotiates with the parents, and the kids go home at night. But they can never work in the garbage dump again.

"Scott brought food to the dump, and I reached into the truck to pull out a bottle of soymilk. There are only about fifty bottles, and I get rushed by about two hundred kids. I have never seen such desperation, *ever,* for this bottle of milk. Do I give it to the starving three year old, or do I give it to the pregnant woman holding two kids? It was overwhelming; I could feel my heart racing with anxiety. And I could feel my anger and rage rising; it was so unjust, so unfair—judgment across the board. The kids hold my hand and take me through the dump, and within thirty seconds, I am covered in flies, as is everyone else. The smell was something that I could not get out of my system for about a month; it was *in* my nose.

"I am talking to a group of children with a translator, and suddenly a young boy grabs hold of my hand. He looks to be eight or nine, but because of malnutrition, he could have been thirteen. It is boiling hot, but he is covered from head to toe in scarves to try to keep the flies off his body. What I could see of his face was matted in dirt. I looked at him, expecting him to say three words in Cambodian: one for water, the other for food, the third for study, meaning take me to the orphanage. But he says nothing. He just looks at me right in the eye and smiles this little tiny smile. I thought this was the most curious thing, so I smile back. He squeezes my hand, lets go, and walks away. But he left something in my hand that was covered in dirt.

"I flick the dirt away, and it was a bright-red heart-shaped charm, surrounded by silver. It was probably from a watchband. It was one of those moments where I was utterly humbled, because there I am, once again, thinking that I am going to save the world, and instead what I get is like, 'Really, honey? Really? Because what I am thinking is that maybe *you* might need a little saving right now.' This kid had come to me and effectively said, 'Remember, it is about the love. That is all that this is. It is about the love.' That heart will stay with me for the rest of my life. It reminds me every day of what my job is.

"I cannot presume to change anything. That is why meditation is so essential; it constantly brings me to the place of acceptance. My job is to come into the experience totally in love and allow whoever I am dealing with to experience that the love that is within me is also within them."

What One Person Can Do

One person *can* make a difference, as we have seen many times throughout history. Usually, the only thing that stops us from stepping out and taking action is our own sense of inadequacy or doubt. Rama had a vision of bringing people together, and, as a result, nearly 10,000 Soviet and American citizens have participated in her Citizen Summit programs. And yet when she began this work, she was a housewife and a yoga teacher with no idea how or if she could do anything.

| RAMA VERNON |

"The Cold War was at its peak. The Korean Airlines disaster had recently occurred, bringing us very close to a nuclear war. As I put my children to bed, they would ask, 'Mommy, are we going to be blown up?' 'No, of course not,' I would reply, reassuring them as much as myself. 'Our government would never let that happen.' And then, through my yoga-teaching work, I was invited to travel with thirty others on a Peace Mission to the Soviet Union. So, quite unexpectedly, I was in Moscow, standing in the center of what Reagan had termed the *Evil Empire,* behind what Churchill had called the *Iron Curtain.* I was raised to believe that our thoughts create our reality, and what scared me most was that I was not alone in my fear, that thousands of Americans shared those same fears, and that if enough of us continued to hold those fears, we would create the very thing that we feared most. I realized that the only way to change such a stereotype that we have been conditioned to believe is to bring people face to face with one another. We could not take the Russians to the United States, so I resolved to bring the United States to Russia.

"It took about five years, developing and building the trust and connecting with the people, and finally we put on the first Soviet/American conference. After that, we were doing trips every month. In the process, I entered into the labyrinth of the Soviet system. I no longer had time to meditate for hours like I used to; instead, this was bringing meditation into action; I was meditating with my eyes wide open. But it was hard. I really got upset with the KGB as, on one trip, we had three concerts organized for Kris Kristofferson, and each time, just at the last minute when he was already on stage, they would close it down. Meantime, they would be wining and dining me somewhere else. When I found out, I was furious. I took heads off in Moscow. I was calling them at midnight really upset. I said, 'Enough! You are not going to do this anymore. You cannot go on with the old patterns. This does not work.' I went to some of the old KGB people and said, 'You have got to stop this *now!*" I raised my voice very, very loud. After that, they said they trembled for months when they heard I was in Moscow. They were scared! That was when I consciously used anger as a tool for change.

"I went to Russia forty-nine times in seven years. On our last visit, one of Gorbachev's people said, 'You have laid down your life, everything, for our people. Some have tried to pull the rug from under you, or stab you in the back, but you kept going and did not let anything stop you. And now our people are free.' Yet, at the same time, there was a Great Depression there. People were flocking to the cities in search of food. There was no heating in our big office. We were sitting in our gloves and coats, and we could see our breath in the air, and I was afraid to even cry because I thought my tears might freeze. I said, 'I feel sad because the people are hungry.' He replied, 'Your mission here was to free our people, not to feed our people.'

"I did not plan to do this. I have always thought that if I can just meditate and find my own peace, that that is the greatest gift that I can give to the world. When the whole Russian thing started, I knew my life would change, that I was stepping to the edge. I kept having this vision that I was going through these jungle paths, cutting away at the underbrush, and I would come to the edge of a cliff. When I looked out, the other side was far away, but when I looked back, the path behind me had closed. I was standing on the edge with a chasm of darkness below, and the other side so distant that it would take a quantum leap of consciousness to reach it. I had this vision for four months over and over.

"I finally gathered all my strength and morale, everything I had in me after years of yoga discipline and meditation—and even then I didn't know if I had the courage. I gathered it all up, and I remember taking this leap knowing I could not possibly stretch far enough to reach the other side. But I had to. So I jumped, and I didn't fall. I do not know how I got to this other place of consciousness, but I crossed an enormous boundary of fear inside myself. You cannot do this work unless you are prepared to give everything. In later years, the Soviet generals who I dealt with called me a brave woman because I went there four times while I was pregnant, and then I brought my three-month-old daughter. But I wasn't brave. My knees would tremble with fear of making a mistake that would hurt the people.

"Going on the front lines became my spiritual practice. What we do in yoga is to take a posture and become familiar with it, and then we go to the next posture, which represents the unknown. Then that becomes the known, and we take another variation, which is the unknown again. So we are always expanding our consciousness until there are no boundaries. When our boundaries dissolve into seeing our world as one global family, then we can never make war on another. If we let human rights violations continue, then we are perpetuating the problem by our inaction."

|||

Political Activism

Political action is deeply affected by our principles and beliefs. The plight of China invading and ruling Tibet is a situation that has aroused many people's anger, a great deal of violence, and innumerable deaths. It has always been close to Kiri's heart, so when the opportunity arose to participate in a peaceful demonstration, she could not resist. Chinese authorities were at base camp in Nepal rehearsing to take the Olympic flame through Tibet. The whole world was going to be watching, and so this was a perfect opportunity to steal the spotlight.

| KIRI WESTBY |

"We were going to Mount Everest base camp. I was to meet up with Tenzin Dorjee, the first Tibetan in exile to return to Tibet and do a high-profile protest. My job was to get him in, no matter what. So a few days later, I am on a flight to China. I am looking for a Tibetan guy holding a bunch of flowers, and he is supposed to be looking for a girl wearing an orange scarf. Our story is that we are boyfriend and girlfriend on a vacation for ten days. There were others in the group, but we did not meet them until later.

"The morning of the protest, we did a lot of meditation. I needed it for what we were about to do. As we walked the hour-and-a-half hike to base camp from where we had stayed, Tenzin was chanting the Tara mantra. We were protesting the Chinese plan to take the Olympic torch to the top of Mount Everest and then run it to Lhasa and past the Potala Palace. We were trying to show that Tibet is not a part of China. We had a banner, which we had carried in pieces and put together at different times in different hotel rooms. One part of the banner said Free Tibet and was written in both Tibetan and Chinese. Just to say that inside Tibet is punishable by ten years in prison. I carried that piece in my bra.

"When we got there, the mountain was all covered in mist. We started praying and doing mantras and whatever people believed in to honor the mountain gods. And then suddenly the clouds parted and the wind stopped and the cameras could work. The sun came up over the ridge and shone down on us. We unfurled the banner, which said One World One Dream Free Tibet 2008, and we sang the Tibetan national anthem. It was transmitted live to New York and Radio Free Asia, which most Tibetans listen to all over the world, and apparently people stood up and took their hats off and started crying. Their anthem had not been sung publicly inside Tibet since the Chinese invasion more than fifty years ago.

"Despite such a well-organized protest, however, we were caught and held in prison in China for five days. They moved us at night in separate vehicles. A female guard kept whispering in my ear, 'You are never going to see your family again. You are going to spend the rest of your life in prison.' That broke me like a stick of butter in less than twenty minutes. They would make us watch as they pulled one of our friends into a separate room, and then we would hear people screaming. We were terrified of being tortured. At one point, I saw everybody getting pulled out of the cars except for me and I heard my friend Shannon scream, 'Stop it—you're hurting me!' That did it. I climbed over somebody, jumped out of the car, and started running around this police courtyard in the middle of nowhere at 3 a.m. like a chicken with my head cut off, screaming their names. I was using all my basketball moves to avoid at least ten police officers who were trying to corner me. I really lost it! But then I connected with another of the protesters, and he just said, 'Think of the ripples that are going out around the world right now. People are hearing about us and saying prayers for us. Think of all the people who are going to hear about Tibet tomorrow morning who may never have heard about Tibet before. Just hold onto the ripples. Don't let this even phase you.'

"From that moment on, I pulled it all back in. I got my head back together. I got reconnected. There followed about fifty-five hours of interrogation. They did not let us sleep, they did not feed us, they kept us in a very hot room and would not let us take off our layers of clothing from base camp, so we were really hot and sweating and I had this horrible rash on my ass after twelve hours of being bumped in vehicles, but during that time, I held it together. I did not break again. I did not cry. During that time, each one of the other people at some point broke, the guards having scared them enough. But I had gone deeper into that quiet place inside, and I did not break again."

|||

Being with What Is

What we have seen in these stories is the apparent contradiction of being with what is, combined with the deep desire for change. One of our meditation teachers said that we absolutely have to be at peace with what is, and that we should also stand up and protest against injustice. This is the marriage of both passive and active, the coming together of being and doing. In the acceptance of what is, there is a spaciousness and non-attachment. If we do not accept what is, if we fight against it, then nobody wins. Within that spaciousness, contemplative action has the chance to bring real change. Being with what is, in this moment now, we are able to enter into places of pain and even torture, and bear witness.

| BERNIE GLASSMAN |

"Auschwitz exemplified a way of getting rid of the others by killing them all. The first time I led a retreat at Auschwitz, I invited people of many traditions, children of survivors, children of SS officers and camp commanders, gypsies, and gays. I brought as much diversity as I could. In our society, we create people as others and some we imprison, some we hang, some we kill, many we avoid. But there we sat together and shared. And by the end of the retreat, we were one family in all of our diversity. Trying to experience the oneness with what had happened there was very powerful. Auschwitz takes you to a place where you rationally cannot figure out what is going on, your mind cannot fathom it, so you drop into this not-knowing and when you open in that place, you experience the oneness."

| FLEET MAULL |

"People come from all over Europe and the United States, Christians, Muslims, Buddhists, Jews, children, people who lost family members at Auschwitz. We have had children of former Nazi guards there. We spend five days in the camp. We form a meditation circle at the selection site and meditate there twice a day, and then we read names of people who have died there. We say a Jewish prayer for the dead several times a day, in different places. We do different religious services, purification ceremonies; we walk around, bearing witness. I think most people who come tune into some flavor of silent sitting, which is the most powerful context for that retreat. It holds everybody. There are other elements of the retreat, but it is really the sitting at the selection site that most profoundly brings everyone together. It is the container that holds us all."

When we bear witness to pain, whether past or present, we are creating the space for healing. The pain is seen and heard; it becomes known. We cannot always apply logical understanding to what we are witnessing; instead, it takes us to that place of not-knowing, but from there, we are able to embrace whatever needs to be embraced. Knowing something creates boundaries of identification—it is a limited place of safety; not-knowing leaves us wide open but far more available and inclusive.

| ROSHI JOAN HALIFAX |

"What does it mean to sit in not-knowing? It means to sit in this seat of absolute openness and beginner's mind, in what Christian mystics refer to as the experience of love or non-duality, or the cloud of unknowing. This not-knowing is such a miraculous and fresh thing. It is not like a mind that is based in concepts or ideas or concretizing our thoughts or beliefs; it is just very open and receptive, like the mind of a child. In this mind of not-knowing, we presence the joy and suffering in this world without being attached to our fixed ideas about how things are. But witnessing such suffering, really being present moment to moment, demands compassionate action, which is the capacity to respond to things just as they are. These three tenants—to sit in the mind of not-knowing, to bear witness, and to act compassionately—enable us to be with every situation. For instance, I have to go to the hospital to visit a friend who is terribly ill. I like to walk into that hospital room with a mind that is a beginner's mind, a mind of not-knowing, and then I can bear witness to his experience without judgment. This is what is. Then I can respond in a way that may bring some perspective to his experience, to help him be with it."

When we see injustice, we can react in one of three ways: do nothing, match such wrong-doing with an equal dose of anger, or compassionately and quietly witness while also protesting the injustice. Meditation connects us so deeply to all other beings that we cannot just sit back and do nothing in the face of unfairness, nor can we respond with any level of violence. The urge to protest and dissent, and yet to do it in a way that creates no further harm, is powerful and unavoidable.

| SYLVIA BOORSTEIN |

"I was arrested for the first time in my life on the eve of the invasion of Afghanistan. I was with a group of clergy in San Francisco holding a peace vigil outside the federal building, and we sat in civil disobedience. The clergy were all wearing appropriate clergy outfits so you knew these were religious people kneeling there. We got arrested for blocking the entry and kept for two hours. But it made the point that, as part of our dedication to seeing the truth about life and suffering and ministering to the ills of people in the world, we also have to take a social stance. We have to go out and protest about political events. We have to stand on picket lines and in peace vigils and go on peace marches and sign petitions. Meditation does not mean to be outside the fray, but to be able to enter the fray with a clear mind, without hate in our heart, without making the other person our enemy; it is to make a statement on behalf of a peaceful world that actually comes from a peaceful heart.

"Meditation is mandated for social action. Our eyes are open; we can see what is happening in the world. It is scary to go out and get arrested, to be handcuffed and have to sit on a cement floor, but meditation gives us strength and support. If you saw your children outside killing each other, you would not just let it happen; you would run out and tell them to stop. In the same way, if we see people killing each other and ruining the world, then we have to run out and say please do not do this, and we have to do it in such a way that the damage does not escalate further.

"I am seventy-one. I am not going to be here by the time the icecaps finally melt, as my children and my grandchildren are going to be. But I can make a difference. We share this one small world, and what happens on the other side of it is also happening to me."

|||

Not Fixing What Is Not Broken

Ultimately, contemplative activism is seeing wholeness in the broken parts, holding the vision of unity even as we protest the ignorance that is intent on destruction. In essence, nothing is broken, nothing needs to be changed, wholeness is present whenever we chose to focus on it. We hold that vision of equality, so that ignorance can have no leverage power.

| RABIA ROBERTS |

"I have come to see that fixing or helping has a kind of built-in disconnect: You are broken, and I am going to fix you, which means I am better than you. To serve the world means I serve with my wounds, I serve with humility, and I serve something that is holy, not because it is broken. The first thing you have to do is show up, just show up to the pain, the disagreements, and the conflicts. We did this in Nicaragua in 1987. We went to the Nicaraguan war to bear witness to the suffering that the people were encountering from the U.S. government–supported contras. We took testimony; we were present, we saw and heard. Meditation trains you to be present to thoughts and feelings and actions as they arise, without commentary, without intervening or interfering. Then we can ask the caring questions: What are you suffering from? What can we do for you? We listen carefully with respect and openness. This is the heart of meditation—you cannot meditate without welcoming what comes, without taking all the walls down, all the knowing, and listening deeply."

Contemplative activism arises from the awareness that we are no different from anyone else, we are all victims of greed and hatred, and yet we also have the same capacity to rise above this to a place of giving and caring. And, in its purest intent, activism is simply to bring awareness, compassion, and beauty to those places that are in need.

| ELIAS AMIDON |

"What I have found with people who are true believers or fundamentalists, who have just come on with their particular view very strongly, is that there is something at the heart of their beliefs that is very precious to them, something very dear. In a way, we are all innocent at heart. There is a tender heart, even if it is inchoate and they are confused, lost, or twisted, there is something they deeply care about.

"We are expressions of this beautiful silence that is behind everything. The Sufis have a word *ihsan*, sometimes translated as 'good acts or action.' But the translation I prefer is *doing the beautiful*. That the gesture of our life is such that, even if it does not change anything, at least each gesture has beauty in it. And that is all we can do. Then the beauty of our life harmonizes with and adds to the beauty of this universe. Meditation is at the heart of this, because meditation is not just a matter of sitting quietly but of opening that primal distinction between self and other, releasing the boundary or border. This can happen by sitting quietly, but it can also happen in the midst of action in the world. That is why I do not see any real division between meditation and contemplative action."

|||

Practice Meditation: Bridging the Gap of Otherness

| FROM ELIAS AMIDON & RABIA ROBERTS |

"All activism involves engagement. We are responding to a call within us to care, to ease suffering and to make our life a blessing to others. Most forms of activism engage us with those we think of as 'other'—people or groups we may disagree with or who make us feel uncomfortable. Contemplative activism seeks to bridge this gap of otherness between people and to nourish personal and communal healing. This practice enables us to apply such an understanding to our own life."

Identifying the Other

"Begin by sitting comfortably in a quiet place. You may use a meditation technique you are familiar with to quiet your mind. When you feel settled, ask yourself: Who is the 'other' in my life? Who do I disapprove of, not trust, or feel unsafe with? This will most likely be someone you would usually avoid coming into contact with."

Making Contact

"Now make a commitment to contact this person or group in an appropriate way. This might involve engaging in conversation with homeless people or

with someone from a group whose beliefs you fundamentally oppose. It might mean making contact with a member of your own family who has caused you pain and from whom you have felt alienated. Whoever you choose, make a commitment of time and place to make contact."

Setting Your Intention

"On the day you fulfill your commitment, begin with a period of contemplation in which you vow to practice deep listening to the other, free of judgments and blame. Breathe calmly and rest in your essential unknowing—the fact that we rarely know the truth of other people's lives as they see it. This is an opportunity for direct experience of the reality of another's life without the need to respond, correct, or fix anything. When you actually meet, you may wish to explain why you wanted to meet, such as your wish to understand them better, without judgment or argument."

Asking Caring Questions

"Now you are ready to bridge the gap of otherness. Here you simply ask what are known as 'caring questions' that gradually reveal what matters most to that person. The key to asking them lies in your ability to listen deeply, without judgment. As you listen, you might become aware of the pain this person has endured, the disappointments or the grief, the desire for happiness this person has been trying to fulfill, or what they value most, and how these values have influenced their actions. If a desire to correct or argue arises within you, notice this feeling and breathe through it.

"This is your practice, your simple presence in the face of what you do not know or understand. Be gentle here—you are not trying to convince anyone of anything. The non-judgmental context of your caring questions opens a space in which any kind of revelation can surface. The essential point of this contemplative encounter is not to change someone's point of view. It is to bridge the gap of otherness that has developed and to allow opportunities for deeper healing to arise."

|||

13

|||

Can Meditation Change the World?

If we divide reality into two camps—the violent and the nonviolent—and stand in one camp while attacking the other, the world will never have peace.

THICH NHAT HANH

In order to ascertain if meditation can actually influence and even change the world, we need to see what is seemingly not right in our world and what, if anything, needs changing. There are some who believe that the world is exactly as it is meant to be and that we are learning important lessons by having challenging difficulties to contend with or that there is a preordained plan bigger than anything any one of us could know. Perhaps all of the above is true, perhaps not.

Whatever the situation, life on our planet does not always seem so divinely planned. Obviously, we experience times of great joy, wonder, laughter, and beauty. We are social creatures and many, if not all, of these good times are due to our relationships and especially to shared love. But there are also many times when we are not so nice, when we treat each other in ways that belie our sociability. We are attacked for being of a different race or color, women and children are raped and abused, we turn away from helping a stranger for fear of those around us, and huge numbers are starving and homeless.

| ED |

"I am a Jew and you are not, meaning that as children, we were only allowed to relate to people who were like us. I wasn't allowed to bring a friend home or to eat in his home if he was not Jewish. I was taught to fear anyone who was different."

Despite such disregard for each other and ingrained prejudice, and even with the injurious capacity of modern warfare methods, if we look back in time we may be surprised to find that we are actually better behaved and nicer to each other now than we ever were in the past, when we were far more barbaric and disrespectful of life.

| ANDREW COHEN |

"Throughout history, the human experience has been extremely brutal. For instance, if we were living at the beginning of the Renaissance in Europe and someone broke the law, then their genitals may be cut off or they would be disemboweled. At the time Shakespeare was writing his plays, people's heads were being stuffed on pikes in order to keep the populace in line. In Roman times, a common entertainment was to watch people be eaten alive by lions. So, despite unspeakable and horrible atrocities in our current era, we are actually becoming more civilized."

As reassuring as it may be that we are kinder to each other now than we used to be, it would seem that some further evolution is needed in order for us to overcome our aversion so we can appreciate and care for each other on a regular basis.

So what is the continuing cause of our disrespect for each other? What is it that creates so much isolation, loneliness, and separation, where we see others who are different from us as the enemy? Why do we treat each other with such disregard and dislike? Is it because we project our hidden fears onto others, thereby making them the problem that needs to be annihilated, rather than seeing that the phobia and intolerance actually lie within ourselves?

| JON KABAT-ZINN |

"We have to learn how to put out the welcome mat for our own shadow side because when we suppress it, we project it onto others and we get the us-and-them syndrome: We are right and they are not, so let's kill them before they kill us."

As much as we have fought the "other" in order to eliminate the enemy or to ensure our own survival, we are now moving into a time where such fighting is actually becoming detrimental to the continued existence of our entire species and is adding to our demise. For us to successfully overcome many of the issues we are facing, whether social, environmental, or global, we urgently need to resolve our own prejudices and to work together, rather than against each other.

| GANGAJI |

"It seems to me that we are on the brink of an evolutionary leap and that what we are calling the human condition is something that has become outmoded. It seemed quite useful at an earlier time, when we really did have to struggle with each other for a piece of food or territory or some shelter. Maybe it is just wired in us, this me-first attitude, or my tribe first, or my nation first, and the idea of attacking others out of fear that something will be taken from us. But we can actually have a cooperative world where we look to each other, because we all need each other for our survival. Before, we needed to overcome each other in order to guarantee our survival; now we need to discover an entirely new way of relating, and we actually need each other to do this."

|||

The Roots of Our Disregard

For us to be able to come together, we need to not only honor our essential interconnectedness, but also to recognize that it is our ego-based selfishness and desire for things to be different from how they are that is a major cause of our disregard for each other. By this, we mean the dissatisfaction with what is and the belief that says if we are not happy or at peace, then there is something wrong with our world and if we can just change other people or our life's circumstances and get them to be a certain way, then we will be happy. If we look closely at our desire for things to be different, no matter how subtle it may be, we find resistance, discomfort, aversion, even conflict. The myth that the grass is greener elsewhere is one we live by for vast amounts of our waking time—the underlying searching, yearning, craving, and longing for a life, partner, and job other than the ones we have.

Society exploits such craving and desire as much as it possibly can. It is hard to read a paper or watch television without feeling some sense of lack: Either we do not have the right clothes, we are not good enough at our job, our hair is the wrong color, we use the wrong deodorant, or we do not know how to make love the right way, and that is why everything is so wrong in our life, and all of this can easily be solved by getting more—it does not matter what it is more of, just more will do: We want, we get, and we still want.

| ED BEGLEY, JR. |

"We can make it a saner and happier world if we just slowed down and had less focus on wanting or needing more stuff. If stuff made you happy, there would be nothing but happy people living in Bel Air and unhappy people living in Fiji where they have nothing, but I have been to Fiji and there are plenty of happy people there. I have never seen a hearse with a luggage rack on top. We have got to get away from stuff and appreciate what is here."

The world we live in revolves around selfishness. We see it in the politics that make land more important than people and leaves the people homeless, that keeps medicines away from those who need them because the price is too high, or that grows crops to sell but not to eat and so the workers go hungry. We see the same traits in our own families when arguments develop and family members stop speaking to each other or in ourselves when we want to turn away from those in need. We rarely reach out beyond our own self-interested desires.

The experience of sitting in quiet reflection soon enables us to see through the enticement of such desire, to see how insatiable most of our needs are, and how they run our lives, often at the expense of our relationships or even our sanity. And while meditation does not leave us completely free of needs, it does free us from the desire to fulfill those needs.

| DEB |

"I was sitting in a meditation group when one of the other participants said to our teacher, Chime Rinpoche, that he no longer wanted to meditate. When asked why, he replied, because he did not want to stop wanting things and that the more he meditated, the less desires he had. Chime laughed and said, "It is not quite like that. I still want things. I still want to be with my wife, I want food on my table, and I want comfortable clothes to wear. The only difference is that if I do not get these things, that it does not bother me, it does not matter.""

Desiring things to be different or wanting more than we have is about the future. Meditation takes us into a deeper place of acceptance of what is in this moment, where the wanting and craving dissolve, for in this moment, we are absolutely complete just as we are.

| PETER FENNER |

"We see the functioning of our conditioned mind. We see how we are habitually engaged in this weird exercise of thinking and feeling that things should be different from the way they are. We fight reality and this produces all of our suffering. Meditation gives us an opportunity to see the insanity of thinking that things can or should be different from the way they are in the moment. This insight lets us close the gap. We say, 'Wow, what is going on here? All there is is this. This moment right now can't be different, because this is how it is.' We see that nothing can be added to this moment or taken away from it. This recognition destroys our fantasies and all of our struggles; we see that right now this is all there is, and we don't actually need anything more than this."

Meditation enables us to no longer be ruled by greed or selfishness but to develop a deeper level of contentment and happiness, independent of anything outside of us. As awareness grows of our own behavior and ego-nature, so desire and seeking pleasure, or the delusion of believing that something or someone can make us forever happy, loses its validity. There is a musk deer in India that has a beautiful smell in its anus, but it searches the whole forest in search of that smell. We are just like that musk deer constantly searching for satisfaction, but through quiet self-reflection, we find the smell was actually within us all the time.

| TARA GUBER |

"Everybody wants whatever they don't have. The gift of abundance is in knowing that it does not make us happy. If I lived in an off-the-grid shack in the middle of the woods with no electricity or communication, and you lived in a mansion with opulence and riches, both of us would have the same chance of being happy, because it is not what we do or do not have, it is not the things that make us happy."

|||

It's All Coming and Going

There is a hidden irony to greed and the desire for things to be different, and that is the fact that nothing lasts, not even pleasure or our latest purchase; everything is constantly changing. We get what we want, but then it is gone. The reality of impermanence is that the world around us has already changed from just a moment ago. Somewhere leaves have fallen, babies have been born, people have died, clouds have passed overhead. Always there is change. Who we are now is not who we were last year, last week, yesterday, even a minute ago. Already our feelings have changed, our thoughts are different, and some of our cells have died while others have been created.

Recently, we were at a memorial service for a dear friend who had died suddenly. It was a celebration of her life and reminded us, yet again, of how precious life is, here one minute and gone the next. Yet it is so difficult to accept this reality! There is a well-known story of a woman who came to the Buddha in tears as her only son had died. She begs him to bring her son back to life; the pain of his death is too much for her to bear. Finally, the Buddha agrees. He says he will bring the boy back to life but only if the woman can get him a single mustard seed from a house where no one has ever died. The distraught woman rushes off and proceeds to go from door to door trying to find a home that has never experienced a death. Of course, she cannot find a single place.

Although there may be sadness with impermanence, there is also great joy, for there is a tremendous freedom in the knowledge that this is the way it is: This is the flow, the rhythm of life, in which all things are coming and going. Impermanence is a characteristic of every situation, every encounter, relationship, mood, or idea, disappointment, or elation. It is our resistance to impermanence and the accompanying fear of what change may bring that tries to make everything appear solid and everlasting.

| MARK MATOUSEK |

"In the smallest, quietest ways, impermanence feels like the ground of being, more beautiful and awe inspiring than scary. The part of the mind that sees itself in meditation is not afraid of impermanence any more than fish are scared of water. It is only the parts of the mind that cannot swim— fear, clinging, self-obsession, control—that sink, defeated by the truth of transience."

Just imagine if everything was permanent. Imagine if we were always the same: There would be no butterflies, no full moon, no ocean tides, no cherry blossoms, and no cherries. Impermanence is our reality, so when we resist it, then we are resisting the very meaning of being here, which is to always be evolving or becoming something more than what we were before.

How Meditation Changes the Picture

| MINGYUR RINPOCHE |

"Who makes problems? We humans. And who is the controller of the human? The mind. And how to control the human mind? Through medi- tation. If you can control the pilot, then the pilot can control the plane."

Meditation can do this because it brings us to a place of clear and caring responsiveness. It is that rare activity that can ease suffering while also giving us the awareness and spiritual intelligence to move beyond the self-centeredness and self- destruction that cause suffering. It removes the obstacles in our mind that prevents us from seeing things as they really are, freeing us to become kinder and more compassionate. In other words, it awakens our full human potential.

| MARK MATOUSEK |

"Albert Einstein described human self-absorption as a kind of optical delu- sion of consciousness. Our obsession with physical survival prevents us from seeing beyond this primitive level, which is why meditation is so mind blowing. Dropping below the animal level, we discover another way of seeing and being that is more vast, inclusive, loving, and durable than the fearful, self-protective mind we use ordinarily. Without meditation, prayer, yoga, or some tool for reaching through the selfish mind to our greater nature, we are doomed to remain in the animal mind."

The equation, therefore, is simple: The more meditation becomes a part of our lives, the more we change and evolve; the more we change and evolve, the more society is transformed and the world moves into a more sustainable, wise, and loving place to be. And all we have to do for this chain of events to occur is to be mindful.

| SYLVIA BOORSTEIN |

"The point of meditation is to keep the mind free of confusion. Meditation, past calming our nerves, past being good for our blood pressure, past allowing us to work out our own internal psychological dramas, which it does, past helping us to get along with our kin and our community, is a way of really deeply seeing the truth that the only way to ameliorate our own suffering and the suffering of the world is to keep our minds clear."

Through the act of paying attention, we are no longer a victim of our own ignorance or subject to self-imposed limitations. Such a deepening of awareness and understanding is essential if we are to end the disregard and violence that destroy so many lives and cause so much unnecessary pain and distress.

| MARSHALL ROSENBERG |

"In 60 percent of the television programs watched by children, the hero either kills somebody or beats him up. History teaches about the good Americans who killed innocent people. I believe engaging in self-empathy supports us to stop and transform the thinking that creates violence. It is a very important part of peace on our planet. We need to take time each day to remind ourselves of the preciousness of compassionate giving and receiving. If we have played violent games with other people—guilt games, shame games, anger games, punishment games—then we can grieve for this in a way that changes us and creates a more caring world."

We have tried many ways to bring peace to the world. We have created organizations like the UN and NATO, have had treaties and summits and endless meetings, but still there are difficulties and disagreements. Egos battle, greed for power dominates over humanity, and old hatred divides one against another. What will it take for us to come together in good-will and to generate genuine peace? Is meditation the missing ingredient?

As meditation enables us to enter and abide in parts of the mind we rarely use, it expands us into higher states of awareness and consciousness. It is this expansion that makes it possible for us to transcend that which separates us. The movement of awareness from self to other than self opens our way of thinking to an unlimited vastness. There are suddenly endless possibilities, we are no longer restricted by a narrow worldview but can step into a bigger, more inclusive picture.

| JOHN HAGELIN |

"Short-sightedness, narrow-mindedness, bigotry, and indifference to nature are all manifestations of constricted awareness, which stems from the lack of experience of our fundamental unity. Modern physics has shown that at the basis of all the diversity of the universe lies the unified field of all the laws of nature, a nonmaterial, self-interacting, self-aware field of infinitely dynamic intelligence—a field of unity. Meditation provides the experience of this underlying unity and simultaneously dissolves the stresses and tensions that constrict our understanding. It changes our experience from awareness dominated by division and diversity to awareness dominated by unity and harmony—the direct cognition that we are all one. In that unified state of awareness, 'Love thy neighbor as thyself' becomes a living reality and a powerful tool for collective consciousness, alleviating acute societal stress, violence, and conflict, thereby providing a practical foundation for world peace."

|||

Can Meditation Save the World?

To make changes in the way we live our lives, how we treat each other, and how the world functions means embodying the awareness that as I am, so the world is; that the world is who I am, just as I am all beings; that everything I think, say, and do affects everybody and everything else, just as they affect me. Change in just one of us affects us all. This awareness demands a new understanding and approach to both personal and world concerns. In light of this, we asked our contributors if meditation could actually save the world, meaning, "Could it change us enough to save us from further destruction and suffering?"

| TIM FREKE |

"The idea that meditation could save the world sounds paradoxical, as saving the world is so active and meditation is seemingly so passive. It makes you stop and think. When we consider how to save the world from environmental disaster, war, overpopulation, famine, and so on, we usually assume we must do things. And, of course, we do need to act to save things. But really it is a transformation of consciousness that is needed so that what we do will work in the way that really influences things for the better, and meditation is without a doubt a very direct way that we can transform consciousness."

Given the on-going conflicts between families and nations, the continual abuse of power, and the resulting hardships experienced by so many, it would appear that we really do need this vital shift in consciousness and a commitment to our own awakening, and that we need it now.

| JACK KORNFIELD |

"We do not need to save the world, because the world as a whole is fine. It is redeeming and saving humanity that is necessary. In doing so, we must end the destruction and harm that we cause to all that is around us. Meditation helps us to awaken into fearlessness, compassion, and connectedness with all life, and this transformation of consciousness is absolutely critical at this time. We have come to the point where we have to do this. The visible suffering that arises from our separation from one another is so enormous that almost everyone feels this need. We know that there is global suffering. We also know within ourselves is the potential for great love and forgiveness and generosity that is a part of our own true nature. And now is the time to transform ourselves and bring that forward."

From this perspective, we can ask what is the world we wish to save? Is it the physical reality of war and destruction, or the mindset that creates such a world in the first place? Is there any point in saving the world if we do not start by transforming the ignorance that got us here? And, more importantly, if we do not awaken to our own true nature, then can we expect to help anyone else to do the same?

| MICHAEL BERNARD BECKWITH |

"When people ask if we can save the world, I ask them, 'What world is it that you want to save?' Is it a world that promotes fear, lack, scarcity, consumerism, sexism, and racism or that stockpiles 'peace-keeping weapons'? Meditation opens the heart to an awareness of oneness, to the inherent goodness within each and every individual regardless of what is manifesting on the outer plane of life. Therefore, we have a responsibility to cultivate a spiritual practice that fosters that awareness. Do whatever it takes to contribute your gifts, talents, and skills not to 'saving' the planet but to *awakening* all beings to their true nature, to their inherent goodness."

Meditation practice not only opens our heart and reveals our deep interconnectedness, but it also enables us to heal and end the war within ourselves. This war is the one that has to be brought to a place of forgiveness and peace so that we can end our war with others. When that happens, then we can see that everything we have ever disregarded, disrespected, or been frightened of was actually a part of us, that our fear was simply a reflection of our separation from our true selves.

| BYRON KATIE |

"The apparent craziness of the world, like everything else, is a gift that we can use to set our minds free. Any stressful thoughts that you have about the planet, for example, or about life and death, shows you where you are stuck, where your energy is being exhausted in not fully meeting life as it is, without conditions. When you question what you believe, you eventually come to see that you are the enlightenment you have been seeking. Until you can love what is—everything, including the violence and craziness—then you are separate from the world, and you will see it as dangerous and frightening. When the mind is not at war with itself, there is no separation."

This transformation of consciousness that is, therefore, so necessary, is seen in the movement from the disregard for each other that we started this chapter with to a place of deep awakening to the truth of non-duality, where such disregard is no longer even an issue.

| PETER FENNER |

"In relationship to the suffering in the world and the suffering of humanity, there is a complete identification with everything, because there is no separation. When consciousness is resting in non-dual awareness, there is no boundary, no judgment of right and wrong, nothing to defend, nothing to protect. Everything is included. In a sense, there is just a state of pure, unbounded receptivity that takes everything in, just as it is. No one is receiving, and it is this 'no one' that has the power to transform the world."

|||

14

| | |

We Are the Change We Are Looking For

Peace comes from within. Do not seek it without.
THE BUDDHA

A revolution is a *re-evolution*, where we take a higher step in the evolution of consciousness; it is also a *revolving*, a turning around of ourselves in response to an inner calling. To be the change and make a real difference in the world means we need a revolution—a compassionate revolution. This is the turning of our energy from being focused on self-centeredness, self-survival, and closed-heartedness to concern for others, generosity, and open-heartedness. If we genuinely want to end war, inequality, and abuse, then we have to practice *ahimsa* and kindness toward ourselves and all others equally, for there will never be peace in the world if we are not at peace within ourselves.

| SAKYONG MIPHAM |

"All of the pain and pleasure that we experience stems fundamentally from the mind. So when we say we want peace on earth, what we are really talking about is reducing the conflict in our own minds."

To consciously activate this change, we need to be honest about our own behavior. If we need more love, then we have to ask how much love are we bringing to the world? If we think there needs to be more compassion, are we the ones who need to be more compassionate? If we are looking for more respect and kindness, than are we showing respect and kindness toward others? If we want a friend, are we being a friend? Some time ago, Ed belonged to a meditation community. At a group meeting, Sarah stood up and announced, "I have no friends here." The teacher replied, "Then be a friend." In other words, are we a part of the problem or the solution?

| SEANE CORN |

"If what is happening on a global level is representative of what is happening on the individual level and if I want to transform what is happening globally, then I have to look within myself and see where I am separating myself from other human beings and from the earth. Where am I living in blame, in hate, in terrorism, in war, in any negative capacity toward another being? For if I am not willing to clean up the fear or the disconnect that is within myself, then I am responsible for what is happening on a planetary level."

Many people believe that they cannot be peaceful or happy while others are suffering or feel guilty if they experience abundance while others are going without. We were teaching a workshop in England. Claire told us, "I cannot be peaceful until my children are peaceful; I cannot be happy unless they are happy." But suffering ourselves because others are suffering does not help those who are already in pain; if we cannot help ourselves, then we will be unable to help anyone. When we find our own peace, then there is one less person suffering. If we look for happiness outside of ourselves, or look for it some time in the future when things have changed, then we will never find it, for it is not dependent on anything or anyone. Rather, happiness is within each one of us; it is always within us, and it can never be found because it was never lost.

| JOHN GRAY |

"The influence we have on others does not come by trying to change them; it comes from focusing on change within ourselves. It looks like this: If I say I want the world to be a healthier, happier, more loving place, then my body has to become a healthier, happier, more loving place. And if I do not have a healthier, happier, more loving body, heart, mind, and soul, then I will have no influence in the world. I can say it, but if I do not literally embody it, then I cannot inspire it in others."

|||

Becoming a True Warrior

In order to create a revolution we need warriors. Normally, a warrior is seen as a tough macho man or gladiator, a brave and courageous participant in war, unafraid of bloodshed or of being wounded for the sake of his cause. But the warriors we need now are engaged in a different kind of battle, the one that is experienced as we endeavor to let go of selfishness and aversion and enter into awareness, heartfulness, and inclusivity.

| JOHN MILTON |

"We are approaching the point where the human-centric perspective is in pretty deep trouble and the only way through this is to reach a place in ourselves where we know our own being and that the sacred core within is what we have in common with every other being on the planet. Until we have made a deep connection with ourselves by appreciating this life then it is very difficult to honor the lives of others."

For heart warriors, the greatest challenge is to keep the heart open at all times to their own pain as well as to the cries of others. Their armory is made up of the qualities of compassion, kindness, generosity, and service. These formidable weapons are used to break through the limitations of exclusivity, greed, and disrespect.

In *Shambhala, The Sacred Path of the Warrior,* Chögyam Trungpa explains that the key to being a warrior is not to be afraid of who we are, to no longer be surprised or alarmed by what we find in our own mind, to know and be at ease with the dark corners in our shadow. This means no longer being embarrassed by ourselves. It is refusing to give up on anyone or anything. We are not timid in our tenderness or reluctant to show our feelings, are not afraid to cry or to embrace the suffering and sadness of others, for we know there is a basic goodness and sanity beneath all the neurosis and ignorance.

| KEN GREEN |

"Mindfulness leads to meekness, which leads to perkiness, to outrageousness, and then to inscrutability. That is the way I have literally learned to walk the path of the warrior. If you let go of your defensiveness, you discover meekness and humility; then you get more liveliness that is very perky and energetic; you can start to be creative and to think and live out of the box, which is really the outrageous part. And then you don't have to prove yourself to anyone, no need to scheme or plan your survival, which is being inscrutable."

As a heart warrior, our responsibility—our capacity to respond—is to be available to all equally with the courage to love unreservedly. "What the warrior renounces is anything in his experience that is a barrier between himself and others," Chögyam Trungpa writes. "In other words, renunciation is making yourself more available, more gentle and open to others." This is possible, not because we are already awake and free of fear, but because we fully acknowledge and embrace fear and use it to encourage fearlessness.

| VICKIE DODD |

"I meditate so that I can be a kinder and saner human being in the world. It keeps me out of trouble with myself, or with others, and allows me to be the caring person that I really want to be. I have always viewed it as a very practical ingredient in my life. I become more ordinary, instead of needing to feel special or victimized. I need meditation in order to be a human being that can walk with sensitivity and generosity."

Self-reflection, prayer, or contemplation does not just make us a nicer person or even a good warrior, but awakens consciousness to itself and its reason for being. This fundamentally changes our relationship with ourselves and our world, creating an inner aliveness we may not have known before.

| ANDREW COHEN |

"What meditation does is directly reveal an absolute sense of purpose and meaning in the discovery of consciousness itself. The fundamental doubt about why am I here, or what is the point, is eradicated. The direct experience of consciousness removes this existential doubt, and that changes everything. The result is that we feel convinced beyond any question that life is good, that existence is good, that being oneself is good, that being a part of the world's process is good. Our life orientation is completely different. Now there is an inherently positive relationship to being alive. That is an enormous shift! It does not mean that all of our neurotic tendencies are automatically gone—they are most likely still going to remain. However, our relationship to them is very different. There is a willingness to engage with them and take responsibility, which is a very positive place to be."

|||

The Revolutionary Power of Meditation

To activate a compassionate revolution is to enter into an exploration of all aspects of our humanness so that we can live sanely in a world that often looks insane, riddled with affliction and conflict. So much hurt and denial, abuse and disrespect, so many atrocities have taken place in the name of religion and politics, or through greed and selfishness, so many misunderstandings between families, races, and countries.

| SEANE CORN |

"People are separating themselves from each other and choosing to live in blame and victimization, rather than in awareness and empowerment. But nothing is happening in this world without our participation; whether it is war, terrorism, repression, or rape, they are all due to our collective thoughts that make us think we are separate. If I can change the part in me that is disconnected—the part that is in blame, shame, or denial—and if I can heal this with love, then I can affect the world. And if I can love this in me, then I can love this in you."

There is an innate and tender place inside each one of us that is loving and happy, and that yearns to share this with others. Without this, kindness would not be possible, compassion would not be possible. For the revolution to be effective, therefore, we have to hold tight to that tender place and give it our priority. In this way our normal self-centeredness dissolves into other-centeredness.

| ROBERT THURMAN |

"Understanding something does not necessarily change our gut reactions, so that is where meditation comes in. When I see my attitude about my own egotism and I realize that I am just one of all beings and I am interrelated with everyone else, then meditation is like a weight that pushes that realization down deeper into my gut until it finds the 'I, me, mine' level where it transforms it. Meditation is what makes my understanding experiential."

Letting go of a me-centered world and stepping into warriorship may feel fearful at first, due to the nature of the ego that creates a solid sense of self and clings to the known and familiar. But releasing the incessant "me" is like off-loading a heavy and demanding weight. What a relief! In this sense, meditation is entirely revolutionary.

| LINDSAY CROUCH |

"I believe that if we sit in silence every day, we are a better human being for it. We spend all this time practicing at playing the piano or practicing our relationships or our jobs or whatever, but we do not think we have to practice kindness or compassion. Meditation is the opportunity to become a more compassionate human being. It is really our only chance."

What would a world full of people engaged in meditation look like? Can we imagine a place where we treat each other with dignity and respect? Where we recognize that our own happiness and well-being is dependent on the happiness and well-being of all others? This may sound like a Shangri-la, but it just takes one person to make a change. From that one person comes another, and another. . . .

Meditation impacts our lives as it enables us to cultivate the psychological, emotional, and spiritual tools that are necessary to resolve issues both within ourselves and in the world at large. And as our every thought, word, and deed radiates outward and affects all others, so it is our responsibility to determine that what we express and the way we behave are of benefit to the greater whole.

| JEAN HOUSTON |

"We must find the meditation that speaks to our innate capacity for knowing, for being, for entering into those wisdom states that give us the intuitive knowledge of what we are and what we must do in this most important time, for what we do now will most profoundly make a difference to our future."

|||

Are You Stinging or Saving?

We began chapter one with a story of a scorpion stinging the frog that was carrying it across a river so that both the frog and the scorpion drown. We told this story to demonstrate how fixed and self-absorbed we can become, unable to change or adapt, even to the point of jeopardizing our own welfare. But, throughout the book, we have seen how quiet self-reflection and meditation can transform this self-centered aspect of our nature by opening our hearts and awakening us to other-centeredness. Then we have the choice to be able to offer generosity in place of selfishness, kindness in place of malice, and harmlessness in place of harm. To illustrate this, here is the end of the story:

Two monks were washing their bowls in the river when they noticed a scorpion that was drowning. One monk immediately scooped it up and set it upon the bank. In the process, he was stung. He went back to washing his bowl, and again the scorpion fell in the river. The monk saved the scorpion and was again stung. The other monk asked him, "Friend, why do you continue to save the scorpion when you know its nature is to sting?" "Because," the monk replied, "my nature is to save."

Coming Next

Due to the many years of meditation our contributors have all experienced, the practice chapters that follow in Part Four are invaluable. There is a depth of insight that even a seasoned practitioner will benefit from and enjoy. Do not hesitate to dive into this ocean of wisdom! The meditations are transformative and have the potential to awaken compassion in every part of our lives.

|||||||||||||||||||||||||||||||||||||||||||||||||||||||||

Part IV

|||

PRACTICE
MAKES PERFECT

IN THE FOLLOWING PRACTICE CHAPTERS, THERE IS A
WEALTH OF UNDERSTANDING AND KNOWLEDGE FROM
OUR VARIED CONTRIBUTORS TO INSPIRE NEW AND
EXPERIENCED PRACTITIONERS ALIKE.

|||||||||||||||||||||||||||||||||||||||||||||||||||||||||

15

| | |

Doing It

Meditation is not a war. It is a way of making friends with ourselves.

RICK FIELDS

The story goes that there was once a famous Buddhist layman named Busol. He was deeply enlightened, as were his wife, his son, and his daughter. A man came to visit him one day and asked him, "Is meditation difficult or not?"

Busol replied, "Oh, it is very difficult—it is like taking a stick and trying to hit the moon!"

The man was puzzled and thought, "If meditation is so difficult, how did Busol's wife gain enlightenment?" So he went and asked her the same question.

"Meditation is the easiest thing in the world," she replied. "It is just like touching your nose when you wash your face in the morning!"

By now, the man was thoroughly confused. So he asked their son: "I don't understand. Is meditation difficult or is it easy? Who is right?"

"Meditation is not difficult and not easy," the son

replied. "On the tips of a hundred blades of grass is the meaning."

"Not difficult? Not easy? What is it then?" So the man went to the daughter and asked her: "Your father, your mother, and your brother all gave me different answers. Who is right?"

The daughter replied, "If you make it difficult, it is difficult. If you make it easy, it is easy. Where are difficult and easy? Only in the mind. Meditation is just as it is."

Yes, meditation is simple: just calming the mind and being still, paying attention and being present. But it is also not always easy! The mind is notoriously resistant to being quiet, and as soon as we try to be still, it seems to do everything it can to distract us. Within a few minutes, our thoughts are wandering, our body starts to itch, ache, or want to move, we remember things we need to do that suddenly seem vitally important, and because we are so distracted, we feel inadequate and think that meditation is not for us.

"Meditation can be intimidating. Sitting there, doing nothing, just breathing can be trickier than it sounds. It may feel strange, uncomfortable, or even put you to sleep. Distractions try their best to pester you. Thoughts of the weekend, family, work, finances, politics, what's for dinner, all invade your aspiring-to-be-still mind. You start to fidget, adjusting your seat, clothes, and hair, anything to have something to do," writes Tara Stiles on HuffingtonPost.com. "Meditation can be like a battle with yourself, your thoughts, your body. But if you stick with the uncomfortable moments, they will start to fade away and cool things will happen."

Learning how to be quiet and calm the body takes patience and perseverance. As we continue, it will begin to feel more natural and ordinary. Remember, music needs to be played for hours to get the notes right, while in Japan it can take twelve years to learn how to arrange flowers. Being still happens in a moment, but it may take some time before that moment comes—hence the need for practice.

| DAVID SHINER |

"There is a point in meditation where it becomes sweet. The beginning may appear hard, it takes discipline, but it is like learning anything: You get up, you get on the horse, you fall off, and you get on the horse again. Swimming is the same thing: You start in shallow water, and then you get into deeper water. If that scares you, then you go back to the shallow water until you get more confident. Practice, practice, practice! Slowly, the joy of being in this quiet space becomes addictive, you are just there, observing. And it transforms itself into so much more, into deeper love for other human beings, deeper respect for life, deeper compassion, and deeper humility. It is like the cream on milk that rises to the top. The real beauty of what we are, the essence of what we are, very slowly starts to bubble to the surface."

Almost everything we do in life is to achieve something: If we do this, then we will get that; if we do that, then this will happen. We are not used to doing anything without an agenda. But in meditation we do it just to do it. There is no ulterior purpose to practicing meditation other than to be here, in the present, without a goal of succeeding, of trying to get anywhere or achieve anything. If our purpose is to try to achieve a quiet mind, then the trying itself will create tension and failure. Instead, we are just with whatever is happening in the moment, whether it is pleasant or unpleasant. No judgment, no right or wrong. Watching whatever arises and letting it go is all that is required. It is more of an undoing than a doing.

| PETER RUSSELL |

"One thing I think is really important is the complete and utter effortlessness of meditation. This is something that is often misunderstood, but if we put any effort into the meditative process, we actually create more tension. We have to completely let go of any wanting, intention, or hoping. I see meditation as coming to a complete and utter acceptance of what is in each moment, as a chance to go into a real 'no-agenda' space. And that can be very hard because we are so conditioned into doing something with a purpose and that the harder we try the better we are going to be at it, which is true in almost every other area of life, but it is the one thing that gets in the way of meditation."

The important point is that we make friends with our practice. It will be of no help at all if we feel we have to meditate, for instance, and then feel guilty if we miss the allotted time or only do ten minutes when we had promised to do thirty. It is much better to practice for a just a few minutes and to enjoy what we are doing than to make ourselves sit there, teeth gritted, because we have been told that only thirty or even forty minutes will have any affect. Meditation is a companion for us to have throughout our life, like an old friend we turn to when in need of direction, inspiration, and clarity. It is to be enjoyed!

| KRISHNA DAS |

"Meditation gives us a taste of what it feels like to feel good for no reason at all, and the more we do it, the less our happiness depends on external things and the more our happiness deepens inside us. It is just so cool because it works."

Stillness is actually a natural state of being; it is what is there when we stop trying, when we release the story. We practice so that we can let go of the busy mind and the stresses and worries that hold us in anxiety and stop us experiencing quiet. Practice is a gathering of our dispersed selves into one place; it brings the mind and heart together in the present moment and acts like an anchor to hold us in presence. It provides a structure for the mind to become focused and clear.

| GANGAJI |

"I invite people to just stop and be still. And in that you discover who you are, because once you discover who you are, you can stop fragmenting into pieces. I know that in any one day there are moments where there is nothing going on, but we link up what is happening from thought to thought without any space. We overlook the spaciousness that it is all happening in."

As the mind settles, insight arises. We see how everything is in constant change and movement, how nothing remains the same; we watch how thoughts and feelings come and go with no permanence. Yet there is also stillness. In this way, we see both change and stillness as reflections of each other. Within that is an infinite spaciousness. We may only touch this spaciousness occasionally or know it fleetingly, or we may find ourselves hanging out there, resting in the quiet moment. As everything changes, so too will this experience. Sometimes it will seem very familiar; other times we will be seeing the same thing only with new eyes.

| DEAN ORNISH |

"There is an old Zen proverb that says, 'Before enlightenment, chop wood, carry water; after enlightenment, chop wood, carry water.' In other words, you may still do the same activities but the intention behind them can be profoundly different, not simply to get what you think is going to make you happy, but rather to have direct experiences of transcendence."

Below, we offer directions on how to create a daily practice: how to deal with distractions, such as endless thinking, how to sit, and finding the right time.

Monkey Mind

I can't relax. I can't meditate. I just can't! My mind will not get quiet; it flies all over the place! My thoughts are driving me mad! Sound familiar?

| CYNDI LEE |

"It is really easy to think that we cannot meditate. People say, 'My mind is so active. . . I'm not getting it. . . I can't do it. . . .' If we went to an exercise class, we would expect to first feel kind of uncoordinated and to not really understand the movement vocabulary, feel tired or maybe stiff, and we would have to push ourselves to go back. But that is natural; we understand that with our body. Well, it is the same with meditation. It takes a while to get it. It takes a while to understand what it is all about, to deal with the mind, and to feel some of the benefits."

In the Eastern teachings, the mind is described as being like a monkey bitten by a scorpion, and, just as a monkey leaps from branch to branch, so the mind leaps from one thing to another, constantly distracted and engaged in discursive activity. Then, when we come to sit still and begin to pay attention, we find all this manic activity going on and it seems insanely noisy. It is actually nothing new, just that now we are becoming aware of it, whereas before we were immersed in it, unaware that such chatter was so constant.

| ELLEN BURSTYN |

"Meditation helps us get behind the ego. It helps us get quiet enough so that we can actually hear the ego at work. All the chatter is the ego's chatter; it is not the essence of our inner being. It is only when we settle down and get quiet that we can hear this voice of the ego and how it clamors for attention. For instance, if we have a moment of absolute peace with no thought at all and we are really focused on the breath and we have achieved that quiet state that we want to achieve, immediately the ego will take credit for it: 'Look how good I can meditate!' To me, meditation is stopping all the associations and chatter in the mind. That takes practice, and I am better at it on some days than others. Sometimes I sit down to meditate and the chatter just goes on and on and my whole meditation gets to be about going back to the beginning where I started. The meditation becomes the attempt to meditate."

The experience of the mind being so busy is actually very normal. Someone once estimated that in any one thirty-minute session of meditation we may have upward of three hundred thoughts. This illustrates the reality of thinking. Years of busy mind, years of creating and maintaining dramas, years of stresses and confusion and self-centeredness, and the mind is not always so ready to be still; it craves entertainment. So it is not as if we can suddenly turn our mind off when we sit down to meditate; that would be like trying to catch the wind: impossible. But having a busy mind does not mean we cannot meditate; it just means we are like everyone else.

It is not possible to fail at meditation. Even if we sit for twenty minutes and our mind is thinking non-stop meaningless thoughts, then that is fine. We just allow thoughts to be thoughts. This will change, as the mind is constantly unpredictable: A busy mind now may be a quiet mind later. All we need to do is keep coming back to the breath or practice, be willing to keep going, and give it time. Our intent is more important than what happens.

| ROBERT THURMAN |

"The first step is to try to focus our mind on something, like counting the breath. When we do, we see all these runaway thoughts that race through the mind, like I wonder if my car will be ready, is my parking meter overdue, will I get a ticket, should I get a new car, is my girlfriend happy? Whatever. Our minds are filled with these preoccupations, and we do not even realize it. But then we see that we can just let them go and bring the mind back to something we want to focus on. That is the first step. It is a beginning, calming, waking-up step. But more important than that is to choose positive thoughts to focus on, such as I want to be more loving to that person who annoys me, I want to be more content, I want to be more friendly, peaceful, happy, and clear, and I no longer need to suffer."

Practicing meditation means slowly and gently training the mind to do something it may not have done before: to be still. The technique gives the mind an activity, such as counting breaths or reciting a mantra, and every time it wanders off on a thinking spree, we simply notice this and bring it back to the practice. The experience of stillness is accumulative: The more we sit, then slowly, slowly, the mind becomes quieter, despite whatever distraction there may be. Ajahn Sumedho, a Buddhist abbot, recounted how he was once teaching meditation in Bombay and right outside the window was a construction site. He had just started the meditation when a pneumatic drill began digging up the road. He could not stop the program, so, "Quite simply, we became the sound."

| PETER RUSSELL |

"I do not think the mind gets in the way of meditation at all; it is simply that this is how the mind is right now. We do not have to start battling the mind or trying to control it. It is the same with sound; we think we cannot be quiet because of the sound of the refrigerator or the sound of the traffic. But actually it is our attitude toward it, because the sound is just a part of being in the present moment, and is, therefore, a part of meditation. It is our resistance to sound that is the barrier to meditation. If we do not resist it, then the mind can be quiet in the middle of all sorts of noise."

In other words, meditation is not a process of trying or forcing the mind to be still. Rather, it is a letting go of resistance, of whatever may arise: doubt, worry, uncertainty and feeling inadequate, the endless dramas, fear and desire. Every time we find our mind is drifting, daydreaming, remembering the past or planning ahead, we just come back to now, come back to this moment. In meditation, paying attention is the point of the practice. To see and let go. To be with what is. Just witnessing. Nothing else is going on.

| DENNIS GENPO MERZEL |

"If trying to grasp at something arises, just notice it, just be aware and mindful that the seeking mind is trying to come back into play and re-identify with the non-seeking. The whole point is to be identified with the process of witnessing, of just being or non-seeking, versus that of seeking or being caught up in the seeking."

The endless chatter is a great distraction, and not just from being quiet but also from being able to really connect with our

inner feelings; it is like a wall of noise blocking out the heart.
As the mind begins to settle, so deeper feelings can arise. As we
embrace these then we have the spaciousness to develop more
altruistic qualities, such as kindness and compassion.

| MAX SIMON |

"The primary reason why I meditate is to quiet down the mind chatter.
Developing love and kindness is really difficult if the whole time the mind
is saying 'That's not true; that's not real.' The technique allows me to get
underneath the conversation. Everybody feels good when they are quiet,
relaxed, and open, so the more that we quiet the mind chatter, the more
good we feel, and then we take it from mediation into life."

Thoughts come and go, but they will settle; the mind does
become quiet, even if only for a moment. Those quiet moments
are like the gaps between the thoughts, and although they may
be brief, they connect us deeply with a great love and openness
within.

| RAM DASS |

"Going inward, going into awareness, not getting caught identifying
with thoughts, you can just be aware of thoughts. I call this being *loving
awareness*."

|||

Labeling Thoughts

One of the ways to become more objective about thinking is to
label the thoughts. Whenever we catch ourselves drifting off
into dramas or daydreams, we can silently repeat: *thinking,
thinking*, and then come back to the practice. In the same way,
if we are getting distracted, we simply label it *distraction, distraction*. It is very possible to go to all sorts of places in the
mind while we sit, create all sorts of images and fantasies, but

each time we label it *thinking* or *distraction*, we can let it all go, including the accompanying emotions, and just be in the present again. There is no need to struggle.

"Notice what pops into your head—like what you want for dinner, whether Benicio is sexier than Brad, if you should ask for a raise. . . . No matter what it is, label it as a *thought*, and then redirect your attention to your breath," writes Nicole Beland on WomansHealthmag.com. "When you catch yourself daydreaming, planning, analyzing, or worrying (which will happen constantly), just let the thoughts drift by and refocus on the air flowing through your body."

We can see thoughts like clouds in the sky, just moving through the sky without stopping and without affecting the clarity or brilliance of the sky, or see them like birds—beautiful, but here one minute and then gone. Watch them fly away. Applying this to feelings as well as thoughts, and we see how everything comes and goes, nothing stays, and nothing is permanent, no matter how strong or insistent the thought or feeling may be.

Witnessing Mind

| ANDREW COHEN |

"It is very difficult without a mirror to see our own nose. In the same way, we are usually so identified with the subjective nature of our experience that it is very difficult to be objective. The basis of meditation is that we assume the position of the witness, we witness our own relationship to ourselves as an objective experience: what was subject, what was felt or experienced as the self, becomes object. In other words, we become aware of many different dimensions of ourselves that we were so identified with that we were totally unable to see them objectively. As we develop our capacity to be aware of our own experience, subject becomes object."

The observer that sees without being engaged is the witness. This is the core of mindfulness meditation. As we develop the witness, we realize that we are not our thoughts, we are not our emotions. We have them, we appreciate them, we honor them, but we are not them. We are that which observes them and witnesses what is, just as it is.

| MICHAEL BERNARD BECKWITH |

"Through the practice of meditation, we become aware that we are aware. We realize that we have a body, but are not the body. We witness the thinking mind, but realize that we are not the thoughts that are passing through. Emotions of all kinds arise, but we realize we are that which witnesses them; our essence remains the witness to the whole panorama of emotions. The more we witness this, the more we see through the ego and actually make it an entertaining ally. We become nonattached to its influence or needs, and as a result, it loses its power."

There is simply the state of being present, of relative freedom from identification with the ego-self. We see how our own selfishness, aversion, or ignorance perpetuates the dramas and maintains the fears, for beneath them is a quiet stillness. In the spaciousness that silence creates, we meet and get to know ourselves; this is a wondrous and beautiful experience. Whether we practice for just ten minutes a day or go into a long period of retreat does not matter. We are removing the barriers that limit us, while opening our doors of perception and awareness.

| PONLOP RINPOCHE |

"Ever since we were born, we have been living in the world of concepts that people have given to us, so we may have never really stepped back and just observed things as they are. When I meditate, it is a process of getting to know myself, witnessing my mind, discovering my true nature, and seeing the nature of the world. When we see something, we just see it; when we hear something, we just hear it. In that state of awakening, we are totally relaxed, but at the same time we have a clear awareness."

We may dip in and out of such spaciousness, but it is always there. Remember, in essence the mind is the clear, transparent sky. Everything in the sky just comes and goes but it does not affect our basic skyness. There is just mind, and as that dissolves into stillness, finally there is no mind!

| DEVA PREMAL AND MITEN |

"Meditation is not just sitting cross-legged in the lotus position for an hour; it is every breath we take and every move we make. And in that, something pure can arise. It is a practice to watch the unknown and to watch the mind and a practice of dedication and nonattachment. We realize that we are not the body and are not our thoughts. They are just two things we get very attached to in this life. In meditation, we can constantly watch this so that it becomes a knowing rather than just an intellectual understanding. We become aware of every sound around us, and, in that awareness, we become the center of the symphony. In the center is emptiness, is presence, an inner vastness. There is nothing going on."

|||

Sitting Right

To sit comfortably, it is best to wear loose, relaxed clothing. Remove glasses or watch, undo any belts, turn off the telephone, and maybe leave a note on the door saying "Do not disturb." In other words, remove anything that might cause a distraction.

For meditation, it is helpful to have a straight back so that the breath can flow in and out unimpeded. Also, an upright back is indicative of an alert and dignified mind, whereas a slumped or rounded back gives rise to feelings of sadness, depression, and hopelessness—not qualities we want to bring to meditation. Traditionally, the posture is sitting cross-legged on the floor, which some people manage to do comfortably. But for many, their bodies are not used to sitting in this way and it can cause discomfort. In which case, an upright chair is just as good.

If sitting on a chair, then use a small cushion to support an upright spine; feet are flat on the floor, and hands are resting in the lap or on the thighs. If sitting cross-legged on the floor, then use one or two quite firm cushions to sit on, as this will lift the spine and buttocks so that the knees fall forward. In this position, the back is naturally upright.

When you first sit down, spend a few moments checking your posture and releasing any tension. Move your body backward and forward a little to get a sense of balance and what a straight back feels like. Head is neither tilted up or down, but just resting comfortably. Eyes are either closed or slightly open but not focused. Despite a perfect posture, aches and pains do occur. If that happens, then move slightly to release the tension, or simply let the discomfort relax by surrendering to it.

| PETER RUSSELL |

"Many people say the thing that disturbs their meditation is they have some discomfort in their body, maybe a pain in the knees or in the shoulder. The normal reaction is to try to push it away, to get rid of it, to ignore it, or wish it was not there. But if you allow it in, you can start to explore it. Okay, there's a sharp bit here, a numb bit here, see how far has it spread. The sensations may get stronger, but the actual hurt comes from the resistance of pushing it away. When we stop resisting, we stop pushing. We are just sitting with it as it is, and then the pain starts releasing, muscles begin to let go. We do not have to get rid of something, rather let it in and let it be. And then the release happens of its own accord."

|||

The Right Time

A lack of time is the main lament we hear from people. Demands from home and work overlap and fill all the spaces. With so much going on—fears, worries, plans, dramas, feelings, resentments, appointments—there seems to be little space for practice. Claire told us, "I am just too busy to meditate; I don't even have time to do what needs to be done. Fitting in meditation is just more than I can handle." This is actually the perfect reason to meditate! Even if it is just for ten minutes a day, it will help us to do what needs to be done.

| DEB |

"I was on a ten-day Zen meditation retreat, and each day we had work assignments. There was never enough time to do the whole job before the next meditation session began, and on one occasion I started to panic. I was trying to finish weeding a flowerbed, and it all just got much and I burst into tears. The teacher came over and took me aside. Very gently, she said, 'You can never have too much to do. You just do what is in front of you, and when you are finished, you do the next thing.' This had the immediate effect of making me take a deep breath and relax. It also radically changed my attitude toward stress."

In order for meditation to be a friend, it helps to have a time specifically for practice, such as when you first get up or before going to bed. Morning people prefer to practice first thing, as that is when they are more awake and focused, but for others it is impractical and a later time in the day works better. You know whether you are a morning or an evening person. And you know the quietest time, maybe when the kids are still asleep. If it is in the evening, it helps to do some stretching or moving first in order to release any physical stress. It is easy to think meditation is difficult if we are trying to be still but our body is full of tense energy. Stretch and relax first.

We can practice as often as we want to or can do: Ten minutes or longer every day, more on days off, even a weekend or week's retreat every few months. If ten minutes in a day is all we can manage, then that is fine. The more often we practice, the better—frequency is more important than length. Meditation is cumulative, so the more we do it, the more we will love it. We can make a commitment to our practice. Even if all we can manage is fifteen minutes once a week, then start there. Getting started is much better than thinking about starting!

| RABBI ZALMAN SCHACHTER-SHALOMI |

"In the old days, there was nothing to fill our minds, no TV or radio, so it was easy to chill out and get empty. But now we are bombarded by so many wavelengths that it is very different. There once was a time when they had coffee vacuum packed, but now it is pressure packed, and when you first open the can, you get a big whoosh of aroma. I believe in pressure-packed meditation, just twenty minutes in the morning and evening and I can really achieve a good state. I don't need longer. This amount can be very effective."

Most important is that we enjoy the time we have. After all, we are going to be the one practicing, and it is much more important that we are happy about what we are doing than doing it according to someone else's specifications. We are not practicing to prove anything or to try to achieve something. It is just there for us to connect more deeply with ourselves, our sanity, and our freedom. And, like learning any new activity, it takes time to get to know the ropes.

| JUDITH SIMMER-BROWN |

"I really think the most important thing we can do is to commit to daily practice. A lot of people talk about meditation, but there is nothing that substitutes for daily practice. Just putting your mind into some kind of set-tled, open, radiant space has a transforming effect that is way beyond any words about it, way beyond any books about it. If you do at least five min-utes a day without fail, then it will grow. Don't think that you need to do an hour a day or it does not count; it is the consistency of the practice that matters. We think going on a big retreat or doing a 10-day silent retreat is going to change our lives, but that is like going into a cave with a bucket of water and throwing the bucket of water on the wall and expecting it to wear away the rock. What really wears away the rock is a daily drip."

Many of us grew up abhorring the idea of discipline, but in this case, it is actually very liberating. Sitting at a certain time on a regular basis is a way of creating order and balance out of chaos. The mind may come up with all sorts of reasons and excuses not to meditate, but we can just acknowledge these and sit anyway. It is a way of showing our care and friendliness toward ourselves.

| DAVID SHINER |

"Meditation has completely changed my life, completely transformed me as a human being. I am not neurotic anymore; I am calm, centered, and quiet. I think real transformation takes a long time, and it comes very slowly and quietly and gently into our lives. Profound transformation does not happen in a weekend course where everybody gets together and you do some sort of deep psychotherapeutic group awareness. For real transformation, you need to have patience and realize that anything of deep and lasting value takes time."

|||

Alone or Together

Whether to practice alone or in a group is a personal decision. We know people who much prefer to sit alone, as they feel able to enter into their own space more easily. But we also lead meditation group retreats and discover that most participants find it very supportive and inspiring to meditate together. The group energy seems to hold the space and allow the participants to go deeper into silence. Those who do like to meditate in a group do not necessarily want to be with any one particular teacher and so often sit with a group of friends at home.

| MARK MATOUSEK |

"One of the best things I have done in my life was to start a weekly sitting group at my house. It is a refuge and sanctuary for friends and deepens my relationships with these kindred souls. It serves as a kind of Sabbath in an otherwise hectic, secular life, an ongoing source of strength and joy from the simplest of practices."

Sitting with others offers a chance for us to grow individually while also sharing that experience in a silent, unspoken way with our companions.

| SUSAN SMALLEY |

"The acronym SIT (Synchronized Individual Transformation) is perfect for describing what often arises when we sit together in meditation or contemplation. Three years ago, my friends and I began a 'Friday morning SIT' at my house. A group of us meet each Friday to sit together in meditation. No one leads the group; no ones teaches. We merely come together, someone reads an inspirational quote from a glass jar full of quotes we have each submitted, we sit together for thirty minutes with a timer to keep track of time, and then go our separate ways. In this weekly ritual, we experience synchronized individual transformations and deepen our friendships as well."

|||

Creating Sacred Space

On the one hand, everything is sacred and wherever we are is no more important than anywhere else; on the other hand, having a place that is special, just for meditation, creates a connection to sacredness in our everyday world.

| DEB |

"Some years ago, I visited the Ajunta caves in India. These ancient rock caves are carved into the side of a deep and very overgrown valley and were only discovered about a hundred years ago when a group of hunters were chasing a tiger. The caves are where Buddhist monks would retreat in the rainy season, and there are numerous rock carvings of them sitting or lying in meditation. When I was in one of the caves, I became aware of how extraordinarily peaceful and quiet I felt. Then I walked outside and reconnected with my ordinary everydayness. Inside serene; outside ordinary. I went in and out a few times to check I wasn't fantasizing it. Same rock; the only difference was that inside years of meditation practice had taken place. It reminded me of very old churches that have that same deep and pervasive quiet due to so many years of prayer and reflection."

Creating a space or area where we sit for meditation, where we can be still and quiet, will empower our practice. We used to have a room for meditation where we could retreat whenever we needed to; now we have the downstairs of our house as a place of quiet.

It could be a room or just a corner, even the cupboard under the stairs. A place where we can have a cushion or chair to sit on, a blanket or shawl, a candle to bring light, perhaps some flowers, some incense, an inspiring or poetic book, or any objects that are important or meaningful to us. Creating the right environment is a way of remembering that this silent space is always accessible. It is an on-going invitation to be still.

This space can also be a place where any member of the family, including children, can go to be quiet and reflective; anyone who is feeling upset or stressed and needs to chill out. We may find it becoming the most important room in the house!

| COLMAN BARKS |

"I grew up on the bluff on the Tennessee River, and I had a place where I would go—actually each member of our family had a place where they would go and it was just theirs, and they would sit there and just watch the river, and I would do the same. I became a kind of river mystic; it was just a deep flow inside me that felt like my first appreciation of beauty."

III

16

|||

Sitting Meditation

It is in the silence I find my life worth living; I find
it interesting. The rest of it is noise.
RUBY WAX

| WAVY GRAVY |

"I do this thing with the children where I say, 'Breathing in, I calm my
body; breathing out, I smile. Breathing in, I know this supreme moment;
breathing out, I know it is a wonderful moment.' When I do that with the
children, they all jump for joy. It is very cool."

If children can do it, so can we! But in our busy and chaotic
lives, we easily miss this treasure that lies within us. All we
need to do is sit still, close our eyes, and become aware of the
quiet stillness beneath the endless chatter in our minds. Others
may laugh and say we are just contemplating our own navel,
but they don't realize that this is actually a very precious gift.

There are various techniques that can help us to be still,
but these techniques are not about trying to achieve anything
or to develop special powers, and no technique is necessarily
any better than any other. Although the techniques may differ,
they all point to the same place, which is the cultivation of
awareness.

| LAMA SURYA DAS |

"Just sitting cross-legged does not help us to become enlightened. Statues sit cross-legged, frogs sit like meditators; I don't think they are becoming enlightened waiting to catch a fly. Rocks just sit there, but I don't think they are enlightened. Awareness is the main component in meditation, a discipline of refining, energizing, animating, and awakening the consciousness."

There are many ways we can bring the mind into a quiet place. Those that gather or focus our attention are the ones traditionally used, the most direct form of which is just watching the natural in-and-out flow of the breath. This internalizes our awareness; it focuses our attention on the inner world rather than the outer one. It also develops mindfulness of our body, thoughts, and feelings.

| TIM FREKE |

"I settle into my body and become aware of all the different parts and what they are doing, like the internal organs and the breath. What is the actual experience of feeling or listening? It becomes an investigation of the moment. I look at the seeing or the hearing or the feeling or the weight of my body or the tension or the relaxation or the breath coming in and going out. Then I sink into the mind and watch the flow of thoughts. What is it to experience thought? What is a thought? What is an idea? Memories come, but what is that? What is the experience of a memory or a fear or a hope? It is endlessly fascinating."

Then there are meditations that develop specific aspects of our being, such as kindness, love, compassion, and forgiveness. These are based on opening the heart. Rather than trying to find these qualities outside of ourselves, they are already within us and we simply need to connect more deeply with them. Each spiritual tradition also has its own meditation techniques, perhaps using sacred teachings as an inspiration or intoning sacred sounds.

| MICHAEL BERNARD BECKWITH |

"There are different meditation techniques that suit different temperaments. There is *contemplative meditation* where a practitioner takes something from one of the scriptures of the world's wisdom traditions, or a poem by Rumi, Hafiz, or Kabir, for example, and contemplates it in silence, until the silence becomes stillness out of which insights begin to be perceived about the piece's inner meaning, to receiving its gift of beauty. Then there is *existential meditation,* like Ramana Maharshi's question, Who am I? A person may be a plumber or a doctor or a schoolteacher, but encoded within them is the desire to discover their original face, their pure essence before the influence of their socialization took place and labels became attached to their simplicity of being. The third meditation practice is what I call *spiritual meditation,* where the practitioner's specific purpose is to enter a state of pure awareness, a consciousness of oneness with God."

Self-inquiry is a time-honored technique used to break through the conceptual limitations of the thinking mind. We do this by asking unanswerable questions that make us step beyond the logical mind to a deeper level of awareness.

| GANGAJI |

"I use inquiry as a way of getting the mind to turn inward to the silence. It could be the question, 'Who am I?' Or it could be 'What am I avoiding in this moment?' Or, 'Where is silence?' 'What is needed in this moment, right in this very moment, what is needed for true peace?' 'What is needed if this was my last moment on earth?' Rather than sending the mind outward to gather information or experiences, it is really sending the mind inward to question our basic assumptions of who we think we are."

|||

CLEAR MIND MEDITATION

The purpose of clear mind meditations is to focus our attention by bringing the scattered and busy mind into a quiet and clear space, and to develop one-pointed awareness. This can be done by following the flow of the breath, as explained below, by gazing at the flame of a candle as taught in many yoga traditions, or by sitting with quiet, open awareness.

Breath Awareness Meditation

| TIM FREKE |

"The greatest discovery for me was that I could sit and watch my breath and that just breathing could become the most fantastically enjoyable experience I could possibly imagine. And I thought, well, if I can get this much pleasure from just breathing, then I'm okay, because as long as I am alive, I am going to have breath. This was huge for me, this sinking into the breath in the body."

To clear the mind, there is nothing simpler than watching the natural in-and-out flow of the breath. This is also known as calm abiding (or *shamatha*) meditation and is the most direct form of sitting practice. As such, it is the foundation for all other practices. We simply follow the breath as it enters and watch it dissolve and merge into our every cell, and follow the breath as it leaves and watch it dissolve and merge into the cosmos.

| PONLOP RINPOCHE |

"I would really suggest *shamatha* meditation. The name itself, calm abiding, suggests that there are two stages here: first is calming your busy mind, your aggressive mind, and your emotional mind; and second is abiding in that state of calm."

The breath is the entry point to the body, so watching the flow of the breath brings our attention inward, enabling external distractions to drop away. This practice focuses our attention and deepens awareness. The breath is always with us, yet it is not ours to own despite it being an intimate part of our every living moment. It is ours only to share, to give away as soon as we have it; we breathe in only to breathe out again. We follow the breath in, and in the moment of breathing out, we merge with all life.

| MICHAEL BERNARD BECKWITH |

"Using the breath as an anchor is important in order to understand the purpose of meditation, because we cannot breathe in the future and we cannot breathe in the past. We can only breathe in the 'now' moment, so awareness of breath keeps us focused on where we are in the present—we cannot save breaths for later on. With breath as the base, if we get caught up in worry, doubt, fear, or even memories of happiness and delight, then coming back to the breath breaks the train of thought and creates a gap where awareness can occur. Deep meditation is paying undistracted attention to reality."

We are not trying to change the breath or to breathe more slowly or purposefully. The mind might become distracted and wander off into different thoughts, but the breath is always there to bring us into the present moment. All we have to do is follow the flow of each breath as it enters and leaves, bringing the mind and the breath together. We constantly come back to that flow.

| NOAH LEVINE |

"I think the best introduction to meditation is the basic breath awareness practice. Just bring attention to the breath, and each time the mind wanders away from it, just gently return to the present. Let any plans and memories be in the background. Perhaps the most important thing is that we do not have to stop the mind in order to meditate, just stop paying attention to it. What we are doing is training our awareness to pay attention to the breath and the body and to let the mind do its own thing in the background. By paying attention to the present-time physical experience, we will be able to expand our attention to even observe the mind itself without getting lost in the stories."

Here are the basic instructions for the meditation. Below the instructions are three additional instructions that can also used to help settle the mind.

Practice Meditation: Breath Awareness

Sitting with a straight back is especially important for this meditation, as you need to be able to breathe easily and freely. Hands are resting in the lap. Eyes are closed or lowered. Establish your posture and take a deep breath and let it go.

Now bring your attention to the rhythm of the breath and simply watch your natural breathing without trying to change it in any way. Let your breathing be normal and relaxed, your attention still and focused.

Let yourself rest in the rhythm of the breath. If you find you are getting distracted or caught up in thinking, simply label your thoughts as distraction or thinking and let them go, or see them as birds in the sky and let them fly away. Do this for at least ten minutes. Just breathing and being.

When you are ready, take a deep breath. Gently open your eyes.

Here are further instructions for this practice to enable you to focus more fully on the breath, rather than getting distracted or restless:

1.   *You can focus your attention on one of three places, whichever is most natural to you: either on your nose tip, watching the point where the breath actually enters and leaves; in the center of your chest, watching it rise and fall with each breath; or in the belly, about an inch below your navel, watching the belly rise and fall. Become familiar with all three places. If at any time you feel restless or caught up in your thinking, then bring your attention to the breath in the belly; conversely,*

if you are getting sleepy or soporific, then bring your attention to the breath at the nose tip.

2. *To help deepen your concentration, silently count at the end of each out-breath: breathe in, breathe out, one; breathe in, breathe out, two; continuing to count in this way up to ten, and then starting at one again. If you lose the count or go beyond ten, just start at one again. When you feel established in this rhythm, after five to ten minutes, you can change to counting at the beginning of each in-breath: one, breathe in, breathe out; two, breathe in, breathe out, and so on, up to ten as before. Changing your focus from the end to the beginning of the breath deepens your concentration. After a further five to ten minutes, if you feel your mind is quiet enough, you can drop the counting and just silently watch your breath.*

3. *Alternatively, with each in- and out-breath, you can silently repeat, "Breathing in, breathing out." This keeps your mind flowing with the breath.*

| ELLEN BURSTYN |

"Just follow the breath and count to ten. But it's a hard thing to get all the way to ten! When I first started doing it, I actually pictured the numbers. It gave me something to focus my visual image on. I just paid attention to my breath and pictured the numbers, got to ten and started over at one. It helped me because it is hard to get quiet without focusing, to get quiet and just breathe without having something to do with your imagery."

|||

Insight Meditation

From breath awareness, insight (or *vipassana*) meditation arises naturally. We rest in stillness, letting the mind be as it is, without any judgment or discrimination. All kinds of thoughts may arise, or feelings, sensations, and images. We watch, without pushing away or holding on. We are simply aware. In between the thoughts or sensations, natural wisdom or insight arises into the nature of our world and ourselves. In particular, we are able to see how all things arise through desire and dissatisfaction, how all things are impermanent and in a state of constant change, and how there is no fixed or solid separate self, simply a state of emptiness that contains all form.

OPEN HEART MEDITATION

| MIRABAI BUSH |

"When we get quiet and still, we are able to see things more clearly, especially how we are all interconnected. We do not stop at our skin; we are all a part of each other. When that happens, it is a letting go of those places that are holding our heart closed and so the heart softens and opens. There is absolutely no reason to keep our heart closed at all, ever."

The second category of meditation includes practices that open the heart by focusing on and developing qualities such as loving kindness, compassion, and forgiveness. As we practice, we go from *trying* to be compassionate or kind to *becoming* it, fully embodying it so that compassion and kindness become natural reflections of who we truly are.

| FRANKLYN SILLS |

"Sitting in stillness enables me to hold the conditions within me as a witness, so my mind settles into a place of listening and deepening, holding a wider perceptual field where things just arise and pass. But I do not sit in a narrow or highly concentrated way. Rather, in a soft and open way, where I am available to the conditions of suffering but they are not me. They are simply conditions. In listening, I hear the suffering of the world and am moved by compassion to act. From stillness, the heart naturally opens."

Loving Kindness

As we saw in chapter eight, loving kindness is a powerful and transformative practice. It awakens our awareness of and care for others while also recognizing there is no essential separation between us. The meditation practice leads us through different stages, from developing this quality toward ourselves and our loved ones, to people we may be having a hard time with, and finally to all beings. This follows the opening and expansion of our awareness from self-centeredness to other-centeredness.

Practice Meditation: Loving Kindness

Spend at least five minutes on each stage of this practice. Settle your body and relax. Then spend a few minutes focusing on the rhythm of your breath, while also bringing your attention to the heart space in the center of your chest.

1. *Now either repeat your name or visualize yourself in your heart so that you can feel your presence there. Hold yourself there, like a mother would hold a child, gently and tenderly. Release any tension on the out-breath and breathe in softness and openness with the in-breath.*

   Feel a growing sense of friendliness and love for yourself. Silently repeat: "May I be well, may I be happy, may all things go well for me, may I be peaceful." Be aware of any resistance—any reasons why you should not be well or are not worthy of being happy. Acknowledge these feelings and just let them go.

   "May I be well": Feel this in your body, especially where you are not well. "May I be happy": Bring in to your heart any unhappy feelings, and accept and love

them. *"May all things go well for me"*: Bring into your heart those places that are not going well and let the loving kindness transform and uplift them. *"May I be peaceful"*: Bring into your heart any stress and worry and transform them into peace.

2. Next, bring your loving kindness to your nearest and dearest—your family and friends. One by one, bring them into your heart as you visualize them or say their name. Direct your loving kindness to them as you repeat: *"May you be well, may you be happy, may all things go well for you, may you be peaceful."* Breathe out any conflicts or disagreements you may have, and breathe in happiness and joy. (If it is easier, you can do just one person each time you practice.)

3. Now, bring your loving kindness to someone you do not know or have no feelings for, a neutral person. Open your heart to this unknown person as you repeat: *"May you be well, may you be happy, may all things go well for you, may you be peaceful."* As you do this, feel how it is not the personality that you are loving, but the very essence of beingness, and this you share: Together, you walk the same earth, you breathe the same air.

4. Next, bring loving kindness toward someone you are having a hard time with: whether a friend, relative, or colleague—anyone where communication is not flowing and there are misunderstandings. Keep breathing out any resistance and breathing in openness as you hold this person in your heart and repeat: *"May you be well, may you be happy, may all things go well for you, may you be peaceful."* Do not get caught up in recalling the story or the details. Hold them gently and tenderly, wishing them wellness and happiness.

5. Now expand your loving kindness outward toward all beings, in all directions. Open your heart to all, whoever they may be, silently repeating: *"May all beings be well, may all beings be happy, may all things go*

well for all beings, may all beings be at peace." Let go of any prejudice or resistance. Feel as if kindness is radiating out from you in all directions, like the ripples on a pond. Breathe out loving kindness, breathe in loving kindness. All beings are worthy of being loved, whoever they are.

When you are ready, take a deep breath and gently open your eyes, with a smile on your lips.

Loving Ourselves

There are variations to this practice that can be used to address specific issues. Below is a practice, offered by psychotherapist Deepesh Faucheux, to heal our more negative issues, such as anger, failure, or self-dislike, as discussed in chapter five.

Practice Meditation:
Loving All Parts of Yourself

| FROM DEEPESH FAUCHEUX |

I invite you to get very comfortable, close or defocus your eyes, and let your awareness come to rest in your body . . . feel your feet on the floor . . . feel your weight in the chair or on the cushion . . . you are neither in the past nor in the future . . . you are simply right here and now . . . there is no place else you have to go, nowhere else to be but simply right here.

And from this place of being completely in the present, take a look at whatever thoughts, feelings, or sensations are present for you. . . .

Simply observe . . . no need to analyze or judge . . . just look . . . just feel. . . .

And gently welcome all of the parts of you . . .

the "good" parts you like . . . the parts you call "me" . . .

the parts you reject . . . the angry part . . . the ugly part . . .
the scared part . . . the bored part . . . the sad part . . .
the hard heart . . . the broken heart. . . .
All of them are welcome here.
And as you look at whatever is present for you, see it as a
big house full of guests . . .
some rowdy . . . some peaceful . . . some ridiculous. . . .
Just look . . . simply inquisitive. . . .
From this place, see if you can invoke a loving attitude . . .
so you are not only accepting all the parts but are also in
loving presence with them . . .
feel your heart . . . allow your heart to stay open.
And from this place, offer yourself a simple prayer:
> *May all of the parts of me be one,*
> *may I be well, in body, mind, and spirit,*
> *may I be at peace.*
(Repeat the prayer three times.)
And from this place of loving presence for the self, notice
what comes up when you say, "It is okay to be happy . . . to
love myself . . . to forgive myself."
Sit with whatever arises for you and simply notice it.
Embrace the "yeses" as well as the "nos."
When you feel ready, notice the weight of your body, sensa-
tions in your feet and hands, and slowly open your eyes.

Forgiveness Meditation

In chapter seven, we discussed the vital role of forgiveness in a
world that encourages revenge. This is a powerful meditation
that releases feelings of separation, guilt, blame, and shame.
It takes us through three vital stages, from forgiving another,
to asking for forgiveness, and then to forgiving ourselves. We
invite you to move into it gently, perhaps just doing one step in
each session, to avoid repressing any feelings. It is important
to acknowledge whatever arises. Forgiveness can take time, so

be patient; your experience will deepen the more you practice this meditation.

Practice Meditation: Forgiveness

Spend five to ten minutes on each stage of this practice. Find a comfortable place to sit, and settle your attention on your breathing. Feel your heart opening and softening.

Gently become aware of any resistance to forgiveness. Do not shy away from this, but see the effect this resistance may be having in you, and how it limits and restricts your feelings. Keep breathing, letting the breath open and soften your heart.

1. *Now focus on one person you wish to forgive and bring that person into your heart. Breathe out any resistance, anger, or fear, and breathe in forgiveness and gentleness. Silently repeat: "I forgive you. For the harm and pain you have caused, through your words and your actions, I forgive you." Let your breath relax you. Be gentle with yourself. Do not get side-tracked by the story or the details of what happened. Let go of all the reasons why this person should not be forgiven, and breathe in forgiveness.*

2. *Now visualize in your heart someone you may have hurt or upset. Silently repeat: "I ask for your forgiveness. I ask for your forgiveness. For the hurt or pain I may have caused you, through my words or my actions, please forgive me." Keep breathing out any resistance. You can put down the story and let go of the pain. Feel your heart opening to receiving forgiveness.*

3. *Now focus on yourself, repeating your name or visualizing yourself in your heart. Hold yourself with care and tenderness. Slowly repeat, "I forgive myself, I forgive myself. For any harm or pain I may have caused, whether*

*through my words or my actions, I forgive myself." As
you do this, you may be confronted with shame or guilt,
or how you have betrayed yourself. Acknowledge this
and then let it go with each out-breath. Keep breathing
in softness, inviting forgiveness. "I forgive myself, I forgive myself."*

*Feel the joy of forgiveness throughout your whole being. You
have forgiven. You are forgiven. Rejoice in the release. When
you are ready, take a deep breath and slowly let it go.*

Meditation, Anywhere, Anytime

Practice does not have to be done in the right posture, at the
right time, or in the perfect environment. In reality, it can be
done anytime and anywhere—including the bathroom, a bus
stop, the train, a park bench, sitting at your office desk, while
the kids are playing. Everywhere is sacred if you think of it as
such. If the bathroom or toilet is the only place where you can
be alone, then do not hesitate. Just lock the door, sit on the
seat, and breathe!

| ED BEGLEY, JR. |

"A mini meditation happened recently when I was in the line at the DMV,
the Department of Motor Vehicles. I didn't bring a book, I didn't have an
iPod or a walkman, no crosswords, nothing, and then I realized this is a
gift! I am in line at the DMV, and so I have this opportunity to breathe in
and breathe out. I am standing in line meditating, and it is no longer about
getting to the end of the line, as it is just happening right now; I am eight
people back in the line and this is where it is. We can get a full meal when
we sit and practice more formal forms of mediation, but then there are
snacks available that we can get in line at the DMV."

|||

Practice Meditation:
As a Last Resort!

Anytime you feel stress rising, heart closing, mind going into overwhelm, just find a place to be quiet, focus on your breathing for ten breaths or until you feel at ease again. As you do this, you can practice one of the following:

1. *Repeat: "Soft belly, open heart" with each in- and out-breath.*
2. *Repeat: "Breathing in, I calm the body and mind; breathing out, I smile."*
3. *Breathing in, repeat: "I am easeful and peaceful"; breathing out, repeat: "I am love."*

Practice Meditation:
Daily Check-In

| FROM MARSHALL ROSENBERG |

We can build into our lives two forms of meditation.

First, at the beginning of the day, is remembering how we choose to live this day, how we want to be, bringing us back to the preciousness of compassionate giving and receiving.

Then, toward the end of the day, we can evaluate that day, seeing whether our behavior nurtured life or not. We do that without self-blame.

Then we can mourn what was not nurturing, or when we have not engaged in compassionate giving and receiving, so we can learn from it, and we can celebrate when we are living in harmony with the life we choose to live.

|||

17

|||

Sounding Meditation

Music without words means leaving behind the mind. And leaving behind the mind is meditation. Meditation returns you to the source. And the source of all is sound.

KABIR

| ED |

"I would sit cross-legged in the ashram in central India and chant the names of Rama and Krishna. This is called the *mahamantra,* or great sacred sound, known in the West as the Hare Krishna mantra. Intoning and repeating the names of the different deities in this way is meant to awaken the divine within and free us from the world of delusion. Chanting in India is very emotional and people are often moved to dance in wild ecstasy. I loved this moment, such a surrendering of the ego-me into the vastness of divinity."

|||

The Healing Power of Sound

Sound has been used throughout the ages and in many spiritual traditions as an expression of devotion, as well as a means of creating harmony and focusing the mind. Unifying our voices creates a powerful form of meditation as it takes us out of the habitual mind and into a place of deep resonance, both within ourselves and with each other. But this unity can easily be lost if the thinking mind intrudes.

| JILL PURCE |

"We have always created community through chanting, such as with church singing to unify with each other and God. When we chant or tune together, we quickly become one, as all the emotions created by separation are eliminated. When we sing words that we understand, however, we are no longer present because we are thinking about what we are singing or we are anxiously trying to remember the words. In the 1950s and 1960s, when the Catholic Church translated the Latin chants into vernacular languages, immediately the ancient Christian tradition of perpetual, contemplative chant became just another stimulus for thought, and thus another source of concern, worry, and anxiety, instead of the aid to liberation and contemplation it had always been."

This changing of Gregorian chant from Latin to local dialects created a previously unknown discord and discontent among Catholic communities as was personally experienced by Deepesh Faucheux during his time as a Catholic monk.

| DEEPESH FAUCHEUX |

"Gregorian chanting was designed to be a meditation; research shows that the Gregorian frequency works on the brain in a particular way to elevate us to a spiritually altered state. When we chanted, I would get very high, even transported. It was always a collective chant done together— what is called *ecclesia*. A group of people with a single purpose of worship attuned together, their behavior, sensibilities, and moods all harmonized. The frequency of the sound integrated the behavior of the chanters, and it smoothed out the rough edges, the anger or fear. When I sang Gregorian, it was like Prozac. It elevated my mood. It made many of the petty things that happened seem just totally unimportant. It actually made life in the monastery bearable, sometimes even blissful, and was the only therapy the monastery needed. Gregorian chant was written for the Latin language, but when they stopped chanting in Latin and tried to do it in the local dialect, many of the monasteries and convents fell apart because the people started fighting with each other. They had lost that shared integrative quality."

Whether through singing or chanting, shared sound blends not just our voices but also our vibrations, which promotes healing on many levels. At the same time, the hormone oxytocin is released during singing, increasing the "feel-good factor." This hormone is best known for its role in inducing labor, but it also appears to influence our ability to bond with others and maintain close relationships. Sounding together loosens the barriers of separation, which allows for a healing of both cells and souls.

| JONATHAN GOLDMAN |

"I have a formula, which is frequency plus intent equals healing: That sound coupled with consciousness creates the outcome of the sound. The mystics and physicists have always known that everything in the universe is in a state of vibration. Therefore, every bone, every tissue, every part of the body is in resonance. This includes our brain waves, breath, and heartbeat, and by attuning together to a particular sound, whether it is an *om,* an *aah,* a vowel sound, or a mantra, our nervous systems attune, resonate, and entrain with each other."

To heal does not necessarily mean to fix a particular part, but it does mean to become whole, where all the different parts of both our psyche and body are brought together in resonance. The health of our mind directly affects our physical health, as unresolved or repressed psychological and emotional issues are often at the root of stress and illness. True healing, therefore, has to start with the mind in order to bring balance and harmony to the body. Sounding is an immediate and effective way to bring healing to the mind.

| JILL PURCE |

"Working to overcome the delusion of separation is the great call of meditation practice. Because separation gives rise to anger, dislike and aversion, desire, greed, and lust, these inevitably insatiable emotions are the cause of anxiety, depression, and the majority of illnesses. Sound affects both the mind and the body through resonance and the introduction of order and coherence. It allows us to work with the cause of emotional and energetic disturbances before they become pathological or affect the physical body.

"The only way we can change is through overcoming the sense of separation. The only way I have found to do this is through meditation and the attention of presence, and there is no question that the most powerful way of meditating is through sound. As we activate ourselves through sound and resonance, we are also providing the very thing that we are using as the means of attention: When we make sound, we are creating that which is the focus of our attention, we are creating a 'circuit of attention.' By creating that which we are attending to and then attending to that which we are creating, we are perpetually in the present, which is the only reality there is. And we attend to it not just with the presence of our awareness, but with our hearing too, because the more of the senses we engage in our attention, the more powerfully present we are."

|||

Making Sound

To benefit from the meditative quality of sound does not mean we have to have a perfect voice or even be able to sing in tune, for often the singing or chanting itself will release a purer tone.

| DEB |

"I was thirteen and in singing class at school. Suddenly, the music teacher told us to stop; he looked around the room and then pointed at me. 'You,' he said, 'will never sing in tune!' That moment inhibited me for years; I was terrified of singing in earshot of anyone else. Until I started to chant, when I found a voice that was hidden inside, which was my heart singing."

There are many ways of making sound and using the voice to discover our inner world. Through the voice and the breath together we can enter into a spontaneous experience of resonance as we release sound from a deeper part of our being.

| CHLOE GOODCHILD |

"The human voice itself, the naked human voice, is a way of accessing inner spaciousness. If we take just one big breath in and let out an almighty unobstructed cry, and keep crying out until we get to the very end of that breath, then at the moment we are literally empty of breath, we will find ourselves in a place where we are on the edge between living and dying. The human voice is a fantastic bridge into a deep state of meditation because it harnesses the emotions and allows a release in a very simple way. It takes us out of the mind and opens the heart, and then we are laughing, crying, and breathing in again, we are coming home again more deeply, falling more and more deeply inside ourselves, letting go and breathing again. Imagine this is the very first or very last breath of our life. In that imagining, we are suddenly at a kind of turning point, on the threshold of a new cycle, we are in unknown territory.

"We have practiced this with people who are dying, with those who are terminally ill, or with ordinary neurotics like ourselves who just want to find a simple, effortless, and accessible way to empty out. It immediately takes us out of the mind and into the emotions, and then it opens the heart, and then before we know where we are we are falling deeply into our own being, surrendering and releasing. We encourage people to do this over a period of time, maybe half an hour, but it could just be five minutes or even just one minute. It brings us up against ourselves in a way that can be both startling and delightful."

Sounding not only enables us to meet and greet ourselves, but it does this by creating an outlet for any distracting inner noise to be released: All our fears and neuroses, excuses and doubts. Making spontaneous free-flowing sound is, therefore, a wonderful precursor to silent meditation as we can sound out any resistance or tension before sinking into the silence.

| VICKIE DODD |

"I use sound to quiet my mind, to quiet the chatter, so that I can go deep enough to listen. I use it with people who have never meditated or who thought they could not. When we sound, then oxygen starts moving and changing the biological system to relieve stress and emotional burdens. Sounding makes the body become more liquid and dissolves thoughts like I can't do this; I'll never know how to do this; I'm tired; what time is it? I'm hungry; I need to go; and I'm uncomfortable. We can sound those thoughts; we can sound unpredictable, chaotic, politically incorrect thoughts. All the different characters inside of us need a voice. Then they can settle down—they have been heard. Anything that is hungry keeps gnawing at us; it is going to get our attention one way or another, so we give it some air. We do all kinds of spontaneous and unpredictable random, chaotic sounding; then we lie down and start breathing. This way, a lot of baggage is released and there might be a moment of nectar that makes it all worthwhile."

|||

Sound and Silence in Meditation

Whereas in silent meditation the mind is free to wander and be distracted, using sound as the focus of meditation creates a deeper experience of silence, as also happens when we do yoga or walking meditation followed by just stopping and being still.

| DON CAMPBELL |

"I spent many years using sound and particularly toning as a vessel for my entry into meditation. I would calm the body, and steady and empty my mind by making a sound that allowed the bones of my cranial sphere to vibrate. Many times, the tonal aspect of a simple hum for five minutes creates a physiological, mental, and emotional place that I call *awakened relaxation.* I was not singing; it was not beautiful; it was not for the outer world. Whether it is chanting a mantra, sutra, or psalms, or singing can-ticles, it is not about what anyone else hears; it is about what you feel completely within your body—how the brain balances, how your pulse changes, how you oxygenate and take deeper breaths, and most especially, it is what happens in the silence that follows."

Although there are many forms of sound that can be used, from the single "ah" sound to more traditional chanting, humming is, without doubt, one of the simplest and most direct sound experiences that we can all participate in.

| DEVA PREMAL AND MITEN |

"Humming is a really easy thing that anyone can do. You do not have to be able to sing, or to know any mantras; you just hum with closed lips. You take a deep breath so that you really are filling your whole lungs, then you hum to the end of your breath, and then you take another deep breath and you hum. If you do that for five minutes, and then you sit in silence for five minutes, you have an experience that is going to be felt during the whole day that follows, because the sound of humming synchronizes the spirit with the body. It is a meditation to unify yourself, to make yourself one. It brings you into a silent space very easily. It is something anyone can do for ten minutes each morning: five minutes humming, five minutes sitting silently."

Sounding does not always imply making a vocal sound; we can be as deeply moved through playing and making music, whether it be a meditative instrument, such as a flute or piano, or one more usually associated with rhythm, such as drums.

| KITARO |

"I love the silence. But for me it is the silence in music. What is music and what is silence? Both are meditation. Sounds are wave and this is meditation, and the silence of meditation is filled with sounds. Drumming is also meditation. Every August full moon at Mount Fuji, I drum all night long for twelve hours, and this is a very deep meditation. The drumming becomes a wave of movement through me; it gives me deep inspiration and strength. The concentration combined with the rhythm means my mind goes in and out, it is changing all the time, sometimes I close my eyes and even in a concert, I am far away. Sometimes a second Kitaro is watching the whole scene, like a third eye. This second Kitaro is watching me as I play my music. When I drum, this Kitaro is the truth and the second Kitaro is watching. In silent meditation, I go into myself more. Sound goes out, and silence goes in."

Making sound also confronts us with our ego, and with our desire to be identified as the singer or chanter, rather than surrendering the ego by becoming one with the sound. In surrendering, we are moved beyond the music, the mere repetition of words, or the intoning of chants to a place of emptiness that is filled with vibration.

| JONATHAN GOLDMAN |

"One of the extraordinary things about making sound is that sound bypasses the rational and goes into the limbic aspect of the brain. So whether we are toning or chanting, we become focused in the present moment; that is all there is. How do we become the sound? By clearing out the ego. Otherwise, we may be making the sound, but we are not one with it."

|||

Listening to Silence

Making a sound or creating music is not all we can do to deepen our meditation; we can also listen. This is not the same as hearing, but is more receptive, as we are receiving the sound into our being. Through listening, we are able to experience the sound of silence itself.

| DON CAMPBELL |

"Meditation occurs in a place of listening after a sound discovery, where the sound and the listening to the sound become a bridge into openness. Whether we are in a hospital bed or a church or a synagogue, whether we are alone or under stress, whether we are in a city or in nature, we can listen. Listening is not to hear. Hearing is just a vessel, whereas listening has a focus to it. The big news is what is going on after the sound has finished. Give yourself a meditation exercise over a month: Each week, go to a different sound experience, like folk singing, a symphony, a jazz bar, a choir, or some place where there is music. Only spend an hour; don't overwhelm. And listen. When you come out of that event, find a place to sit and meditate and notice what is going on. It is the extra value after the experience."

|||

Practice Meditation: Listening to the Inner Voice

| FROM RABBI TIRZAH FIRESTONE |

"One really good way to meditate is the shema, which means 'to listen' in Hebrew. It is the central prayer in Judaism: 'I hear you God.' It is a proclamation of oneness. So I might say to repeat the shema. *But as* shema *means 'listen,' then first say the prayer and then just be quiet and listen. Be quiet for five minutes. After you say the prayer, just listen to what the still small voice is saying to you right now. And then go on with your day."*

|||

Chanting Sacred Sounds: Mantra Meditation

| KRISHNA DAS |

"Repetition of the divine name changes us. It is like sending a seed out in the wind. The seed lands on a roof and slowly, over the years as the seasons change, the shingles of the roof begin to break down and the seed takes root. The plant grows and soon destroys the roof and then the whole house. That house is like our conventional self, the self we think we are, and the walls and the roof of the house create this false sense of who we are. Through chanting the names of the divine, that false image of ourselves is destroyed; we are no longer who we think we are. There is just vast space with no illusion of separateness."

A mantra is a sacred sound, a series of sounds, or a phrase that, when repeated either silently or out loud, brings us to a place of stillness and calm and opens the heart to an outpouring of joy. Mantras are traditionally chanted in Latin or Sanskrit language and usually consist of a repetition of the names of the divine, as this has the effect of taking us out of our normal, thinking mind and into an open and clear space that holds us in the present moment.

| JILL PURCE |

"The beauty of chanting mantras is they are sounds that have no discursive meaning, even if the individual words themselves can be translated. Mantras trick the mind into assuming it is entering into the familiar territory of language and concepts, which allow us to feel safe in the world of objects and perceptions, but instead leads us into presence, into the nature of mind itself. Words lull us into thinking we are in our normal landscape. Mantras are not words in that sense at all, however, and so they provide a way of allowing us to go beyond language, time, and thought, into the nature of mind itself."

The use of a mantra is common to all religions and spiritual traditions. Sanskrit mantras or sacred sounds were experienced by the sadhus, or "holy ones," while they were in deep meditation and taught their disciples. A mantra may be the name of a spiritual being, such as Mother Mary, Jesus, Hare Krishna, or Namo Buddha. Or it may be a word or phrase that has special meaning, such as "Be at peace." In both Buddhism and Hinduism, *Om* is a favorite sound, as it means "the sound of the universe": *Om Shanti* is "peace," *Om Mani Padme Hum* means "the jewel in the heart of the lotus" or "the awakened mind," and *Om Namah Shivaya* is homage to Shiva, the destroyer who dispels negativity.

A mantra has a soothing and healing effect on the mind, as well as lifting us to greater levels of awareness. For instance, the recitation of the name of Krishna is said to take us out of the material world and into the joy and salvation of Krishna Loka, "the land of milk and honey." In mantra meditation, we can use any of these sounds, such as repeating *Om* as we breathe in and *Shanti* as we breathe out, or a word or short phrase that has a special heartfelt or sacred meaning to us. Keep it simple and easy to repeat. Treat it like a friend that we keep close to us.

| RAM DASS |

"Each person can use the mantra 'I am loving awareness.' Just repeat this and become loving awareness. Then we share that loving awareness with all others."

Repetition is considered the most direct way to calm the mind. For a busy mind, it encourages one-pointed awareness, and for a sleepy mind, it gives us something to focus on; by repeating the mantra, we can let go of any need for external entertainment. In this way, the mind is released from its habitual or agitated thinking patterns, and in the process, we become absorbed and anchored in the sound, discovering the stillness within. Past and future dissolve. It is like a broom that sweeps our mind free of clutter.

We can repeat the mantra silently or out loud, either during our meditation session or at any time during the day. Deb loves chanting quietly to herself as she is shopping in the supermarket; it stops her buying stuff she doesn't need! It can be very helpful if we need to stay clear and balanced; if we are in a difficult situation, then we can just silently repeat the mantra. Mantra meditation is like spiritual food; it awakens our creative process, nourishes our spirit, and opens our heart—what more could we want?

Practice Meditation: Mantra

To practice mantra meditation, sit comfortably with your back straight. Take a few deep breaths and relax and settle your body. Then begin to repeat the mantra, either silently or intoning it out loud if you are alone. Repeat it in rhythm with your breathing.

Use the mantra as an anchor to keep the mind focused and quiet. Whenever you get distracted or drift off into thinking, just bring your mind back to the sound.

You can also use a rosary or mala—a string of 108 beads— as a way of keeping your mind focused. With each repetition of the mantra, move one bead. If you know how long it takes to do one round of the mala, then you can do as many rounds as you wish for your meditation session and you will not need to time yourself with a clock.

|||

18

|||

Moving Meditation

*Each step we take creates a cool breeze, refreshing our body
and mind. Every step makes a flower bloom under our feet.*
THICH NHAT HANH

Alistair was having a hard time sitting. We were leading a meditation retreat in Ireland, and Alistair's posture was askew; he would start out sitting upright but within five minutes would be bent over. Every so often, we would quietly say, "Straighten your back," and he would try, but it did not last long. However, when we interspersed sitting with walking meditation, he was in his element. At the end of the five days, we asked how everyone had done and if there was anything they would like to share. Alistair simply said, "Thank you for introducing me to my feet."

Although meditation may be an experience of conscious oneness, of merging into a greater whole and dissolving boundaries, it is not a matter of either ignoring or forgetting the body. There are many stories of ascetics denying their physical needs in an attempt to purify their bodies and minds, and the Buddha himself also practiced such austerity before he realized that spiritual awakening was not separate from his physical self. Rather, within the body, is everything we have ever experienced, like an airplane's black box, and we can use that knowledge to inform our present reality. By bringing greater awareness to the body as the ground of our being that connects us to all life, we discover an infinite source of information and insight. We sit, sing, or walk our meditation practice in the body; through it, we experience every sensation and feeling and embody our awareness in the relative world.

| REGGIE RAY |

"Meditation is a way to become a full human being, a mature human being, a person who is in possession of themselves and experiences this world in a complete way. When you bring awareness into your body, you enter into a realm of mystery and openness around feeling and sensation. In effect, you turn off the thinking function, and the body itself begins to guide you in your life. Insights arise, but also new ways of feeling and experiencing the world, and that is really what it means to grow as a human being."

Mindfulness is more than just being aware of our thoughts and feelings or how we relate to others; it also applies to the body and our movements, such as walking or even how we pick up a cup of tea. Do we reach out and grab the cup, or do we pick it up with respect? Eating is a physical action that we are usually unaware of as we are so often distracted by conversation or watching television. Eating silently and with awareness, as practiced on meditation retreats, extends our mindfulness into our everyday world. In the same way, different moving meditations awaken awareness of our physical presence so that we inhabit our body and actions with greater consciousness.

| LINDSAY WAGNER |

"To me, meditation is surrendering myself—or the self that I think I am—to the inherent connectedness to the source of all of creation. It isn't restricted to just the quiet times. It is my goal to be very still when I am still, and not to lose touch with that connectedness when I am moving. It constantly reminds me and strengthens my awareness of that connectedness."

Movement and emotion arise from the same Latin root: *emovere*. To be emotionally moved by something is to be physically affected by it. If we are sad or depressed, then our movements will be heavy and slow; if we are angry, they become jerky and dramatic. Moving the body beyond its habitual limitations loosens energy on both the physical and psycho/emotional levels. In other words, releasing tensions in the body also releases them in the mind.

Feelings and memories get locked in the joints, muscles, and ligaments, often from as far back as childhood. The joints enable us to move with grace and fluidity; they also join up our thoughts and feeling with our actions. If that connection is restricted or blocked, then the energy cannot flow freely and there is a lack of emotional ease. So through moving the body, greater freedom comes to the mind. In this way, the body becomes our teacher.

| TAMI SIMON |

"For me, it is easier and more effective if I work through my body—I can unravel things pretty deep and quick. I breathe right into those tight places and ask them to show me what they are holding; I see the images and hear the story that comes into awareness. Our body is the smartest teacher we have, and it wants us to reclaim our open-heartedness and connection to the earth and the things that really matter. If we listen to our body, it is asking us to enter a natural meditation, it tells us to lie down when we are tired, it tells us when we need to stop, to slow down. Moving meditation is the ideal way of slowing us down enough so our body can speak to us."

Moving meditation is found in such practices as hatha yoga, tai chi, or qigong, or in walking, running, dancing, and even firewalking. For instance, during long periods of sitting meditation, such as on a retreat, the periods of sitting are always combined with periods of walking meditation as a way to not only move and stretch the body but also to experience extending the meditation into the rest of life. As with using sound, through movement we are giving the mind something to do so that it can become still. The challenge here is that our eyes are open and there can, therefore, be greater distraction. But as we surrender to the movement so the boundaries between stillness and movement dissolve.

Yoga

The word *yoga* literally means "yoke," or "that which unites." It is the uniting of the body, mind, and spirit, encouraging a full experience of the intricate relationship between the mind and body, and how to bring this relationship into balance and harmony. Developed thousands of years ago, yoga has many different aspects: ethics, discipline, relaxation, meditation, devotion, and knowledge, as well as movement.

Hatha yoga, a system of physical movements, is the form of yoga practiced the most in the West. Hatha uses different postures, or asanas, to stretch, invigorate, balance, and tone the body. As the body finds greater equilibrium and harmony, so does the mind. The word *asana* means "seat" and implies that the movement prepares us to be able to sit for meditation.

| RICHARD FREEMAN |

"My initial impression of yoga was that I would just do a few asanas, a few postures, to kind of un-stress all of my nerves and then I would just sit down and go into deep meditation. If only it were so simple! My appreciation of this practice has grown over the years. I still see it as dissolving back into meditation and awareness, but it is also a way of taking the refined insight gained in meditation out through my nervous system and into the things that my nervous system connects to in the world. It helps me find and face the little knots or misunderstandings in my own perception or the denials that happened years ago in my childhood that stop me from experiencing things fully."

Although some forms of hatha yoga are nowadays taught in an energetic fashion, traditionally it was done slowly, with awareness. Ed trained in India, where he was taught hatha as a meditative flow. The system of asanas was developed so that each posture relates to a different attitude, which is expressed both physically and mentally. The movement makes the spine more supple, releases tension, and brings the mind inward. The effect develops over a period of time, subtly changing the way we move and walk, as well as the way we think, feel, and behave. It is ideally suited to relieving stress, and indeed it is taught in many stress-reduction clinics. But it is especially important in helping us to recognize our limitations and to go beyond them. Without pushing or straining, we breathe and move through our resistance in a posture, simultaneously watching the mind going beyond its own restrictions.

| RICHARD FREEMAN |

"Yoga is almost a way of looking for trouble. You may be feeling pretty good, but then you start doing postures and all of a sudden you discover there is a holding pattern that goes way deeper into your very being. You have to breathe into it and observe it as it is. The postures and the breathing, or *pranayama*, are like a fine toothcomb that take out all the buried stuff you don't need anymore. If you had just sat in meditation, you may not have found that pattern as it arises through the movement."

As each different posture stretches the mind as well as the body, we gradually find ourselves moving into a different position where our reference points have shifted and both mind and body have opened to a new understanding. This becomes a meditation in movement, and also deepens our sitting meditation experience.

| KALI RAY |

"When we begin to apply the real principles of yoga, it is a relaxation in action. There is an 'economy of movement' as we only move what we need to and every movement counts. We use the body as a tool for concentration and focus. Being aware of the movement in every posture shows us how to be aware of every movement or action in life. The body is like an instrument used by a musician, a play between the breath and the posture in a steady rhythm. We start to feel this rhythm in life as a rich, meditative flow. There are many different principles of this flow, but they are all aiming to become more aware, and this greater awareness is meditation. The intention is to experience the meditative flow through the body, breath, and mind in harmony, so that in the rest of our life we are at ease and the mind is calm. Then, when we come to sitting meditation, we are ready to look at our mind, to see what emotions, feelings, and thoughts are there and to discover their true nature. If we continue with our lives without having any connection between what we do in meditation and what we do in life, then we will not see much change."

In this way, yoga enters into every aspect of our lives and becomes a living meditation finding expression through the body. As the body opens, we open. As the body flows, our own resistances release and relax into that flow.

| CYNDI LEE |

"I teach the *vinyasa* form of yoga, traditionally defined as 'things going in a logical sequence.' There are three parts to this: rising, abiding, and dissolving. The dissolving of one thing is the arising of the next . . . we inhale and exhale: That is a vinyasa. Every day and night is a vinyasa; every life is a vinyasa; every ebb and flow of the tides is a vinyasa. We can observe the same flow with any kind of feeling—it arises, it dissolves. It's like a Hallmark card: 'One door closes and another one opens.' At the end of the day, it is not about how long we can sit on our mat or whether we can wrap our legs around our neck; it is how much we can open to ourselves and other people."

|||

Walking

Walking meditation is usually practiced by alternating it with sitting meditation, as it brings the mind and body into a unified whole. This is particularly the case during longer sessions of sitting.

| DEB |

"We are on a retreat in Thailand. Watching the flow of the in- and out-breath, I walk, lifting, moving, and placing. Breathing and walking. Breathing and walking. From one coconut tree to the next, then back again, the ground between is soft. Eyes downcast, I place my bare feet carefully, mindful of the black ants, spiders, and beetles. Around me I am vaguely aware of others doing the same, breathing and walking, each in their own spaciousness."

Walking meditation is not the same as going for a walk through the woods or by the beach, lovely as that may be, but is a more focused, deliberate, and conscious walk. The eyes are open but lowered just to the ground in front so that the mind does not drift or get distracted. Entering into the rhythmic movement of walking meditation, of just placing one foot in front of the other, allows the mind to find a natural stillness.

| MAURA SILLS |

"Walking meditation is probably more effective for me than most other meditations, as the thinking mind starts to drop away when I come into body and feeling, it slows me down. It also softens that sense of me, I, and myself. I start to pay attention to movement in relationship, to make contact with the earth, to feel my body in space; I pay attention to the conditions in my body, to the air. It is about relationship. You cannot go walking with your eyes closed; you have to have some sense of external awareness as well as inner awareness. The relationship of the two is essential."

Silent walking meditation has been used in many places around the world as a means of peacefully demanding an end to violence, and also as a way of contrasting the busyness of life, as seen in PDMs.

| MAX SIMON |

"We do something called a PDM, which is a public display of meditation. We get groups of young people together, and we walk in single file, in silence, and sit in silence in public places. One time we did this was in front of Louis Vuitton, the designer clothes store on Rodeo Drive in Beverly Hills. We had thirty-five young people walking until we were in front of the shop, standing still shoulder to shoulder. When I said PDM, everyone dropped down on the street and settled into mediation for fifteen minutes. Then at the signal everyone got up and we walked to the next spot and did it again.

"We do it that precisely so that the participants can see how they show up and how they are really able to step into a place of power when they are centered. Afterward, we debrief. Many say how amazed they were to get quiet, sometimes for the first time, even with cars whipping by at sixty miles an hour. Some people say that they feel more comfortable in their own skin because to deal with the distractions—at one point, we had paparazzi snapping photos of us, and people walking by asking us what we were doing—we had to come into a centered space that enabled the external distractions to melt away."

|||

Practice Meditation: Walking

This can be done for anything from ten to thirty minutes. Traditionally, it follows a sitting meditation practice, but many people enjoy it so much that they practice it at any time. It can be done outside or inside, wearing shoes or barefoot. It can be done continuously, or in a space of maybe thirty to fifty steps with a marker at each end that you walk between. This eliminates any concern about where you are going and decreases distraction.

Walking meditation is a practice of balancing the outer world with your inner world, with your feet as the bridge between the two. As your mind becomes quieter and there is just walking, with nothing else going on, then you will find yourself merging into the rhythm, feeling each small movement and the effect it has on your whole body.

Stand upright with your hands held together lightly in the front so that your arms stay relaxed without causing tension in the shoulders. Your eyes should be lowered, but not your head, so you can see the ground in front while not being distracted by anything going on around you and without getting a stiff neck.

Begin to walk, bringing your awareness to the movement. As you walk silently, repeat, lifting . . . placing, with each step. You can move slowly or a little faster if you need energizing. Stay mindful and aware, keeping shoulders and neck relaxed, your movement flowing and your breathing natural.

Become aware of the meeting point of your shoes or skin with the ground: Notice the bumps and dips, the texture and quality of the ground. Lifting . . . placing.

Be aware of the relationship between yourself and the world you are moving in. If you turn around, then stop for a moment first and notice the difference between moving and stillness. Walk . . . stop . . . turn . . . stop . . . and walk again. Lifting . . . placing.

At the end of the walking, close your eyes and stand completely still for a few moments, watching your breath and feeling the sensations in your body. Experience the stillness. Then open your eyes and enjoy your day!

Firewalking

We were teaching in Sweden at a large summer gathering. At the end of the week was a firewalk, a walk over red-hot embers, led by Peggy Dylan. Although the experience was new to us, it was immediately clear the quality of meditation such a mind-opening experience demands, as it takes us far beyond our self-imposed limitations and fears into a vast spaciousness that the ordinary mind can barely comprehend.

| PEGGY DYLAN |

"In its purest form, meditation is the transcendence of our belief structures about reality, while experiencing the underlying force of the infinite that flows through everything. The only place to firewalk from, the only place to step onto the coals from, is the moment of touching that infinite place. Even though we cannot consciously comprehend what we are doing, when we step onto the fire our bodies are in a state of connection with all that is; we are touching the same place we go to in meditation, the place of stepping into the unknown.

"People have walked on fire for thousands of years in many different ceremonies, and the purpose has always been to use the walk as a prayer, or as a way of transcending whatever is ill to create greater well-being, which is also the purpose of meditation. It is used to gather power and energy, to gather a sense of capacity that comes when we transcend our human restrictions, as we step through the barrier of fear before we take that first step onto the coals. We have no idea what is going to happen when we walk on fire. But there is also no way to know what is going to be happening in five years or even five minutes. What we can know, and what the firewalk teaches us, is that when we step forward in trust, faith, and courage, then there is a benevolent aspect of the universe that steps with us. This is precisely the same thing that happens in meditation.

"In that place of trust, no matter how challenging the world looks or how challenging our personal lives may be, we can just feel the fear. I will take a group of four hundred and collectively we drop into that fear. We acknowledge the fear, acknowledge the sense of failure, the sense of 'I can't,' 'I won't,' and 'I've always failed in the past.' And then we transcend it into hope, capacity, and a positive form of movement.

"One of the beauties of firewalking is that you cannot pretend those are not hot coals; you stand in front of the fire and it is real. Your delicate feet are real feet. You are stepping through fear and knowing in your body that what you think will happen does not have to happen. In other words, there can be exquisite positive outcomes from events that you previously thought would have a negative consequence. This is indelibly printed on the subconscious. 'I can do remarkable things, I can step through fear and manifest beauty, manifest joy, manifest healing, and it is in the body.'"

|||

Running

Exercise of any form has the potential to bring the mind into the body and, in so doing, to create an inner quiet. Deb experiences this when she swims. For her, it is a wonderful meditation; the quiet of the water, the movement of her body, her mind is completely still. Running is another form of exercise that can be experienced as a meditation.

| SAKYONG MIPHAM |

"The truest form of meditation is sitting, because your body is in a natural balance between being awake and being very still. When you are doing running or moving meditation, the mind has to become very precise in order to fully embody the movement. When I am long-distance running, my meditation is a combination of the movement of the legs, the feet, the breathing, the sense of being centered, and the immediacy of the situation. Some people listen to music while they run, but I am very focused on being present. When you are present with the pain, or whatever is going on, then there is a fullness of the whole experience. You are very alive in that process, as opposed to non-meditation running, where you just put your mind somewhere else and let the body go along.

"Meditation as a way of strengthening, focusing, and enlightening the mind is only one of the steps. The next step after sitting is meditation in action, so that you embody the practice. This is more challenging as you have more activity going on at the same time as stillness. You have more chance to not be mindful or focused. Often we are very caught in the past or the future; we are daydreaming or planning. When you bring your mind back and draw it into the center of your heart, you become more synchronized and awake to your immediate environment. When running and entering 'the zone,' you are completely synchronized and the mind opens. Time becomes irrelevant.

"In Tibet, we say the mind is like a rider on a horse; wherever the horse goes, the mind has to go. In an untrained mind, they say the rider is helpless; he doesn't have any legs and arms and, therefore, is unable to control the horse. We can experience this when we are sitting and our mind is just wandering everywhere. The horse is taking us all over the place. When we are running with awareness and our minds are focused in the present moment, then everything becomes totally awake. We are in control of the horse! Consciousness is going throughout our whole body. As we become more mindful, we become vital and powerful. It is a wonderfully clear space."

|||

Dancing

Dance has been used throughout all the spiritual traditions as a form of losing the self and opening the heart to merge with the divine. It is seen in the Sufi whirling dervishes, the Tibetan dancing lamas, the ecstatic dance accompanying Hindu devotional chanting, or in Jewish circle dancing. It brings us together as one, releasing the boundaries that separate us from each other.

| DEB |

"We were eating dinner at a small taverna on the Greek island of Rhodes when we heard the waitress talking about a dance to be held that night. It was midnight before the entire village had assembled on a flat, grassy outcrop normally used for playing football: Small children, lanky teenagers, farmers and shopkeepers, grannies and old men clinging to walking sticks, they all came. Tables had been spread with food and drink. A small band began to play, and over the next two hours, we watched both the young and old take hands and dance, sometimes in circles, sometimes in winding lines, sometimes in pairs or groups of eight. I experienced the power of this collective dancing when one of the teenagers with rings in his nose and tattoos coving his arms, who had at first looked completely bored and disinterested, stepped into the middle of the circle and led a snake-like dance around the field, his eyes alight with joy."

To dance is to feel the gift of life in our veins, to directly experience the joy of each breath. This is particularly true of free dance, where the body moves of its own volition, self-consciousness dissolves, and in its place comes an awareness of each part of the body and its relation to the whole. Dance enables our self-imposed limitations, inhibitions, fears and self-obsessions to be released; in their place, we find a greater sense of freedom and joy.

| GABRIELLE ROTH |

"Stillness is my rhythm. In my teens, alone in my bedroom with the radio turned up as loud as possible, I danced my pain—all the sadness and anger that was not allowed or expressed in my family or my culture. Much later, I would realize that I was seeking a way to get out of my head and the fastest way to still my mind was to move my body. Put the psyche in motion and it heals itself. Normally, the mind is thinking one thing, the body is moving in a different direction, and the heart is doing a third thing, so there is a huge disconnect. We live in the chat room above our necks, but we need to find our roots and our center.

"Dance allows me to live in meditation, for awareness to infuse every moment of every day. When my feet are connected to the earth, they dance on the skin of the great mother, listening to her every song. Her intelligence comes up through the soles of my feet into the heart of my body and talks to me. When we listen to our feet, we hear her song and it becomes a part of us. She is alive and vibrating and moving in patterns and cycles.

"In the dance, we can go so deeply into our bodies that we bypass the concept of a separate self and move into the big body that holds us all as one. We are not in a body, but it is in us, in the amazing unified field of holy otherness that is who we really are. This is my meditation and it moves my memories, my tears, my fears, my instincts—the fragile threads that hold me and you and all of us in a web of divine intelligence. It calls us to extend so far past an individual self that we become everything in one deep, expansive breath."

|||

Practice Meditation: Dance

Little instruction is needed here. Choose your favorite music and let it move you. Try different rhythms: fast, melodic, staccato, soft, and slow. See what it feels like to open your chest, to lift your arms, to spin or bend, to move quickly or slowly. Keep breathing throughout. Let your emotions ebb and flow with the music. Dance your feelings, your relationships, and your parents. Dance your illness or your pain. Dance your anger; dance your fear. Then dance your joy and laughter! Dance who you really are.

And then stop and be still. Stand or sit and just breathe gently and enter the stillness that is always there behind the movement.

Creativity and Meditation

In the quiet space of meditation, spontaneous inspiration and vision can arise as the creative mind finds expression through the contemplative mind. This aspect of moving meditation is where we take that creativity into an outward expression so that others may also access that experience and, through it, find themselves.

| JANE FONDA |

"The wise ones all spoke to us in parables, in poetry and metaphor, because that is the form that penetrates and transcends our defenses. We go to some deep part of ourselves; it is non-linear and non-cerebral, which is what meditation is."

Many creative acts are solitary, such as writing and painting, which can be the doorway to reflection and insight. In order to find the right words or expressive image, the creator has to go deeper within to a place of non-ego, a surrendering to the creation itself. As writers, we often look back at what we have written and wonder where the words have come from as we have little memory of having written them. It is as if we had dissolved into the creation of the writing.

| COLEMAN BARKS |

"Rumi says, 'Listen for presences inside poems. Let them take you where they will. Follow those private hints and never leave the premises.' When poetry is spoken, we can meet on a deeper heart level. Poetry and music and movement are all ways we can experience our shared inwardness."

All the arts have their own form of expression. Painting, in particular, is where the painter surrenders to the act of painting in order to find himself.

| ROBERT VENOSA |

"When I sit down to paint, I enter into a deep meditation because I truly lose myself, I lose who I am, and I become a part of the painting. I believe any creative act is a form of meditation, any act where you lose yourself to the act. Artists and meditators go to the same place; we are getting to that source in the center, but through different paths. Artists seek the knowledge of themselves through their art. I am looking at who I am through my painting; it is basically a mirror, a reflection of who I am, and the deeper I go in my painting, the more it advances and evolves, the more I am opening up, and in that is the discovery of my deeper self."

As the act of creation takes us into a meditative state, so the physical act of painting can be a direct experience of meditation itself, where there is no separation between the painter, the brush, the paint, the canvas, and the breath.

| MARTINA HOFFMANN |

"Whenever I enter the creative process, I find myself in this very peaceful state where I have no sense of my ego or my body. When I meditate, I intentionally follow my breath. When I paint, I follow my brush. So I go to that same space. I allow myself to be an open vessel to whatever information is available: visual, emotional, or spiritual. As in meditation, I sit down, I settle myself, and I focus. Then I pick up my brush and I start watching my brush or watching my breath. It is the same thing."

|||

Practice Meditation:
Creative Writing

Have a pad of paper and pen beside you. To experience the creative power of meditation, start by sitting quietly and watching your breath for at least five minutes. When your mind is settled and relaxed, move gently to pick up the paper and pen.

You can write in two ways. One way is to create a simple question, and then let your writing flow freely in response. It may be a question about your health, your feelings about your work, or about a particular person, or whatever is relevant for you. Having asked the question, let your response arise spontaneously from the meditative mind. It does not have to be word perfect; this is just for you.

Alternatively, pick a theme or image to write about. Perhaps a bird on a branch, a beach with waves lapping, or a forest of tall trees. Whatever image comes to you, let the words describing it flow freely, without judgment, so that you are creating the image completely anew for yourself.

When you are done, lay down the pad and pen and just sit quietly for another few minutes, letting the rhythm of your breath take your deeper within yourself.

|||

Contributor Bios

|||

Patch Adams is a renowned medical doctor, clown, social activist, and founder of a free hospital. *See* www.patchadams.org

Elias Amidon leads interfaith wilderness retreats with Rabia Roberts and directs the Spirit in Action program. He is a lineage holder of the Sufi Way. *See* www.sufiway.org

Judith Ansara is a teacher of applied human consciousness, psychotherapist, coach, seminar leader, and movement artist. *See* www.sacredunion.com

Anne Bancroft is the author of numerous books, including *Zen: Direct Pointing to Reality*; *Weavers of Wisdom*; and *The Buddha Speaks*.

Marc Ian Barasch is the author of *The Compassionate Life*; *Healing Dreams*; and *The Healing Path*. He is founder/director of the Green World Campaign. *See* www.greenworld.org

Coleman Barks is the renowned author of numerous Rumi translations. *See* colemanbarks.com

Michael Bernard Beckwith, featured in *The Secret* with over 4 million copies sold, is the founder of the Agape Spiritual Center, with over 8,000 members. *See* www.agapelive.com

Ed Begley Jr. is an actor nominated for six Emmy's and an environmental activist devoted to green living. *See* www.edbegley.com

Russell Bishop is a coach and consultant. He is senior editor-at-large and contributor to the HuffingtonPost.com. Contact russell@bishopandbishop.com

Sylvia Boorstein is a psychotherapist and the co-founder of Spirit Rock Meditation Center. Her books include *On Being a Faithful Jew and a Passionate Buddhist*. *See* sylviaboorstein.com

Joan Borysenko is the co-founder of the Mind/Body Clinical Programs at Beth Israel Deaconess Medical Center. Her many books include the bestseller *Minding the Body, Mending the Mind*. *See* joanborysenko.com

Gregg Braden is a renowned pioneer in bridging science and spirituality. His books include the *New York Times* bestsellers *The God Code* and *The Divine Matrix*. *See* greggbraden.com

Sarasvati Burhman is a senior faculty member at the Rocky Mountain Institute of Yoga and Ayurveda. *See* www.rmiya.org

Ellen Burstyn is an Academy award–winning actress and five-time nominee, and author of *Lessons In Becoming Myself*. *See* www.ellenburstyn.net

Mirabai Bush is the co-founder and director of The Center for the Contemplative Mind in Society, and co-author of *Compassion in Action*. *See* www.contemplativemind.org

Don Campbell is the founder of the Institute for Music, Health and Education, and author of eight books, including the bestseller *The Mozart Effect*. *See* www.mozarteffect.com

Michael Carroll is a corporate consultant and coach and the author of *Awake at Work* and *The Mindful Leader*. *See* www.awakeatwork.net

Andrew Cohen is a spiritual teacher and a founder of the award-winning magazine *EnlightenNext*. His many books include *Enlightenment: A Call for Evolution Beyond Ego*. *See* www.andrewcohen.org

Seane Corn is the National Yoga Ambassador for YouthAIDS and co-creator of "Off the Mat and Into the World" campaign. *See* www.seanecorn.com

Lindsay Crouse is an award winning actress and teaches Tibetan Buddhism and spiritual partnership. *See* www.lindsaycrouse.org.

Richard Davidson is a Vilas Professor of Psychology and Psychiatry, a researcher at the University of Wisconsin, and a pioneer in mind-body medicine. *See* psych.wisc.edu/faculty/bio/davidson.html

Steve Demos founded White Wave, Inc., the makers of Silk Soymilk, and is co-founder and chairman of NextFoods, the makers of GoodBelly fruit drinks.

Deva Premal & Miten have sold over 700,000 chanting CDs. *See* www.devapremalmiten.com

Vickie Dodd is the author of *Tuning the Blues to Gold* and a teacher of sound healing *See* www.sacredsoundsschool.com

Peggy Dylan is the founder of SUNDOOR School of Transpersonal Education and the International Firewalking School. *See* www.sundoor.com

Deepesh Faucheux is a psychotherapist and Zen practitioner and a trainer of therapists. He currently teaches transpersonal psychology at Naropa University, in Boulder, Colorado.

Peter Fenner is a pioneer in the field of non-dual psychotherapy and the author of *Radiant Mind: Awakening Unconditional Awareness*. *See* www.radiantmind.net.

Rabbi Tirzah Firestone is an author, psychotherapist, and spiritual leader of Congregation Nevei Kodesh in Boulder, Colorado. *See* www.tirzahfirestone.com

Jane Fonda is an Academy award–winning actress and five-time Oscar® nominee. She is also a social and political activist, fitness instructor, and Zen practitioner. *See* www.jane-fonda.net

Debbie Ford is the founder of the Ford Institute for Integrative Coaching and author of the *New York Times* #1 bestseller *The Dark Side of the Light Chasers*. *See* www.debbieford.com

Matthew Fox is a member of the Dominican Order, the founder of the Friends of Creation Spirituality, and the author of 28 books, including *Original Blessing*. See www.mattewfox.org

Richard Freeman is a senior student of Sri K. Pattabhi Jois and the founder/ director of the Yoga Workshop in Boulder, Colorado. *See* www.yogaworkshop.com

Tim Freke is a respected authority on world mysticism and author of over 20 books, including *The Jesus Mysteries* and *Lucid Living*. *See* www.timothyfreke.com

Gangaji is an international non-dual spiritual teacher and the author of *You Are That* and *The Diamond in Your Pocket*. *See* www.gangaji.org

Robert Gass is a psychologist, leadership coach, and corporate consultant. He is also a chant master and recorded the bestselling *Om Namaha Shivaya*. *See* www.sacredunion.com

Grover Gauntt is a sensei, a founding teacher of the Zen Peacemaker Order, and head teacher of the Hudson River Zen Center in Yonkers, New York. *See* www.zenpeacemakers.org.

Mark Gerzon is the author of *Leading Beyond Borders* and president of the Mediators Foundation for conflict resolution. *See* www.mediatorsfoundation.org

James Gimian is the author of *The Rules of Victory: How to Transform Chaos and Conflict*, and publisher of *Shambhala Sun* magazine. *See* www.shambhala.com

Bernie Glassman is the founder of the Zen Peacemakers, the Greyston Bakery, and the Maitri Center. He is also the author of *Infinite Circle: Studies in Zen*. *See* www.peacemakers.org

Jonathan Goldman is the director of the Healing Sounds Association and author of *The Seven Secrets of Sound Healing*. *See* www.healingsounds.com

Joseph Goldstein is a cofounder of the Insight Meditation Society in Barre, Massachusetts, and the author of many books, including *Insight Meditation*. *See* www.dharma.org

Chloe Goodchild is the founder of *The Naked Voice*, and has performed for film and television sound tracks, with two Grammy nominations. *See* www.thenakedvoice.com

John Gray is the author of the bestseller *Men Are from Mars, Women Are from Venus*, and is an international teacher, seminar leader, and relationship counselor. *See* www.home.marsvenus.com

Ken Green is an award-winning film producer currently producing a multimedia adaptation of the *Tibetan Book of the Dead*. *See* www.goldensunfoundation.org

Tara Guber is the founder of Yoga Ed., dedicated to the development of health/ wellness education programs for yoga and creative play. *See* www.yogaed.com

John Hagelin is a quantum physicist and educator, and has pioneered Unified Field-based technologies to reduce crime, violence, and to promote peace. *See* www.hagelin.org

Roshi Joan Halifax is abbot of the Upaya Zen Center in New Mexico, director of the Project on Being with Dying, and founder of the Peacemaker Institute. *See* www.upaya.org

Andrew Harvey is a spiritual scholar and teacher, and author of over 30 books, including *The Direct Path* and *Hidden Journey*. *See* www.andrewharvey.net

Gay and Kathlyn Hendricks are authors of many books, including *Five Wishes; The Corporate Mystic;* and *Conscious Living;* and co-founders of The Spiritual Cinema Circle. *See* www.hendricks.com

Nirmala Heriza is the author of *Dr. Yoga*; a yoga cardiac specialist at Cedars-Sinai Medical Center; director of LA Integral Yoga Center; and president of the United Council on Yoga. *See* www.dr-yoga.com

HH The Karmapa is the seventeenth head of the Karma Kagyu school of Tibetan Buddhism. *See* www.karmapa.org

Martina Hoffmann is a painter and sculptress and teaches art internationally with her partner Robert Venosa. *See* www.martinahoffmann.com

Jean Houston, PhD, is the co-founder of Foundation for Mind Research, founder of the Mystery School, and a prolific author. *See* www.jeanhouston.org

Jon Kabat-Zinn is the director of the Stress Reduction Clinic and the Center for Mindfulness in Medicine, Health Care, and Society at Massachusetts Medical School, and is the bestselling author of *Full Catastrophe Living*.

Byron Katie is the founder of The Work, and bestselling author of *A Thousand Names for Joy: Living in Harmony with the Way Things Are.* *See* www.thework.com

Father Thomas Keating is the founder of the Centering Prayer movement and of Contemplative Outreach. He is the author of many books, including *Crisis of Faith*. *See* www.snowmass.org

Constance Kellough is a publisher, management consultant, and author of *The Leap: Are You Ready to Live a New Reality?* *See* www.namastepublishing.com

Kitaro is a Grammy and Golden Globe–winning musician whose record sales have soared to over 10 million worldwide. *See* www.kitaromusic.com

Jack Kornfield is a teacher of the Insight Meditation Society and Spirit Rock Meditation Center. His books include the bestselling *A Path with Heart*. *See* www.jackkornfield.org

Krishna Das is an internationally respected Indian chant master, with over 10 award-winning chanting CDs. *See* www.krishnadas.com

Cyndi Lee, founder of the OM yoga center in New York City, is also the author of *Yoga Body, Buddha Mind*, and the *OM Yoga in a Box* series. *See* www.omyoga.com.

Noah Levine is the author of *Dharma Punx* and *Against the Stream*. *See* www.noahlevine.com

Michelle and Joel Levey, co-founders of InnerWork Technologies, work with leading corporations. Their books include *Wisdom at Work*. *See* www.wisdomatwork.com

Joseph Marshall III, from the Rosebud Sioux Indian Reservation in South Dakota, is the author of many books, including *The Wisdom of Crazy Horse*. *See* www.thunderdreamers.com

Mark Matousek is the bestselling author of *Sex Death Enlightenment* and *When You're Falling, Dive*. He is the co-chair of VMen—men ending violence against women—with Eve Ensler. *See* www.markmatousek.com

Fleet Maull is a sensei, author, and founder of Prison Dharma Network, the Peacemaker Institute, and National Prison Hospice Association. *See* www.prisondharmanetwork.org

Mark Mawrence has worked extensively as an executive and corporate consultant in the arenas of strategy, branding, marketing, and communications.

Dennis Genpo Merzel is a Zen master, founder of the Kanzeon Zen Center, and the author of, among others, *The Eye Never Sleeps* and *The Path of The Human Being. See* www.bigmind.org

Dan Millman is a former world champion athlete and author of *The Way of the Peaceful Warrior.* The movie, *The Peaceful Warrior,* was based on his book. *See* www.danmillman.com

John Milton has pioneered The Way of Nature and its programs, Sacred Passage and Nature Quest. *See* www.sacredpassage.com.

Mingyur Rinpoche is a master of the Karma Kagyu lineage of Tibetan Buddhism and author of the bestseller *The Joy of Living. See* www.mingyur.com

Edgar Mitchell is an Apollo 14 Astronaut, the sixth man to walk on the moon, and the founder of Noetic Sciences. *See* www.edgarmitchellapollo14.com

Shanida Natarja has a PhD in Neurophysiology and is the author of *The Blissful Brain: Neuroscience and Proof of the Power of Meditation. See* www.blissfulbrain.com

Dean Ornish, MD, president of Preventive Medicine Research Institute and Medical Director of HuffingtonPost.com. His books include the best seller *The Spectrum. See:* www.pmri.org

Ponlop Rinpoche is lineage holder of Tibetan Buddhism. His books include *Mind Beyond Death.* He is the founder of Nalandabodhi International. *See* www.nalandabodhi.org

Jill Purce pioneered the sound healing movement and has taught internationally for nearly four decades. *See* www.healingvoice.com

Ram Dass is a renowned spiritual teacher, co-founder of the Seva Foundation, and author of numerous books, including the classic bestseller *Be Here Now. See* www.ramdass.org

Kali Ray is the founder of TriYoga®, now taught in over 30 countries. *See* www.triyoga.com

Reggie Ray is the founder of Dharma Ocean Foundation and author of *Touching Enlightenment. See* www.dharmaocean.org

Bonnie Reiss served as Senior Advisor to California Governor Arnold Schwarzenegger (2003–2007) and is an Operating Advisor to Pegasus Capital Advisors.

Linus Roache, nominated for a Golden Globe in 2003, is now starring in NBC's *Law and Order.* He is managing director of EnlightenNext in New York City.

Rabia Roberts is a peace worker and social activist, and co-director of the Spirit in Action program. *See* www.boulderinstitute.com.

Marshall B Rosenberg is director for the Center for Nonviolent Communications. His many books include *Nonviolent Communication: A Language of Life. See* www.cnvc.org

Gabrielle Roth is a theater/music director, the creator of the 5Rhythms®, and the best-selling author of *Maps to Ecstasy. See* www.gabrielleroth.com.

Peter Russell is a scientist and the author of many books, including *The Global Brain; Waking Up in Time;* and *From Science to God. See* www.peterrussell.com

Sakyong Mipham Rinpoche is the spiritual director of Shambhala International and author of the bestselling *Turning the Mind into an Ally* and *Ruling Your World. See* www.mipham.com

Jeff Salzman, co-founder of CareerTrack Training, is currently Director of Boulder Integral. *See* www.integrallife.com

Rabbi Zalman Schachter is the founder of the P'nai Or (Children of Light) religious fellowship and the Alliance for Jewish Renewal. *See* www.rzlp.org

David Shiner is a clown, actor, playwright, and director of Cirque du Soleil. *See* www.cirquedusoleil.com

Franklyn Sills is the author of *Being and Becoming*; *The Polarity Process*; and *Craniosacral Biodynamics.* See www.karuna-institute.co.uk

Maura Sills is the co-founder of the Karuna Institute UK, director of Psychotherapy Training, and a prime developer of Core Process Psychotherapy. *See* www.karuna-institute.co.uk

Judith Simmer-Brown is on the faculty for Religious Studies at Naropa University and is the author of *Dakini's Warm Breath: The Feminine Principle in Tibetan Buddhism.* See www.naropa.edu

Max Simon is a world-renowned speaker, author and coach. *See* www.getselfcentered.com.

Tami Simon is the founder and CEO of Sounds True Publishing, a multi-media publisher with a clear mission to disseminate spiritual wisdom. *See* www.soundstrue.com

Susan Smalley is a professor of Psychiatry and the director of the Mindful Awareness Research Center at the Semel Institute of Neuroscience and Human Behavior at UCLA. *See* www.marc.ucla.edu

William Spear is the author of *Recovering Original Ability* and director of the Fortunate Blessings Foundation. *See* www.fortunateblessings,org

Ajahn Sumedho is the abbot of Amaravati Buddhist Center and senior most Western disciple of the late Ajahn Chah. *See* www.buddhanet.net

Lama Surya Das is the founder of the Dzogchen Foundation and author of *Awakening the Buddha Within* and *Awakening the Buddhist Heart. See* www.surya.org

Mary Taylor is the author of four books on yoga as it relates to a healthy life. *See* www.yogaworkshop.com

Robert Thurman is a professor of Indio-Tibetan studies at Columbia University, New York City, and President of Tibet House US. He has been named one of the 25 most influential Americans by *Time* magazine. *See* www.bobthurman.com

James Twyman is a best-selling author, filmmaker, and musician, and author of many books, including *The Moses Code. See* www.emissaryoflight.com

Robert Venosa, a visionary artist, has been exhibited worldwide and is represented in major collections. His artwork is on Santana and Kitaro CD covers. *See* www.venosa.com.

Rama Vernon is a yoga teacher, past editor of the *Yoga Journal,* and international mediator. *See* www.americanyogacollege.org

Lindsay Wagner is an Emmy award–winning actress, advocate, and humanitarian. She teaches Quiet the Mind & Open the Heart workshops. *See* www.lindsaywagner.com

Alan Wallace was ordained as a Buddhist monk in 1975. He is the president of the Santa Barbara Institute for Consciousness Studies. *See* www.sbinstitute.com

Wavy Gravy, 1960's icon and activist, is co-founder of Seva Foundation to combat blindness and of Camp Winnarainbow. *See* www.wavygravy.net

Kiri Westby has traveled the world since the age of eleven and has been working for human rights since 2000.

Marianne Williamson is a bestselling author with four books #1 on the *New York Times* list, including *A Return to Love.* Her latest book is the *Age of Miracles. See* www.marianne.com

Other Books by Ed and Deb Shapiro
Voices from the Heart

Other Books by Deb Shapiro
Your Body Speaks Your Mind

CDs
Meditation: Four Steps to Calmness and Clarity
Yoga Nidra
Samadhi
Metta

Acknowledgments

||

Our thanks to David Nelson; this book would not have been possible without him. To Editorial Director Michael Fragnito, for his support and clear vision; to Kate Zimmermann, our caring and intuitive editor at Sterling; and Megan Perritt, our great publicist. Our gratitude to Susan Mears, our friend and agent, who has always been there for us. Thanks to Johanna Walker, for her diligent transcribing; Wendy Zahler at Marianne Williamson's; Susan McTigue, at Ellen Burstyn's; and the assistants of many of our contributors—you know who you are. And a special thank you to Ponlop Rinpoche, Robert Thurman, Rabbi Zalman Schachter-Shalomi, Jean Houston, Sylvia Boorstein, Joan Halifax, and Nirmala Heriza, for their kind help.

Index

Page numbers in **bold** are quotes from contributors